TRADE BLOCS?

The Future of Regional Integration

edited by Vincent Cable
and David Henderson

THE ROYAL INSTITUTE OF
INTERNATIONAL AFFAIRS
International Economics Programme

Published in Great Britain in 1994 by the Royal Institute of International Affairs
Chatham House, 10 St James's Square, London SW1Y 4LE.

Distributed worldwide by The Brookings Institution, 1775 Massachusetts Avenue,
Northwest, Washington, DC 20036-2188, USA.

British Library Cataloguing in Publication Data
A CIP catalogue record for this book is available from the British Library.

ISBN 0 905031 81 4

Printed and bound in Great Britain by Redwood Books.

CONTENTS

CONTRIBUTORS

Ichiro Akimune	Senior Research Fellow, Sumitomo Life Research Institute, Tokyo
Dr Vincent Cable	Head of International Economics Programme, Royal Institute of International Affairs
Professor David Currie	Director, Centre for Economic Forecasting, London Business School
Professor David Henderson	Former Head of the Economics and Statistics Department, OECD, Paris
Masayuki Nohara	Senior Research Fellow, Sumitomo Life Research Institute, Tokyo
J.M.C. Rollo	Chief Economic Adviser, Foreign and Commonwealth Office, London
Kimitoshi Sato	Senior Research Fellow, Sumitomo Life Research Institute, Tokyo
Professor Alasdair Smith	Professor of Economics and Dean of the School of European Studies, University of Sussex
Dr Benn Steil	Senior Research Fellow, International Economics Programme, Royal Institute of International Affairs
Dr Stephen Thomsen	Research Fellow, International Economics Programme, Royal Institute of International Affairs
Dr John Whitley	Senior Research Fellow, Centre for Economic Forecasting, London Business School
Masami Yoshida	Senior Research Fellow, Sumitomo Life Research Institute, Tokyo

ACKNOWLEDGMENTS

This volume was prepared as a result of a collaborative research project on 'trade blocs' between the Royal Institute of International Affairs at Chatham House in London and the Sumitomo Life Research Institute in Tokyo. Thanks are due to SLRI and, in particular, Mr Miyamoto for his support of the project. We would also like to express appreciation to Jim Rollo, former Head of the International Economics Programme at the RIIA, who helped to launch the project with SLRI.

Amongst those who helped with critical comments on the papers were Heidi Sherman, Chief Economist at Shell, and, at Chatham House, Susie Symes, Head of the European Programme, and Richard Grant, Head of the Asia-Pacific Programme.

In the production of this volume we would like to thank Gillian Bromley and Margaret May for patient editorial work, Hannah Doe for overseeing production and Fionnuala O'Flynn for general administration.

September 1994   Vincent Cable
                                                                      David Henderson

ABBREVIATIONS

ACP	African, Caribbean and Pacific countries
AFTA	ASEAN Free Trade Area
ANCERTA	Australia-New Zealand Closer Economic Relations Agreement
APEC	Asia-Pacific Economic Cooperation
ASEAN	Association of Southeast Asian Nations
BBC	brand-to-brand complementation
BIS	Bank for International Settlements
CAD	Capital Adequacy Directive
CAP	Common Agricultural Policy
CEE	Central and East European Countries
CFSP	Common Foreign and Security Policy
CIS	Commonwealth of Independent States
COB	Commission des Opérations de Bourse
CUS(F)TA	Canada-US (Free) Trade Agreement
DTI	Department of Trade and Industry
EAEC	East Asia Economic Caucus
EC	European Community
ECB	European Central Bank
ECJ	European Court of Justice
ECOFIN	Council of European Economic and Finance Ministers
EEA	European Economic Area
EFTA	European Free Trade Association
EMI	European Monetary Institute
EMS	European Monetary System
EMU	Economic and Monetary Union
ERM	Exchange Rate Mechanism
EU	European Union
FDI	foreign direct investment
FIBV	Fédération Internationale des Bourses de Valeurs
FSU	former Soviet Union
FTA	free trade area
GATT	General Agreement on Tariffs and Trade

GDCF	gross domestic capital formation
GDP	gross domestic product
GSP	Generalized System of Preferences
G6	Group of Six
G7	Group of Seven
G10	Group of Ten
HTS	harmonized tariff system
IIT	intra-industry trade
IOSCO	International Organization of Securities Commissions
ISD	Investment Services Directive
LDC	less developed country
Mercosur	Common Market of the South
MFN	most favoured nation
MNC	multinational company
MNE	multinational enterprise
MOU	memorandum of understanding
NAFTA	North American Free Trade Area
NASDAQ	National Association of Securities Dealers Automated Quotations System
NIE	newly industrializing economy
NTB	non-tariff barrier
OECD	Organization for Economic Cooperation and Development
PCA	partnership and cooperation agreement
PPP	Purchasing Power Parity
QMV	qualified majority voting
REI	regional economic integration
RTA	regional trade agreement
SAARC	South Asian Association for Regional Cooperation
SBD	Second Banking Directive
SEC	Securities and Exchange Commission
SEZ	Special Economic Zone
SFA	Securities and Futures Authority
SIB	Securities and Investments Board
SII	Structural Impediments Initiative
SITC	Standard International Trade Classification
VER	Voluntary Export Restraint
WTO	World Trade Organization

1 OVERVIEW

Vincent Cable

The changing context of regional arrangements

There has been a recent upsurge of interest in economic regionalism. In some cases regional integration is taking place spontaneously, through market forces, impelled by the dictates of economic geography. In others, formal structures are being created in the shape of free trade areas, customs unions, common markets and various types of preferential association. These approaches – which differ considerably in their motivation and effects – have unfortunately attracted the all-purpose designation of 'trade blocs'. This term carries connotations both of confrontation and of a uniformity of style which may be quite wrong. Indeed, in the concluding chapter of this volume, David Henderson argues that the idea of 'trade blocs' has often detracted from understanding the significance of economic integration and the benefits to be derived from it. This overview considers some of the various, diverse, forms which regional integration takes.

Recent developments

There has certainly been a quickening of interest in the creation of formal structures for regional integration. In Europe, the European single market ('1992') process, the Maastricht Treaty, and the European Economic Area (EEA) and EC enlargement negotiations; in North America, the completion of the NAFTA accords; across the Pacific, the launching of Asia-Pacific Economic Cooperation (APEC); in East Asia, the creation of the ASEAN Free Trade Area (AFTA) and the East Asia Economic Caucus (EAEC) proposal; in Australasia the Australia-New Zealand Closer Economic Relations Agreement (ANCERTA); elsewhere, the attempts to breathe new life into Latin American integration through Mercosur (and as many as 25 other regional liberalization initiatives): all these developments attest to a widespread belief in the value of regionalism.

The context of the debate on regionalism, however, has changed since the opening of the 1990s. Then, the GATT multilateral negotiations were floundering while the EC was speeding towards yet deeper integration through implementation of the single market and the Maastricht Treaty; and NAFTA was being negotiated in an environment of optimism. The idea of regionalism as an alternative to globalism in trade was strong and feared by those excluded, especially from the putative 'fortress Europe'. Since then, the Uruguay Round has been completed, albeit with difficulty, while far from regionalism proving a simple and easy alternative, both the Maastricht Treaty and NAFTA have provoked enormous political hostility (but were ratified) and the EMS has collapsed (though not necessarily permanently). Both regionalism and globalism have come up against the same obstacles: nationalism and powerful sectional interests.

Regionalism has not, overall, had a particularly successful history. After a flurry of interest in the 1960s and 1970s, triggered in large part by the successful establishment and enlargement of the European Community, a large number of regional arrangements in Africa, Latin America, the Caribbean and the Middle East were tried and either failed completely or failed by far to match expectations. ASEAN and the South Asian Association for Regional Cooperation (SAARC) have survived but to date have little concrete to show for their integration efforts. The regional structures built up under communism in Eastern Europe have largely disappeared with communism and the Soviet empire. These experiences are worth remembering since it is not regionalism, as such, but rather certain approaches to it which have been successful.

Bhagwati (1992) has distinguished between the 'First Regionalism' of the 1960s and the 'Second Regionalism' of the present. The First Regionalism never flourished outside the EC (and EFTA), for two reasons. First, the energies of the United States were channelled not into promoting regionalism in the Americas or the Pacific basin, but into promoting multilateralism and non-discrimination, though it acquiesced in the formation of the EC and the use of GATT's Article XXIV to sanction the Common Market, largely for political reasons. Second, the developing (and communist) countries which embraced regionalism used it to promote industrial import substitution through the economies of scale offered by a regional market. They all failed to overcome the difficulties associated with the political allocation of industries and the sharing of the high costs of industrial protection.

Under the Second Regionalism both these factors have changed. The United States has come to support regional integration in North America and, more cautiously, in a wider hemispheric and Pacific context. Motives for this shift in US attitudes have varied from time to time and from one advocate to another, opinions differing as to whether regionalism is an alternative, a complement or a catalyst to multilateralism. But the experience of successful – wider *and* deeper –integration in Europe has undoubtedly been a key influence, whether European integration is seen as a threat to the United States or as a positive role model. On the second point, development strategies in developing and former communist countries have been radically reappraised in favour of open and market-based economies. A powerful factor behind the accession of Mexico to NAFTA (and the pursuit of membership by Chile and Argentina) and the current attempts of East European countries to join the EC is to create an irreversible commitment to, and strong external support for, market reform.

Rationale

The current attempts to forge regional arrangements have, in their theoretical underpinnings, elements of continuity with, and also major elements of difference from, the earlier experiments. Continuity is provided by the basic framework of customs union theory as originally set out by Viner, which acknowledges both the economic efficiency gain from regional trade liberalization and also the ambiguous overall benefit because of the costs of trade diversion. Moreover, ideas of economies of scale from larger markets – an important element in thinking about the EC single market – were prominent in early thinking about European integration (and in the failed Latin American and East European experiments which tried to achieve economies of scale through 'planners' preferences': see Balassa, 1975). Alasdair Smith's chapter in this volume (Chapter 2) shows how these building blocks are now being supplemented by new theoretical insights derived from imperfect competition and growth theory which point to the potential gains to participants from economic integration in general and regional economic integration in particular.

There are some respects in which the context of the Second Regionalism is different. One is the large, perhaps predominant, role now exercised by capital movements and by companies which operate transnationally. Such capital mobility was both a cause and an effect of the deepening of economic integration in Europe and, arguably, has been the driving force behind closer integration in East Asia, where there has been little preferential regional trade liberalization. Stephen Thomsen's chapter (Chapter 5) looks at the way in which FDI is acting to reinforce regionalism as well as (and more than) economic integration at a global level.

A second, and related, new phenomenon has been the progress of financial integration, prompted by the deregulation of financial markets and competition between them, the liberalization of capital flows and the growth in trade in financial services. The process of financial integration is both global and regional, and Benn Steil's chapter (Chapter 6) discusses the EC dimension in particular.

A third element is that as neighbouring economies become more integrated through trade and capital movements they may more closely approximate an optimum currency area, so that the issue of monetary union may arise. Debate rages in the EC as to whether that stage has been achieved for all or some members (de Grauwe, 1993; Eichengreen, 1991); with a few small exceptions (notably the East Caribbean) this has otherwise not been a major feature of regional integration. The chapter by David Currie and John Whitley (Chapter 7) looks at (eventual) European monetary union from the standpoint of the possible gains to be reaped from enhanced macro policy coordination in a regional context.

The debate over monetary union in Europe has highlighted another set of questions now looming larger in the economic integration debate, focusing on the extent to which the most effective route may lie less through clearly defined, cohesive, 'blocs' than through shifting groups of countries: what in Europe is called 'variable geometry'. The European enlargement debate dealt with in Chapter 3, by Jim Rollo, and the discussion of monetary integration by Currie and Whitley highlight the blurring of boundaries taking place in Europe. APEC is an assemblage of Asian, Pacific and North American countries which seems to have discovered 'variable geometry' by accident, encompassing a variety of different kinds and levels of integration (NAFTA; ASEAN-AFTA; ANCERTA; 'Greater China'; regional growth poles like the Singapore-Johore-Riau 'triangle'). The possible enlargement of NAFTA to encompass new members – an eventuality which is provided for in the Agreement – will soon lead to the question of how to reconcile membership with other potentially overlapping regional groupings (the Andean Group: Mercosur; the Caribbean Community; the Central American Common Market).

The blurring of boundaries affects not just membership of regional arrangements but also the nature of the barriers to integration. As the more obvious, visible, barriers to trade are scrapped, further integration may be frustrated by different national rules and standards which were earlier not seen as trade policy instruments at all. This is especially the case for trade in services, which does not involve physical cross-border shipments. The question of how to advance trade liberalization in this deeper way is the central concern of the EC Single Market Act. The principle of 'mutual recognition' and the associated idea of 'competition among rules' have emerged as a more effective way forward than attempted harmonization (Woolcock et al., 1993). In Chapter 6 Steil gives a practical illustration of the dilemmas posed in one particular sector. The APEC work programme referred to in the chapter by Masami Yoshida et al. (Chapter 4) anticipates such questions in an Asia-Pacific context.

The EC experience, especially, has thrown up another new set of issues, also related to the optimum choice of activities to be delegated to the regional integration process (rather than to global, national and sub-national entities): the 'subsidiarity' debate. By considering the extent and significance of the 'spillovers' or externalities from independent national decision-taking, it is possible to identify those areas where it would be advantageous, or disadvantageous, for decisions to be made collectively at a regional level. A recent study of the EC

suggested that the Community has achieved about the right degree of centraliza-
tion (or regionalization) of decision-making in competition policy, but has gone
too far (relative to national discretion) in respect of labour market policy and
environmental policy (Begg et al., 1993). NAFTA, by encompassing some
regional responsibility for national environmental and labour policies, may also
have gone beyond what is justified on the grounds of spillovers.

A further dimension to the 'subsidiarity' debate concerns the extent to which
liberalization initiatives are most competently dealt with regionally, rather than
multilaterally or globally. Several of the chapters in this volume try to cast some
light on this issue. One recurring theme is the issue of whether regionalism
enables global economic integration to proceed faster and/or go deeper than it
otherwise would if it relied solely on multilateral mechanisms (i.e. GATT or the
OECD in its 'Codes of Liberalization'). Does it, on the contrary, undermine the
willingness of negotiators to seek multilateral solutions by making them seem
less necessary (because of the perceived alternative of a regional market) or less
compelling (by distracting energy and commitment from the regional integration
process), or by driving multilateral partners further apart (through discriminatory, trade-diverting, trade policies, and through diverging forms of regional
harmonization of rules and standards)? Thomsen takes a benign view in Chapter
5. Chapter 4, however, reflects the perception of the EC as fundamentally
'discriminatory' in character and a spur to regional integration elsewhere driven
by fears of a 'fortress Europe'. In Chapter 2, Smith traces some of the ambigui-
ties in the external effects of EC integration. In the event, the (more or less)
successful conclusion of the Uruguay Round has laid to rest some of the worst
fears that a stronger emphasis on regionalism would prevent progress in multilateral liberalization.

Different approaches to regional arrangements

From the chapters in this volume on different regions and sectors, and from the
theoretical literature, it becomes clear that regionalism or the 'regional bloc'
concept encompasses a variety of quite different approaches to integration,
reflecting different objectives and having different effects. It may be useful to
review some of these differences and to ask which taxonomy of regionalism is
the most useful.

Market-led versus institutionally driven regionalism

Chapter 4 makes use of the distinction between regional integration led by
market forces and that driven by institutional developments to differentiate
Asian regionalism from the EC (and NAFTA). A recent OECD report on

regionalism (Woolcock et al., 1993) makes essentially the same distinction, between 'market-led' and policy-driven integration. The contrast is drawn between, on the one hand, the growth of Asian integration which has occurred spontaneously, through business decisions without an intergovernmental framework (and, indeed, in spite of some governmental hostility, as between China and Taiwan) and, on the other, the growth of integration within formal treaties which embody the liberalizing (and discriminatory) elements of regionalism.

There are in practice several distinctive features of market-led integration, which occurs mainly in Asia. Despite minimal formal, institutionalized, trade liberalization, intra-regional trade expanded from 20 per cent of the total (for nine East Asian countries) in 1970 to 30 per cent in 1990. One feature is that it is driven primarily by cross-border private capital flows searching out profitable opportunities. Trade barriers may come down in their wake or may remain and create a rationale for FDI, which is highly protected in the host country market, as in Indonesia or China, for example. A second is that integration is most intense in cross-border zones where firms can take best advantage of low transport costs and other cost differentials to outweigh the continuing penalties of trade barriers within the region (or where there are special localized agreements, as in the case of Mexican *maquiladora*, or where smuggling and circumvention of regulations is possible, as in south China). A third feature is that while liberalization is taking place, it is unilateral (or part of a global multilateral process) rather than regionally negotiated.

In practice the distinction between 'market-led' and 'institutionally driven' integration can be overdrawn. In Western Europe, EFTA countries outside the EC are just as involved in intra-European trade as EC members are. The potential havoc created by the recent decision of Switzerland (neither an EC member nor a member of the EEA) to bar transalpine lorry trade is a potent reminder of the extent to which intra-European trade has rested on informal, market-based understandings. Thomsen's chapter cites a study by Wijkman on how sub-regional 'trade blocs' are emerging within Western Europe based on market-led, geographical factors rather than on trade policy. Moreover, the upsurge of cross-border mergers and acquisitions in the 1980s was as much a cause as an effect of the 1992 'deepening' of the Community. And, as Steil makes clear in Chapter 6, it was market competition between European capital markets which precipitated European legislation, rather than the other way round.

Complementary versus competitive economic structures

One of the main distinctions between European and Asia-Pacific integration is that the former has (consciously) involved integration between countries at comparable levels of development and similar factor endowments, while the latter involves the opposite. (NAFTA is a hybrid case, with US-Canada integration resembling the first model and US-Mexico the second.) Chapter 2 suggests that the question of whether integration is between economies at the same or different levels of development is important, since the effects on the pattern of output and the distribution of income are more significant in the latter case than in the former.

There are two strands of argument advanced by those who are rather pessimistic about the gains which could accrue from integration among countries at different development levels. The first, derived from conventional customs unions theory, is that competitive rather than complementary structures maximize trade creation and minimize trade diversion. The other, derived from the concept of growth poles (and the experience of, for example, southern Italy), suggests that close economic integration would lead to polarization such that the poorer or more peripheral regions would be impoverished by the union (and a large call would be made on subsidies from the more highly developed). This pessimistic view is not, however, borne out by experience either of regional integration or of trade more widely. There are balancing mechanisms – notably wage rates – which favour the poor regions. In the EU, the experience of Portugal, Spain and Ireland (and, arguably, Scotland and Wales) has been reassuring; they have performed at least as well as the European 'core'. Smith's review of the recent literature (Ben-David, 1991; Barro and Sala-i-Martin, 1992) suggests that evidence now points to the growth-disseminating effects of integration rather than to a widening gap, let alone impoverishment of peripheral areas.

The profile of integration in the two archetypes is quite different. Integration between economies with competitive structures and similar levels of development generates intra-industry trade (and investment flows) based on economies of scale and product differentiation in ways described in Chapter 2. There is little incentive to labour migration; despite relaxation of barriers to cross-border mobility, other EU nationals make up only 2.5 per cent of the German labour force, 2.0 per cent of the British and virtually none of the Italian. By contrast, 'complementary' union generates inter-industry trade based on different factor endowments as in a Heckscher-Ohlin framework. The trade between Japan and Singapore on the one hand and their low-income neighbours on the other is predominantly of this kind, as is trade between Mexico and the United States. Complementary regional structures are likely to reinforce already strong incentives to labour migration (though this is resisted strongly in Japan, Singapore and Hong Kong and, less effectively, on the US-Mexican border), and to give rise to capital flows from savings-surplus to savings-deficit economies which are 'factor-oriented' rather than 'market oriented' (Masami Yoshida et al., Chapter 4).

Different trade policy issues are thrown up within each of these two archetypes. For competitive economic structures characterized by intra-industry trade, market access issues do not arise predominantly from radically different levels of protection designed to safeguard different factor-based cost structures but from different product and technical standards and rules: the stuff of 1992. But for complementary economic structures the policy agenda reflects the impact of different factor endowments: witness the resistance in the United States to 'social dumping' from low-wage Mexico in labour-intensive industries and in Mexico to FDI from the United States in 'sensitive', and usually capital-intensive, industries.

'Open' and 'closed' regional arrangements

Chapter 4 defines 'open regionalism' as a 'negotiating framework consistent with and complementary to GATT' and cites APEC as a model of this approach. But, as the authors point out, 'openness' has (at least) two different meanings: openness in the sense of non-exclusivity of membership and openness in the economic sense of contributing more to the process of global liberalization than it detracts from it (through discrimination). In practice, the two issues are linked since exclusion matters more if membership has substantial discriminatory effects.

Ex ante, it is not possible to predict whether the discriminatory and trade-diverting effects of common commercial policy will outweigh the trade-creating effects of liberalization. *Ex post*, the empirical literature is close to being unanimous that the EC has functioned in a trade-creating sense for manufactures but has been trade-diverting for agriculture (Balassa, 1975; Mayes, 1990; Jacquemin and Sapir, 1989). Dynamic gains (which are potentially larger than the static effects) in any case have external spillover effects.

There is continued debate as to whether the 'deepening' 1992 process has led to more or less 'openness'. The scrapping of national barriers under Article 115 of the Treaty of Rome has made access a little easier for non-EU suppliers, as has the simplification of procedures. But it is not always clear whether the adoption of Community rather than national restrictions (on cars, for example) brings about a less or more restrictive outcome (Smith, Chapter 2). Smith also points out that while the single market has made public procurement discrimination more transparent, access barriers to non-EC bidders are lower, and the 'mutual recognition' of standards has a net effect of increasing access to all suppliers. Conversely, a global rather than a regional approach to trade negotiation does not necessarily give rise only to liberal outcomes. One consequence of the Uruguay Round negotiations has been to precipitate a move to a more restrictive anti-dumping regime in the EC (through majority rather than qualified majority voting): arguably a move that would not otherwise have occurred.

The 'open'/'closed' distinction is in some ways unsatisfactory also because of the difficulties of defining the counterfactual case. We do not know and cannot tell, for example, whether the EC's notoriously protectionist Common

Agricultural Policy is now more 'closed' than policy in Europe would have been on average had the Community not existed or were it to dissolve. The persistence of even higher levels of agricultural protection in EFTA countries (or, for that matter, in Korea and Japan) does not suggest that the alternative would necessarily have been greater openness.

We also need to distinguish between the declared objectives of regional integration and what has actually occurred. Yoshida et al., in Chapter 4, (rightly) cite some of the more mercantilist objectives of the EC – including the creation of 'European national champions' – but in practice industrial policy has evolved towards greater 'openness': public-sector support for industry has declined (for budgetary reasons); competition policy has operated so as to emphasize the benefits of competition rather than the creation of 'champions' (as witness the landmark De Havilland case); and the interventionist 'Cresson clause' in the Maastricht Treaty was emasculated.

There are, in fact, few clear-cut examples of 'closed' regionalism. The common markets of Central America and the Andean Group (and Comecon) were 'closed' in the sense that they were specifically designed to facilitate import substitution. They failed.

Deep versus shallow integration

Another distinction – sometimes described as 'trade liberalization versus integration' (Woolcock et al., 1993); sometimes as 'shallow versus deep integration' – is implicitly but not explicitly addressed in the chapters in this volume. It captures most effectively the rationale for the development of the EC subsequent to the establishment of a customs union and differentiates the EC approach from those in other agreements, notably NAFTA and APEC. (In practice, however, the distinction is not so neat; the Australasian Closer Economic Relations Agreement has elements of 'deep' integration without full freedom of trade, and in pre-1913 Europe there was free capital and labour movement without free trade.)

The main differences (or additions) which deepening is said to involve are several. First, it goes beyond a concern with tariffs to tackle non-tariff barriers to access: government procurement, technical standards and frontier procedures. Second, 'deepening' is more intrusive, forcing governments to surrender sovereignty over national norms and practices which may be impediments to trade. Third, it involves a comprehensive, all-embracing, approach to liberalization going beyond the narrow 'request and offer' approach of 'shallow' integration. Fourth, it carries dispute settlement beyond bilateral negotiation to incorporate a genuine surrender of sovereignty to courts and supranational institutions.

Deep integration, however, is not to be equated with uniformity or 'harmonization'. In the EC, an approach to harmonization is being evolved – through mutual recognition – which maximizes market access and may give an advantage to companies which originate in countries with the most transparent and least protectionist standards. By contrast, the harmonization of rules, as Steil shows in relation to capital market liberalization, does not necessarily result in the choice of best practice. Attempts to achieve harmonized common environmental and social standards in the EC (now being emulated in NAFTA) may themselves represent barriers to trade since they artificially eliminate cost disparities and they are therefore elements of disintegration. Deep integration can also act strongly against multilateralism. The Japan-US Strategic Impediments Initiative (SII) negotiations arguably involve a form of 'deep integration' in relation to so-called 'structural impediments'; but their chief effect is to entrench bilateralism, and to increase the extent of trade tension.

It is possible that deep regional integration may lead to divergence between the regions involved and to 'systems frictions': tension not between closed trade blocs but between different, possibly incompatible, systems of rules and standards within regional groupings. Several examples have been cited of how, for example, NAFTA and the EC are reinforcing divergent approaches. First, the US-led and EC approaches to financial services liberalization are different and, arguably, divergent, the former stressing 'national' treatment based on host country regulations, the latter seeking to achieve 'mutual recognition', which in effect underlines home country regulations: in the EC, but not in NAFTA, a company supplying a foreign (within-region) market has no need to comply with the regulatory requirements of that market. Arguably, the EC approach is a more effective way to integrate economies (and is being considered as a model for both GATT and APEC), but it is taking the EC in a different direction from NAFTA. There is a sharp contrast, too, in the approaches of the EC and the United States (and NAFTA) towards the practices of local and regional authorities, the former being much more prescriptive. Yet another potential cause of divergence is monetary union, which may reduce currency fluctuations and policy spillovers within the EC while increasing them with other partners.

Impacts of regionalism

The chapters that follow bring together some of the evidence about the impact of regionalism. In general, the evidence seems rather ambiguous and, on balance, downplays the role of regionalism in trade flows.

First, is there any evidence that intra-regional trade (or investment) is growing faster than trade (and investment) in general? Chapters 4 and 5 judge this to be the case. Both Thomsen and Yoshida et al. quote recent data suggesting that both in the EC and in East Asia intra-regional trade has been growing faster than inter-regional trade. But different data sets produce different conclusions. Intra-EC trade grew relative to EC trade outside the region between 1963 and 1973 and after 1985, but not in the intervening period; and Asia-EC trade has grown faster than intra-EC trade in the 1980s. The evidence for the contribution of formal regional integration arrangements to the regionalization of trade is inconclusive, as is that relating to FDI flows. Both intra-EC FDI and extra-EC FDI quadrupled in the late 1980s.

Second, is there any evidence that regional integration schemes, as such, have successfully fostered a redirection of trade flows on a regional basis? Thomsen argues forcefully that the growth of regional trade is due to geography, not to regionalism. This bears out the conclusions of a Japanese study based on a gravity model which explains EC, US-Canada and US-Mexico trade in terms of geography and leaves only intra-East Asian trade requiring further explanation – ironically, since that region is the one that has seen no formal regional arrangements. This conclusion bears out the well-established results from other gravity models, which suggest that economic integration among neighbours will, in general, be 'naturally' more efficient than that achieved over long distances (Thomsen). One analyst recently concluded that three decades of European economic integration had just about re-established the 'natural' level of trade before it was disrupted by war in 1914 (Sapir, 1993). Europe has a history of attempted economic integration going back centuries, if not millennia, involving trade and common money. Just as the formation of the EC owed much to the burying of wartime Franco-German enmities, much recent integration experience in Europe and elsewhere has involved the stripping away of previous artificial impediments to trade among neighbours: the 'distortions' introduced by a colonial past (British and Portuguese accession to the EC); ideological separation (association with or admission to the EC for East European countries; the growing integration of the 'communist' Chinese and both the Vietnamese and Russian economies with the rest of the Pacific basin); and autarkic forms of economic nationalism (abandonment of Mexico's 'revolutionary' economic policy as part of the NAFTA process). The end of the Cold War and a greater degree of consensus around the idea of economic liberalization have, as one of their many consequences, removed many of the artificial barriers to trade among neighbours. Formal arrangements have, therefore, catalysed neighbourly integration but cannot be credited with all, or even most, of it.

Third, is there any evidence of the welfare- or growth-stimulating effects of regional integration? Much of the analysis is *ex ante* rather than *ex post* and in the case of the EC single market has produced a very wide range of estimates (the current state of depressed activity in the EC suggests at least that the more extremely optimistic assessments of the growth-stimulating effects of the 1992 programme were excessive, or at least premature). Smith cites arguments to the effect that the dynamic benefits of integration are much more substantial than the static effects calculated from partial equilibrium models, though estimates are highly speculative (Baldwin, 1989).

Fourth, is there any evidence relating to the impact of regional integration on third parties? As already noted above, analysis based on the traditional trade creation/diversion framework is broadly reassuring – particularly if the external spillovers from the dynamic growth effects are considered. But it is not inevitable that regional arrangements should go together with more external liberalization. Counter-examples include the establishment of the Common Agricultural Policy: evidence suggests that trade diversion was the dominant aspect.

Regionalism versus multilateralism

A continuing concern about regionalism is that it reduces the motivation for and commitment to multilateralism. An essentially negative perspective on contemporary regionalism is set out in recent papers by Bhagwati (1992) and Wolf (1994). These address the underlying philosophy and interests of the players within the European Union which may have, at best, a partial concern with economic liberalization. Wolf argues that the Maastricht Treaty was a key turning point, reinforcing the tendencies in Europe towards a recentralization of state power at a European level. Bhagwati points to other elements of mercantilism: the idea of a large, 'self-sufficient' (protected) 'home' market within the region; the vested interests of groups benefiting from regional trade diversion; and the wish of applicant members to capture some of the benefits of the protected market (a point reiterated below by Rollo in the context of East European applicants' motivation).

Several counter-arguments exist to offset these concerns: that regionalism is breaking down economic nationalism and increasing awareness of economic interdependence; that it is a useful laboratory for new approaches to deeper integration which can be applied multilaterally (in relation, for example, to product and technical standards, services, government procurement, state subsidies, competition policy and dispute settlement); that it makes negotiation easier by reducing the number of players; and that it encourages the codification and formalization of rules and regulations affecting trade, making them more transparent and less capricious and discretionary, if not always more liberal.

The question of whether regionalism and multilateralism are conflicting or complementary processes is in substantial part an empirical one. This project took place against the background of some decisive events which provided further evidence. Had either NAFTA or the GATT process (or both) failed, the verdict on this would have been different. In the event, they both succeeded, at least in surmounting the immediate hurdles of the Congressional ratification of NAFTA and achieving inter-governmental agreement within GATT. (At the time of writing, the GATT agreement was being threatened at the ratification phase in both the US Congress and European courts, though in both cases this appeared to be a surmountable obstacle.) Both singly and together, the two agreements represent a net gain for liberalism; and there has been no major question of incompatibility or inconsistency between them.

With the benefit of hindsight, the very weakest proposition that could now be advanced is that the regional and multilateral processes have not been mutually exclusive. Indeed, we can say more. The political momentum acquired by President Clinton in securing the NAFTA Treaty – which was seen as a victory over protectionism – was important in reinforcing the GATT negotiations. And, in the event, neither the channelling of EC energies into the Maastricht negotiations nor the vested interests in trade diversion created by the EC's agricultural (and textile) policies was sufficient to prevent a GATT agreement being reached (or to stop enlargement negotiations with the EFTAns and East Europeans). The Marrakesh agreement on liberalizing public procurement within GATT is further evidence of an (EC) regional liberalization initiative acting as a forerunner of, and not as an impediment to, wider liberalization. There is, moreover, not a simple dichotomy between regionalism and GATT multilateralism; a good deal of multilateral liberalization (for services, for example) has been achieved in an OECD rather than a GATT context.

Looking to the future, there are new issues crowding onto the trade agenda, some of which will advance the cause of trade liberalization and others of which will hamper it. But these new issues cut across the regionalism versus multilateralism debate and are only indirectly part of it. For example, the attempt to achieve harmonization of environmental process standards and labour standards in pursuit of a 'level playing field' and 'fair' trade runs wholly contrary to the liberal idea of patterns of free trade reflecting relative cost differences. But this attempt is being pursued with comparable energy in both regional and global fora and is producing resistance in both (from Mexico in NAFTA and from the United Kingdom in the EC) for the same reasons. It is not possible to argue with any conviction or consistency that regionalism provides conspicuously more or less fertile soil for 'bad' policy. On the other hand, consideration of the trade implications of competition policy is being advanced within regional groups (the EC and APEC), between them (in the form of a NAFTA-EC understanding) and in GATT in terms which are broadly comparable.

Conclusions: where regionalism goes from here

The project has generated a variety of chapters which underline the complexity of the phenomenon known in general terms as 'regionalism' or 'trade blocs'. Together they highlight the growing sophistication of the theory of economic integration; the mushrooming of empirical literature; the several different approaches to regionalism and possible taxonomies; and the new issues being thrown up by large-scale capital movements and by so-called 'deep integration', both of which take integration further than would be entailed by membership of customs unions.

A major concern underlying this project has been whether regionalism will undermine multilateralism and, in particular, GATT. Recent events have been reassuring on this point; but the Uruguay Round agreement is not yet operational. There are important lacunae (for example, financial services). There is much uncertainty about the procedures and general orientation of the new WTO. It is not yet clear whether the GATT process has been strengthened sufficiently to hold at bay aggressive bilateralism (as in the US-Japan dispute) or protectionism directed against low-wage and/or non-OECD players (such as China or the East Europeans). And the ability of GATT – soon to become the WTO – and the OECD to carry forward the liberalization process from 'shallow' to 'deeper' levels in the wake of regional agreements still has to be tested.

One important, normative question which runs through this volume is how the GATT system needs to be strengthened so as to ensure that regionalism is 'open' and supportive of multilateral liberalization. The authors do not suggest that there is anything inherent in regionalism which prevents it being 'open' rather than 'closed'. But the time is ripe for a clearer definition of the principles which must be followed in order to ensure that the former rather than the latter prevails. At present the main safeguard for multilateralism is provided within Article XXIV of GATT which, while legitimizing customs unions and free trade areas, tries to minimize trade diversion by insisting that the common tariff of a customs union 'shall not on the whole be higher or more restrictive than the general incidence of the duties and regulations of commerce applicable ... prior to the formation of such a union', and for a free trade area that 'the duties and other regulations of commerce' shall not be 'higher or more restrictive' than those previously in effect. Various additional or more specific safeguards have been suggested by Bhagwati, Low and Wolf which, if adopted, could meet most of the concerns expressed:

(1) *Parallel liberalization.* Countries within a union should liberalize their external protection pro rata with the progressive elimination of internal duties. One practical way to make this principle effective would be to require that the lowest tariff of any union member before the union must be part of the common tariff.

(2) *Unique associations.* Countries should be limited to only one preferential arrangement in order to prevent the emergence of a complex, mutually conflicting, politically inspired network of regional groups and to encourage the choice of whichever grouping best advances the liberalization process.

(3) *Open-endedness.* Conditionality for membership should be open-ended in the sense that applicant members may be required to accept existing rules but no more.

(4) *Non-discrimination in rule-making.* The MFN principle should apply to substantial rule making (as, for example, in the application of EC competition policy to non-members in EFTA and NAFTA).

(5) *Multilateral accountability.* It should be a requirement that the regional arrangement should not merely obtain initial Article XXIV approval from GATT but be subject to continued surveillance.

(6) *Stronger GATT disciplines on 'instruments of commercial defence'.* One of the greatest fears of outsiders regarding the EC has been that the bargaining strength of the Union makes it easier to use anti-dumping and other 'commercial defence' instruments. The fact that the EC has recently relaxed its internal criteria for activating anti-dumping measures (moving from qualified majority to majority voting) excites considerable fears in this regard. The implication is that stronger GATT rules to discipline anti-dumping measures and the use of VER-type instruments are an essential guarantor of open regionalism. The Uruguay Round makes modest steps in this direction.

The conclusion, which is developed in considerably more detail by David Henderson in Chapter 8, is that 'open regionalism' is possible as well as desirable but that progress on regionalism calls for comparable and parallel progress to strengthen multilateral disciplines.

References

Albert, Michel, 1991, *Capitalisme contre capitalisme,* Seuil, Paris.

Balassa, Bela, ed., 1975, *European Economic Integration,* North-Holland, Amsterdam.

Baldwin, Richard, 1989, 'The growth effects of 1992', *Economic Policy,* 4, 9, pp. 247–81.

Barro, Robert and Sala-i-Martin, Xavier, 1992, 'Convergence', *Journal of Political Economy,* 100, pp. 223–51.

Begg, David, et al., 1993, 'Sensible centralisation', in *European Economic Perspectives,* CEPR, London.

Ben-David, David, 1991, 'Equalising exchange: a study of the effects of trade liberalisation', NBER Working Paper 3706.

Bhagwati, Jagdish, 1992, 'Regionalism and multilateralism: an overview', paper presented to World Bank and CEPR conference on 'New Dimensions in Regional Integration', Washington DC, April.

de Grauwe, P., 1993, 'The political economy of monetary union in Europe', CEPR Discussion Paper 842.

Blackhurst, Richard and Henderson, David, 1993, 'Regional integration agreements: world integration and the GATT', in Kym Anderson and Richard Blackhurst, eds,

Regional Integration and the Global Trading System, Harvester Wheatsheaf, Hemel Hempstead.

Eichengreen, Barry, 1991, 'Is Europe an optimum currency area?', NBER Working Paper 3579.

Jacquemin, A. and Sapir, A., 1989, *The European International Market: Trade and Competition*, Oxford University Press, Oxford.

Low, Patrick, 1993, *Trading Free: The GATT and US Trade Policy*, Twentieth Century Fund Press, New York.

Mayes, David G., 1990, 'The external implications of closer European integration', *National Institute Economic Review*, 4, November, pp. 73–85.

Sapir, André, 1993, 'Regionalism and the new theory of international trade: do the bells toll for the GATT? A European outlook', *The World Economy*, 16, 4, July, pp. 423–38.

Wolf, Martin, 1994, 'Towards an integrated Europe', in *The Resistible Appeal of Fortress Europe*, published by the Trade Policy Unit of the Centre for Policy Studies, London with the American Enterprise Institute for Public Policy Research.

Woolcock, S. et al., 1993, *Study on Regional Integration*, OECD TD/TC(93) 15, December.

2 THE PRINCIPLES AND PRACTICE OF REGIONAL ECONOMIC INTEGRATION

Alasdair Smith*

1 Introduction

In this chapter, I consider what we can learn from the study of economic integration about the possible impact of regional integration agreements on the global economy. The study of economic integration is in part conceptual and theoretical; however, like the broader study of international trade, it is in the end the study of the real world, and the theory is suggestive rather than conclusive. I therefore devote a considerable proportion of the chapter to asking what we can learn from existing experience of economic integration, of which the European Community is the most important exemplar.

I start with the basic concepts of customs union theory and their implications, but then consider why the analysis of economic integration has moved beyond these classic ideas into the realms of imperfect competition. I pick up a question to which I return later in the discussion: the implications of economic integration between countries at different levels of development. Here recent literature on trade and growth and on economic geography has started at least to ask some important questions, even if not yet to supply the answers.

The discussion of trade diversion and of external trade creation opens up the question of how harmful the effects of a regional integration agreement are on the rest of the world: here theory is not of much help and the example of the EC is open to more than one interpretation. There is no doubt that there are problems with the EC as a trade policy-maker, and these may be generic problems with regional integration agreements in the global system. The EC's slowness to move on trade policy issues may have contributed to its somewhat protectionist reputation, but neither this nor the still more notorious Common Agricultural Policy justifies a conclusion that the formation of regional integration agreements is protectionist *per se*. There are very clear dangers, but there are also disciplines.

* I am grateful for the comments of project participants and of David Henderson on an earlier version. Parts of section 2 of the paper draw on Smith (1992).

2 The economics of integration

2.1 Trade creation and trade diversion

The traditional analytical basis for the measurement of the effects of economic integration is provided by the concepts of trade creation and trade diversion, developed by Jacob Viner. When trade barriers are reduced between partner countries, trade between them will increase; 'trade diversion' refers to the replacement of trade with other countries by trade with partners, while 'trade creation' refers to trade replacing home production or associated with increased consumption. There can also be 'external trade creation' if the integration process leads to a reduction in trade barriers with the rest of the world.

Trade creation increases national economic welfare, as higher-cost local production is replaced by lower-cost partner imports; trade diversion reduces welfare, as lower-cost imports (subject to tariffs) from third countries are replaced by higher-cost (but tariff-free) partner imports. To particular interest groups, however, trade diversion, offering protected markets in partner countries, may be more attractive than the loss of home market implied by trade creation.

2.2 Trade creation and trade diversion in the European Community

In the case of the European Community, even a glance at changes in trade flows suggests that much of the growth of intra-EC trade in manufactures since 1956 derives from trade creation, since the growth of intra-EC trade in manufactures has been accompanied by rapid growth in external trade. The notable exception is agricultural trade, where there is much trade diversion.

More careful accounting is needed, however, as it is not appropriate to compare the 1956 trade pattern with the 1990 trade pattern and attribute all changes between the two dates to the effects of European integration. Rather, what has to be done is to isolate out the effects of integration from all the other effects associated with the passing of time: the natural development of trade flows, the growth of income, global trade liberalization and happenstance. Mayes (1978) provides a useful survey both of methodology and of the results of European integration, while the more recent survey of Winters (1987) focuses on the narrower issue of the effects of UK accession to the Community on trade in manufactures. The studies which these works examine employ a wide range of methods, differing considerably in the degree of sophistication with which the non-integration effects are filtered out of the calculation, and producing a wide range of numerical estimates of the effects of integration. However, almost all of the estimates surveyed by Mayes suggest that the formation of the European Economic Community generated substantial trade creation and much less trade diversion.

2.3 The nature of intra-EC trade

The traditional study of trade creation and trade diversion used a model in which markets were treated as perfectly competitive, so that price reflected marginal cost. Over the past fifteen years much analysis of international trade has moved away from that assumption. One motivating force for the move was the realization that real-world trade patterns are seriously incompatible with the predictions of the perfectly competitive model. The prevalence of intra-industry trade among developed countries, trade which is hard to explain in terms of the standard textbook treatment of comparative advantage, has been a major spur to analytical development.

Some intra-industry trade is purely a statistical phenomenon, as the collectors of statistics allocate to the same category goods that are in reality quite different: the finer the goods classification used to report trade flows, the lower the proportion of intra-industry trade. But even at the finest classifications, there is still much intra-industry trade. The most plausible explanation of intra-industry trade is the coexistence of product differentiation and economies of scale. Consumers perceive differences and have preferences between different brands of goods; and no one producer can satisfy the full range of varieties because of the cost disadvantages of attempting to do so. The study by Balassa and Bauwens (1988) of intra-European trade flows in manufactured goods confirms that product differentiation is a significant influence on intra-industry trade. There is more intra-industry trade in industries where there seems to be a higher degree of product differentiation.

Product differentiation implies imperfect competition, as each producer has market power in its individual varieties. Intra-industry trade is not the only feature of trade patterns that suggests that imperfect competition matters. Much of world trade is in the products of oligopolistic industries in which a few firms have large market shares; obvious examples include the car, chemicals, consumer electronics and steel industries. In concentrated markets, dominant firms must have a considerable degree of market power, even ignoring product differentiation. The increasing importance of multinational corporations is another indication that imperfect competition has to be considered, for a key element in the explanation of the existence of such firms is that they have firm-specific advantages to bring to their hosts, and firm-specific advantages suggest market power.

These facts imply that the traditional theory of customs unions, based on the concepts of trade creation and trade diversion, and mirroring the traditional approach to the study of trade policy, is not a satisfactory approach to the analysis of the effects of economic integration in the modern world. It is often said that the traditional theory is 'static' and that we need also to consider 'dynamic' effects; but 'dynamic' is an imprecise term. It is better to say that when we are considering industries in which product differentiation, imperfect competition, economies of scale and externalities matter, these features of the market should be incorporated into our analysis of the economics of integration.

2.4 Integration with returns to scale and imperfect competition

An early contribution to the incorporation of economies of scale into the study of economic integration is Corden (1972). Corden analysed the effects of the integration of the market for a homogeneous good in which each country has at most a single producer before integration and of which supplies are available from the rest of the world at a given price. The analysis is confined to cases where it is possible to assume that price is determined by the world market price plus transport cost and tariff. This analysis identifies new possible effects of integration: cost reduction, as a firm previously confined to its home market expands to supply the partner market also, and trade suppression as imports are replaced by home production which has become economic as a result of integration. Corden's approach, although based on strong simplifying assumptions, provided the basis for the studies of North American integration by Wonnacott and Wonnacott (1967) and of European integration by Williamson (1971).

A different approach was taken by Owen (1983). The core of his analysis is a somewhat informal argument that integration will make efficient firms more willing to invest and drive out the inefficient by increasing the size of the market wrested from them. Owen finds evidence for his hypothesis in the development of several major European industries and suggests, for example, that the gains from Italian exports of washing machines to Germany, Britain and France were of the order of 54 per cent of the value of the trade, or 16 per cent of the value of Italian production. These are larger numbers than would typically be found in a study of the gains from trade that ignored economies of scale.

Smith and Venables (1988) offer an approach that is more general than Corden's and more formal than Owen's. Firms are assumed to have economies of scale and to sell differentiated products. The model is used to analyse the effects of two interpretations of the intra-EC non-tariff-barrier reduction implied by the EC's 1992 single market programme. One is a simple reduction in the costs of intra-EC trade, while the second couples the trade cost reduction with an assumption that the EC becomes a single market in the sense that firms will be unable to set different prices in different national markets; and the size of the results obtained depends not only on the policy assumption made. The effect of the first policy is to generate an increase in intra-EC trade, as trade costs, and therefore prices, fall. There is a further price-lowering effect from increased competition, and this also lowers profits. If firms exit the industry in response to the lower profits, the reduction in consumer prices is moderated, but there are still positive consumer gains. The welfare gains are greatest in those industries with the most economies of scale and with much intra-EC trade. As Smith and Venables do not explicitly model external trade barriers, the welfare effect cannot be divided into trade creation, trade diversion and other effects. Since sales patterns in virtually all goods display substantial home-country bias, with firms having much larger shares of their home markets than of other European markets, the alternative policy variant implies a shift to a more competitive market environment, and in this case Smith and Venables find in the more concentrated industries welfare gains that are several times larger than those associated with the first policy variant.

This second variant is not a policy change in the normal sense, but a policy change accompanied by an assumed, but essentially unexplained, change in firms' behaviour. There seems to be considerable variation in prices across national markets in Europe, but the basis of this variation is not well understood, and it is therefore not obvious that the single market programme will remove whatever gives rise to the variation. If intermediaries are prevented by differences in national regulation from buying goods in markets where prices are low in order to sell them in markets where prices are high, then the single market will make a difference, by removing this barrier to convergence of prices. On the other hand, in so far as the price variation is the consequence of different national currencies limiting cross-border competition, the additional gains of the second policy variant may not be available until European monetary union is achieved. These gains are therefore best thought of as gains that would result *if* the single market programme were to have a substantial effect on market structure as well as on trade costs, rather than as gains that will necessarily flow from the programme. However, some empirical support for this approach is provided by Sleuwaegen and Yamawaki (1988), who found that 'EC-wide concentration rather than national market concentration is becoming important in determining the national price-cost margin in industries where the market is geographically integrated and the importance of intra-Community trade has been increasing' (p. 1472).

Norman (1989) has extended the Smith-Venables analysis to EFTA countries and found related results. Because home firms are not so dominant in many sectors in small EFTA countries, the pro-competitive effect of market integration is not so strong as in the Smith-Venables analysis of the EC. This is a point to bear in mind in thinking about the extension of trading 'blocs' to include smaller peripheral economies.

The work of Smith and Venables focuses on the pro-competitive effects of trade liberalization and suggests that such effects can be quantitatively very important, especially as the trade policy agenda (at least within regional groupings) broadens to include regulation, competition policy and non-tariff barriers.

2.5 Trade, growth and geography

Recent years have seen a resurgence of interest in the study of economic growth. The growth theory of the 1960s focused on the role of saving and capital accumulation, using models with constant returns to scale. In such models, the principle of diminishing returns to capital implies that the per capita growth rate of the economy must converge to the rate of technical progress and no explanation is offered of the different per capita growth performance of different countries. More recent work has attempted to provide economic explanations for the sources of economic growth. One approach (Romer, 1986; Lucas, 1988) has centred on the idea that the accumulation of physical or human capital gives rise to 'spillover' effects, while the approach of Grossman and Helpman (1991) centres on R&D, which they treat as a normal economic activity into which there is free entry. Without spillover effects, entry into R&D drives down the rate of return and pushes the economy into a steady state without per capita output growth, in a manner analogous to the role of capital in the traditional growth model. But if R&D contributes to the stock of generally available knowledge capital, a public good, as well as to the development of privately appropriable blueprints for new projects, then the economy becomes capable of sustaining a permanent growth of per capita income, with the growth rate determined by saving behaviour. When knowledge spillovers are confined within national boundaries, a country's pattern of specialization is one in which history may matter – a country with a head start in technology may maintain that lead.

Crafts (1992) suggests that the empirical evidence points to a modest role for such spillovers, and not one that would give rise to self-sustaining growth in output per worker. He finds evidence that capital accumulation does indeed play a more important role in explaining growth than it is given in the traditional Solow model of economic growth. Although he finds support for the hypothesis that there is upward 'convergence' between the income levels of poorer countries and those of richer countries, the experience of growth within the OECD after 1945 was much more variable than models of convergence would lead one to expect, suggesting that their predictive power is quite low.

Much of the experience of economic growth remains to be explained by other factors, including the differential prevalence of rent-seeking behaviour and differences in national industrial relations systems.

The relevance of this to economic integration is that it raises the question whether the closeness of economic relations between countries may be an important determinant of economic convergence. Convergence in the neoclassical growth model is determined by the dynamics of capital accumulation with diminishing returns; but the possibility of spillover effects being transmitted through trade in goods, or through labour or capital mobility, suggests that other channels may be important too. Grossman and Helpman identify several channels through which R&D may be affected by international trade: trade may impede economic growth if a country's expanding export sector draws human capital away from R&D; international diffusion of knowledge will tend to raise growth, and trade may facilitate that diffusion; but intense competition with large or advanced countries may depress the national R&D effort.

On the basis of the links between trade and growth, Baldwin (1989) argues that the Smith-Venables approach to the measurement of the gains from European economic integration is too conservative. Increased output will, he argues, generate additional saving and investment which will contribute further to output growth. With increasing returns to scale or with effects feeding through R&D, there could result a permanent increase, not in income, but in the growth rate of income. Baldwin suggests that these effects might double the estimates of the welfare effects of economic integration as well as adding significantly to the growth rate of income. Both his theory and his numerical estimates are speculative, even by the standards of the trade; but at the very least they serve to make the point that there is still much to explore about the 'dynamic' effects of trade liberalization.

The extent of convergence and the impact of regional integration on convergence are in the end empirical matters, since theoretical investigation is necessarily inconclusive. Convergence among industrial countries has speeded up in the period since 1950 as international trade liberalization has proceeded (indeed, much of the divergence between US growth and growth in the rest of the world took place during the preceding forty years of increasing protectionism), to the benefit of the trade liberalizers (such as Western Europe) rather than the protectionists (such as Latin America). One interesting recent piece of research casts light on the possible effects of European economic integration on regional disparities. Ben-David (1993) finds that the dispersion of income in the six original members of the Community was large and persistent before the Second World War but decreased with postwar trade liberalization; also that the decrease in the dispersion seems closely linked to the growth of intra-EC trade, with convergence becoming eventually as rapid as that between states in the USA. On the other hand, income dispersion among a group of countries that experienced limited trade liberalization, but without the complete elimination of tariff barriers that occurred in the EC, showed no tendency to diminish. This result is not unlike that of Barro and Sala-i-Martin (1991, 1992), who found stronger evidence of convergence among the states of the United States than among separate countries. These observations seem both to confirm the role of trade liberalization in convergence and to suggest that the thoroughgoing liberalization implied by a true common market may be more effective.

Governments often seem to take it as self-evident that special efforts should be made to attain or maintain competitiveness in high-technology sectors. Can this concern be justified? The simplest argument in its favour is that the countries and the regions which specialize in the production of such high-technology products are better off than those that produce more traditional products: California is richer than Pennsylvania, Japan than China. But this simplistic argument begs the question of what is cause and what is effect. Skilled and highly educated labour commands much higher rewards in the world market than unskilled labour, and it is used in high-technology industries; but the high wage cost of such labour is a signal of its high opportunity cost. The artificial fostering of high-technology development itself seems unlikely to create a self-sustaining high-wage economy.

In our earlier discussion of imperfect competition, we saw the relevance of economies of scale internal to firms. There may also be scale effects external to firms but internal to industries, as firms benefit from being part of a larger industry. It is the existence of such spillover effects which raises the possibility of self-sustaining development in which 'history matters', and in which government policy can affect the rate of growth. However, even then we need to be cautious about confusing economic growth with economic welfare: areas of slower growth can reap the benefits of high-technology production elsewhere as the prices of high-technology products fall.

Perhaps the most persuasive single piece of evidence of the importance of external economies is the tendency of production to concentrate in particular locations, the focus of the recent literature on 'economic geography'. The concentration of the American microelectronics industry in one particular part of California and one particular part of Massachusetts strongly suggests that there are gains to producers from proximity to other producers in the same or related lines of business. This suggests that spillovers are localized and that there are possibilities for the 'creation of comparative advantage'. More generally, Krugman (1991a) draws attention to the fact that highly-skilled American labour is concentrated in California and the north-eastern seaboard, even though the American education system is of reasonably uniform quality throughout the country and labour is both free to move and, by European standards, remarkably willing to move throughout the whole United States. Such local spillover effects seem to provide a more promising basis for interventionist policy than the 'strategic trade policy' argument associated with Brander and Spencer, which turns out to be very sensitive to the details of how markets are assumed to function, details that it seems most unlikely governments will know; moreover, attempts to assess the empirical significance of the argument have generally suggested that the effects are small (Krugman and Smith, 1994).

The concerns of 'economic geography' need to be incorporated in the analysis of the effects of integration. Krugman and Venables (1990) offer a simple model in which economic integration may narrow or widen the gap between central and peripheral regions: a reduction in transport costs increases trade, but competitiveness may be influenced more by considerations of market access (if some transport costs remain) which favour the core, than by comparative cost which favours the periphery. Krugman's (1991a) comparison of the distribution of industry in the United States and in Western Europe raises the possibility that the deepening of European integration will give rise to much more polarization in the location of economic activity in Europe.

2.6 Trade and income distribution

Increasing attention is being given to the possible impact of trade on income distribution. The classic theorem of Stolper and Samuelson suggests a strong effect of trade on factor prices. The 1970s and 1980s have seen rapid growth of international trade and in the United Kingdom and United States a substantial widening of income differentials within the labour force. Throughout Western Europe there has been a considerable increase in unemployment, which can be interpreted as an alternative manifestation of labour market pressure on unskilled workers. With such a clear conjunction of theoretical prediction and empirical outcome, it is natural that competition with the abundant unskilled labour of the developing countries is identified by many as the cause of the relative (and, in the US, absolute) decline in the income of unskilled workers in developed countries. Closer analysis raises doubts about the causal links, and the case for scepticism is well put by Krugman and Lawrence (1993). The extent of the displacement of unskilled employment in the United States by trade seems simply too small to explain what has happened to wages.

However, Wood (1994) argues for a more careful accounting still to allow for the heterogeneity of products. Goods produced in developed countries are not the same as those imported from developing countries, even if statistics allocate them to the same 'industry'. This can imply a much larger impact of trade on the employment and wages of unskilled workers in developed countries than would be deduced simply from the volume of trade. The point is easily illustrated by example. Statistics of trade between the EC and Central and Eastern Europe show a high degree of intra-industry trade, for example in textiles, clothing and footwear. If Polish exports of clothing and shoes to Italy are matched by a more or less equal flow of clothing and shoes from Italy to Poland, the apparent effects in factor markets will be negligible. If, however, the reality concealed by the statistics is that high-quality goods embodying the labour of highly skilled designers and marketers are flowing in one direction, while the goods flowing in the other direction are the products of low-skilled mass-producers, the impact on factor markets may not be negligible: there will be in Italy an increase in the demand for skilled workers and a reduction in the demand for the unskilled.

Again narrowing the focus to issues of economic integration, the question becomes one of the relation between the heterogeneity of countries within a regional integration arrangement and the stresses to which the arrangement will be subjected by inequalities. Surely a main reason for the comparative success of EC integration is the fact that integration between economies at approximately similar levels of development does not have a large impact on income distribution.

2.7 The lessons of economic integration

What can we learn from this brief survey of the analysis of economic integration? Should it lead us to be pessimistic or optimistic about the effects of the development of regional integration agreements?

First, we should note the lessons of the traditional theory, that integration is more beneficial the more trade it creates and more harmful the more trade it diverts. In the literature there are speculations about the circumstances most favourable to each of these two phenomena: for example, economic similarity and geographical proximity might seem conducive to trade creation. Bhagwati (1992), however, is surely right to downplay this approach as being unduly and unnecessarily speculative: what really matters is that trade diversion is related to the level of external trade barriers, so the simple message is that we should be wary of preferential trade arrangements that leave high external barriers in place, or worse still lead to the erection of such barriers.

The implications of intra-industry trade for economic integration are clearly of great importance. First, as we have seen above, it brings issues of competition and market structure to the forefront of attention (though the importance of these factors will vary from sector to sector and may be less in the case of the incorporation of smaller peripheral countries into a trading group than among the core of the group formed by larger countries). Secondly, the political problems of adjustment to the growth of intra-industry trade are much less than those associated with 'comparative advantage' trade because producer groups in each sector gain from export opportunities as well as suffering from import competition.

The study of the EC's single market programme raises another question about the nature of economic integration. Much of the progress to be made in the liberalization of trade may have to do with the harmonization of regulation and the removal of non-tariff barriers, but these are forms of trade liberalization that the multilateral GATT/OECD system has not tackled to any great extent. That such non-tariff issues are being tackled at the regional level (in NAFTA as well as the EC) may suggest that this is the more appropriate level on which to make progress.

The implications of recent work on trade and growth for the study of economic integration are potentially important but highly uncertain, as we still understand so little about the fundamental forces underlying economic growth. One suggestion, however, is that regional trade liberalization within integration agreements might be as effective as or more effective than global liberalization in promoting convergence. To be specific: European convergence might be fostered as much by the incorporation of Eastern Europe in the European Economic Area as by its adherence to a revitalized GATT. The most important aspect of the issue may be the question of which kind of integration embodies the clearer commitment to open markets.

3 Regional blocs as global actors

The different strands of analysis considered in the previous section have each suggested in different ways that the key question may be whether regional blocs will push policy in a more protectionist direction. Will the blocs bring together protectionist interest groups and enable them to act together in a more effective fashion? Will intra-bloc liberalization create pressure for external protection? Will regional blocs be effective participants in a multilateral system? Is it possible to have 'open regionalism', where a group of countries agree on a trade liberalization which they then apply to all countries, in or out of the group?

There is a small amount of formal analysis relevant to these issues: for example Kennan and Riezman (1988) investigate the impact of the size of a country on its aggression as a trade policy-maker, but this is some distance away from producing results applicable to real-world blocs. Krugman (1991b) considers explicitly the effects of regional blocs on global protection, and his model is extended by Bond (1992) to allow asymmetric growth of regional integration agreements and asymmetric patterns of inter-bloc trade. The setting is one in which there is free trade within a bloc, and each bloc sets optimal tariffs with respect to the rest of the world, taking others' tariffs as given. Bond finds that whether welfare grows or falls as bloc size increases depends on the trade pattern, and that there will be a tendency for blocs to increase their size relative to other blocs in order to gain market power.

This kind of formal analysis is of interest, but is of limited value in interpreting and predicting the behaviour of real-world institutions which are driven by political forces that are unlikely to be well represented by a model of national welfare optimization. Nor has the formal analysis of political economy reached a stage where it has useful results to offer us. It seems more productive to look for guidance from real-world experience of the political economy of protection in trading blocs. Let us then turn to the case of the EC and ask what we can learn from it.

3.1 Protectionist effects of European integration

The simplest ground for fearing that regional integration will have a protectionist effect is the analysis of trade diversion, which implies an automatically negative effect on the rest of the world from the formation of a bloc, even if the bloc does not have higher external trade barriers on average than did its constituent members. The Common Agricultural Policy of the EC is a paradigmatic example of trade diversion and is the origin of much of the rest of the world's fears about the protectionism of the EC. The CAP is harmful to European consumers as well as non-EC farmers, and it is not particularly beneficial for many EC farmers. In spite of its economic costs and its budgetary costs, the CAP has proved remarkably resilient: it was the major obstacle to the completion of the Uruguay Round of trade negotiations in GATT, and it is the single biggest obstacle to the freeing of trade between the EC and Eastern Europe. Not only does the EC start off from a point that is unacceptable to its trading partners, it has (at least partly because of the internal politics of the Community's mode of negotiating) been very inflexible. And this is a *Common* Agricultural Policy: the first genuinely EC-wide economic policy.

It is not necessarily the case that a bad EC policy is the result of European integration. Many non-EC countries in Europe, such as Austria, Switzerland and Norway, have agricultural policies that are more irrational and costly than the CAP. The fact that we see a trading bloc acting in a protectionist fashion does not mean that blocs *per se* are protectionist (apart from their trade-diverting effect). However, the political economy of protection gives reasons to suppose that there may be some systematic tendency for integration to have protectionist tendencies: for the standard reason that producer lobbies are stronger than consumer lobbies, it is easier for a liberal state to offend its consumer lobby and agree a protectionist common policy than for a protectionist state to offend its producer lobby by agreeing a liberal common policy. The CAP probably *is* worse than the policies that a non-integrated Western Europe would have adopted.

A further point about political economy arises from the behaviour of the EC as part of the GATT system. Though the member states, not the EC itself, are the signatories of GATT, the Community negotiates as a single entity. The division of responsibility between Council and Commission makes the EC a difficult body to negotiate with. The EC's negotiators come to Geneva with a negotiating position that has already been hammered out by intra-EC negotiation, and they may therefore be reluctant to make concessions that will upset the intra-EC agreement. Thus the EC tends to be inflexible in negotiation. This problem was particularly clear in the Uruguay Round negotiations on agriculture, where the inflexibility of the EC's position was surely linked to the difficulty of achieving an intra-EC consensus on the desired direction of reform. Contrast the position of the US administration, which is given 'fast-track' negotiating authority by the legislature to get the best deal it can, and then submit it for ratification or rejection as a whole.

A further problem may arise from the additional adjustment pressures created by intra-bloc liberalization. Bhagwati (1992) points out that much of the protectionist threat from blocs arises from the possibility that trade creation and increased competition within the bloc creates a demand for increased protection from extra-bloc competition, and that selective and contingent protection, such as anti-dumping action, responds to such demand. Indeed, the EC has been a very active user of anti-dumping and of VERs against Japan, South-East Asian NIEs, other less-developed countries and East European countries. From time to time, the EC has argued strongly for the legalization of the discrimination that characterizes unofficial trade policies like VERs but is not permitted in GATT-sanctioned safeguard action.

3.2 Liberalizing effects of European integration

GATT rules on the permitted tariff levels of a customs union are intended to ensure that the formation of a union does not lead to increased external protection. The EC's single market process is interesting in this respect precisely because, being concerned with non-tariff barriers, it is not regulated by the GATT provision. There is an important aspect of the single market process that is peculiar to the reduction of non-tariff regulatory barriers to trade: the emphasis on mutual recognition of standards as the principal means of removing border barriers has in itself a strongly deregulatory effect, as the least demanding national standard will tend to become the European standard. Whether common standards are arrived at by negotiation or by regulatory competition, there is an effect on external as well as internal suppliers. As the German market is opened to French beer, it is opened also to American beer (because the French market is already open to American beer). When European car manufacturers are required to obtain only one set of certifications to give their products access to the whole EC market, so Japanese manufacturers will enjoy the same benefit.

A further important aspect of the EC's single market programme is that it is supposed to require a more rule-based regime. Though it is, of course, an open question to what extent this stated objective will be met in practice, there should be some such effect. Single states can introduce important policies in very informal ways: by bureaucratic actions or by informal understandings. When, however, policy-making involves negotiations between states within a bloc, policy almost necessarily becomes more rule-based. In the trade policy context, given the scope for covert protectionism through informal action, a move towards a more rule-based regime is likely to be a move towards less protectionism. Indeed, governments embrace rule-based regimes precisely in order to give themselves more ability to resist particular interest groups and pursue the 'general' interest. In this respect the EC's position compares favourably with that of the United States, whose 'aggressive bilateralism' is founded on a lack of faith in the GATT system of rules. Whatever merits there are in the different positions, it is surely the case that the USA's embrace of bilateralism makes its policy-making more subject to interest-group pressures.

3.3 Rhetoric and reality in trade policy-making

One of the most sensitive implications of the European single market programme is that if there is to be a truly single market, without any impediments to intra-EC trade, so that all goods from third countries will circulate freely inside the EC on equal terms, regardless of the point at which they enter, as Articles 9 and 10 of the Treaty of Rome actually lay down, then national trade policies must either fade away or be replaced by EC-wide policies. There is obvious political pressure not simply to let existing external protection be eroded away by the effects of the internal market programme. Equally, however, there are considerable difficulties in arriving at a common policy; difficulties which are illustrated below by the development of EC trade policy towards cars.

When the EC has sought to replace national trade restrictions with EC-wide barriers, the United States has made quite loud noises about the unacceptability of the EC's taking particular actions. Quite evidently, the United States has had a deliberate policy of objecting to EC trade policy actions as if they were new restrictions, even when the action consisted of the replacement of national restrictions with an EC-wide restriction of similar effect. (This is a defensible line for the United States to take: it is in its interests to take every possible opportunity to reduce protection; and, of course, it has to worry about the trade-diverting effects of even an unchanged level of average protection.) Another clear example is the EC's directive on public procurement which, in the process of opening up intra-EC procurement, has had to codify the extent of discrimination against non-EC suppliers. The United States has, quite naturally and properly, objected to the discrimination; but its objections create an impression that the EC has undertaken a restrictive measure, rather than replacing a set of national measures with an EC measure that is probably less protectionist towards non-EC suppliers than the replaced national measures. The very existence of the protests creates an impression that is almost certainly unjustified. It is thus important to distinguish between rhetoric and reality in trade policy-making, as the rhetoric may give a misleading impression of how protectionist policy really is.

3.4 EC trade policy on Japanese cars

The European car market provides a fascinating and instructive case study of European Community trade policy-making, discussed in detail by Smith and Venables (1990). As we have seen, the elimination in the single market process of non-tariff barriers has major implications for external trade policy when different countries have different external policies; as a result, the single market programme faces major political and economic difficulties as it confronts the implications for the car market. There is the further issue of how EC trade policy should respond to 'transplants' arising from Japanese direct investment in Europe. There was a long period of intra-EC negotiation preceding the negotiation with the Japanese to produce the 1991 'consensus', which managed to create an EC-wide VER to last until 2000, to maintain some national restraints on Japanese car sales and to fudge the treatment of 'transplant' production.

The example of the car market nicely displays the general themes discussed earlier in this section: the naturally liberalizing and market-opening effects of the single market process; the ponderous decision-making procedures within the EC; the misleading impression in some quarters that the replacement of national trade policies by an EC-wide policy of broadly equivalent effect is evidence of 'fortress Europe'; and the generation of some undoubted pressure for external protection by the increased internal competition. Perhaps the key issue, however, is exposed by the 'transplant' problem. National trade policies, many of doubtful legality and lacking in transparency, are being replaced by a negotiated agreement at least some of whose provisions are open. There is, further, a commitment to full liberalization by the end of 1999. However, the issues raised by the transplant problem suggest a very real possibility that the EC will be pressured into quite serious departures from its most fundamental rules concerning free movement of EC-produced goods. I argued above that a move towards regional integration agreements, especially where the bloc becomes involved in internal deregulation as well as in strict trade policy issues, should be a liberalizing move. But this argument may be much weakened if we experience blocs being as willing to embrace 'grey area' protection as individual states.

3.5 European protection in the longer run

The discussion of the principles of economic integration has exposed the issue of regional inequality within a bloc as a central concern. As in the case of the impact of blocs on protection, theory in itself is inconclusive and we have to turn to real-world examples for elucidation if not for definitive answers. In the case of the EC, the most interesting questions are raised by the prospect of increased trade with Central and Eastern Europe (CEE), a closer formal association between the CEE countries and the EC, and eventual CEE membership of an enlarged

European Union. The future intra-European trade pattern will be an important influence on trade relations between the wider Europe and the rest of the world.

The path of economic change in Central and Eastern Europe is by no means predictable, and the effects on international trade are therefore also unpredictable. Rollo and Smith (1993) discuss the difficulties in present EC-CEE economic relations arising from the rapid growth of trade in products such as food, textiles, and steel about which the EC is 'sensitive'. Hamilton and Winters (1992) suggest that the rapid growth of EC-CEE trade should continue as the CEE countries become reintegrated into European and world markets, and also provide evidence to support the proposition that the CEE countries, being relatively well endowed with human resources, should expect to have comparative advantage in fairly advanced sectors. West-East trade in Europe might then be more like West-West trade than like North-South trade in the global economy.

If indeed East-West trade in Europe is of an intra-industry character, there might be less protectionist pressure within the EC, for the two reasons discussed above: producer groups in particular sectors may see export opportunities as well as import competition; and there may be less pressure in the labour market on unskilled workers than there would be if the CEE countries concentrated heavily on exports of products of low-wage labour. Even on the most optimistic scenario, however, there will be some sectoral pressures and some pressures on unskilled labour in Western Europe. There are subsidiary concerns raised by the study of trade and growth and of economic geography: will the linking of an advanced West with a backward East speed the convergence of the East towards the West? What will be the respective roles of (adequately supplied) human capital and (very scarce) physical capital in that convergence? Will integration tend to cluster activities in a small number of regions, and will these regions be in the prosperous West? We do not have answers to these questions – the theory cannot provide them, and the real-world experiment is only beginning. That experiment will be of interest not only in Europe itself, but also in respect of its wider lessons for the effects of integration among heterogeneous countries.

References

Balassa, Bela and Bauwens, Luc, 1988, 'The determinants of intra-European trade in manufactured goods', *European Economic Review,* 32, pp. 1421–37.

Baldwin, Richard, 1989, 'The growth effects of 1992', *Economic Policy,* 9, pp. 247–81.

Barro, Robert and Sala-i-Martin, Xavier, 1991, 'Convergence across states and regions', *Brookings Papers on Economic Activity,* pp. 107–58.

Barro, Robert and Sala-i-Martin, Xavier, 1992, 'Convergence', *Journal of Political Economy,* 100, pp. 223–51.

Ben-David, David, 1993, 'Equalizing exchange: trade liberalization and income convergence', *Quarterly Journal of Economics,* 108, pp. 653–79.

Bhagwati, Jagdish, 1992, 'Regionalism and multilateralism', *The World Economy*, 15, pp. 535–55.

Bond, Eric, 1992, 'Optimality and stability of regional trading "blocs"', typescript, Penn State University.

Corden, W. Max, 1972, 'Economies of scale and customs union theory', *Journal of Political Economy*, 80, pp. 465–75.

Crafts, Nicholas, 1992, 'Productivity growth reconsidered', *Economic Policy*, 15, pp. 387–426.

Grossman, Gene and Helpman, Elhanan, 1991, *Innovation and Growth in the Global Economy*, MIT Press, Cambridge, MA.

Hamilton, Carl and Winters, L. Alan, 1992, 'Opening up international trade in Eastern Europe', *Economic Policy*, 14, pp. 77–116.

Kennan, John and Riezman, Raymond, 1988, 'Do big countries win tariff wars?', *International Economic Review*, 29, pp. 81–5.

Krugman, Paul, 1991a, *Geography and Trade*, MIT Press, Cambridge, MA.

Krugman, Paul, 1991b, 'Is bilateralism bad?', in Elhanan Helpman and Assaf Razin, eds, *International Trade and Trade Policy*, MIT Press, Cambridge, MA.

Krugman, Paul and Lawrence, Robert Z., 1993, *Trade, Jobs and Wages*, NBER Working Paper 4478.

Krugman, Paul and Smith, Alasdair, eds, 1994, *Empirical Studies of Strategic Trade Policy*, University of Chicago Press for NBER, Chicago.

Krugman, Paul and Venables, Anthony J., 1990, 'Integration and the competitiveness of peripheral industry', in Christopher Bliss and Jorge Braga de Macedo, eds., *Unity with Diversity in the European Economy: the Community's Southern Frontier*, Cambridge University Press for CEPR, Cambridge.

Lucas, Robert E. Jr., 1988, 'On the mechanics of economic development', *Journal of Development Economics*, 22, pp. 3–42.

Mayes, David G., 1978, 'The effects of economic integration on trade', *Journal of Common Market Studies*, 17, pp. 1–25.

Norman, Victor, 1989, 'EFTA and the internal European market', *Economic Policy*, 9, pp. 424–65.

Owen, Nicholas, 1983, *Economies of Scale, Competitiveness and Trade Patterns within the European Community*, Oxford University Press, Oxford.

Rollo, Jim and Smith, Alasdair, 1993, 'The political economy of Eastern European trade with the European Community: why so sensitive?', *Economic Policy*, 16, pp. 139–81.

Romer, Paul M., 1986, 'Increasing returns and long-run growth', *Journal of Political Economy*, 94, pp. 1002–37.

Sleuwaegen, Leo and Yamawaki, Hideki, 1988, 'The formation of the European common market and changes in market structure and performance', *European Economic Review*, 32, pp. 1451–75.

Smith, Alasdair, 1992, 'Measuring the effects of "1992"', in David Dyker, ed., *The European Economy*, Longman, London, pp. 89–99.

Smith, Alasdair and Venables, Anthony J., 1988, 'Completing the internal market in the

European Community: some industry simulations', *European Economic Review*, 32, pp. 1501–25.

Smith, Alasdair and Venables, Anthony J., 1990, 'Automobiles', in Gary Clyde Hufbauer, ed., *Europe 1992: An American Perspective*, Brookings Institution, Washington DC, pp. 119–58.

Williamson, John, 1971, 'Trade and economic growth', in J. Pinder, ed., *The Economics of Europe: What the Common Market Means for Britain*, Charles Knight, London, pp. 19–45.

Winters, Alan L., 1987, 'Britain in Europe: a survey of quantitative trade studies', *Journal of Common Market Studies*, 25, pp. 315–35.

Wonnacott, Ronald J. and Wonnacott, Paul, 1967, *Free Trade Between the US and Canada: The Potential Economic Effects*, Harvard University Press, Cambridge, MA.

Wood, Adrian, 1994, *North-South Trade, Employment and Inequality: Changing Fortunes in a Skill-Driven World*, Oxford University Press, Oxford.

3 THE EC, EUROPEAN INTEGRATION AND THE WORLD TRADING SYSTEM

J.M.C. Rollo*

1 Introduction

The European Community is the one true trading bloc in the world at this moment. Alone among other groupings, such as NAFTA or APEC, it is a set of nation-states with a largely common commercial policy, is a customs union and is moving towards free internal trade in goods and services and free movement of labour and capital. At an international level it acts as one of many aspects of commercial policy. The need to reach intergovernmental agreement within the EC has made it difficult for third countries to reach negotiated settlements with it in multilateral negotiations. (The time taken to reach an agreement in the Uruguay Round of GATT as well as the difficulties at the end of the Tokyo and Kennedy Rounds are examples.) The Community has also formed preferential trade agreements with other countries and groups of countries, notably EFTA, Turkey, the countries of Central Europe, and the African, Caribbean and Pacific countries under the Lomé Convention. This lack of flexibility at multilateral level and preferential trading arrangements with neighbouring countries and states with historical relationships with EC members are perhaps the most obvious features of bloc-like behaviour. The Community's sheer size, however, is also a factor. The difficulty of solving trade disputes with a grouping which represents 20 per cent of world exports (see Table 3.1 below) obviously looms larger than with smaller groupings. Only the United States and Japan begin to have the same preponderance on world markets. Size is also relevant in considering the effect the Community has on its preferential trading partners. Recent trade policy reviews of Sweden and Norway (GATT 1990, 1991) have contrasted rhetorical support for the multilateral system with the high proportion of trade which goes to preferential partners. The point is not just the fact of EC-EFTA trade but also that EFTA was set up as a response to the original EEC. The existence of an effective trade bloc encourages others to form similar combinations. More importantly, as the original trading bloc integrates more successfully

* This paper is based on research undertaken while the author was Director of Economics at the Royal Institute of International Affairs. The opinions expressed are the author's own and should not be taken as an expression of official government policy.

Table 3.1 The new European economy

	Population 1992 (m)	GDP 1992 ($bn)	GDP per cap. 1992 ($)	Total exports 1992 ($bn)	World export market share[a] 1992 (%)
EC					
Belgium	10,025	218.7	21,815	30,850[b]	1.1
Denmark	5,170	142.1	27,485	18,029	0.6
France	57,372	1,324.9	23,093	86,416	3.1
Germany	80,569	1,775.1	22,032	196,357	7.0
Greece	10,300	79.2	7,689	3,420	0.1
Ireland	3,547	48.8	13,758	7,264	0.3
Italy	57,782	1,223.6	21,176	75,226	2.7
Luxembourg	340	10.4	30,588	—[b]	0.0
Netherlands	15,178	320.4	21,110	33,192	1.2
Portugal	9,846	83.9	8,521	4,529	0.2
Spain	34,085	573.7	16,831	18,548	0.7
United Kingdom	57,848	1,040.5	17,987	83,412	3.0
Total	342,062	6,841.3			
EFTAns					
Austria	7,884	184.7	23,427	44,432	1.6
Finland	5,042	109.6	21,737	23,982	0.9
Iceland	260	6.6	25,385	1,528	0.1
Norway	4,286	113.1	26,388	35,103	1.3
Sweden	8,678	245.8	28,324	56,116	2.0
Switzerland	6,905	240.5	34,830	65,531	2.3
Total	33,055	900.3			
Mediterranean					
Cyprus	715	7.1	9,888	1,009	0.0
Malta	360	2.6	7,239	1,390	0.0
Turkey	58,467	114.2	1,954	14,715	0.5
Total	59,542	123.9			
Central Europe					
Czech Republic	10,383	25.3	2,438	12,321[b]	0.4[b]
Hungary	10,202	30.7	3,006	10,705	0.4
Poland	38,365	75.3	1,962	14,046	0.5
Slovakia	5,346	10.2	1,917	Cz[c]	Cz[c]
Total	64,296	141.5			
The Balkans					
Albania	3,338	1.0	285	190	0.0
Bulgaria	8,952	11.9	1,330	2,592	0.1
Romania	22,865	24.9	1,087	4,469	0.2
Slovenia	2,017	12.7	6,318	n.a.	n.a.
Total	37,172	50.5			

Continued

Table 3.1 concluded

	Population 1992 (m)	GDP 1992 ($bn)	GDP per cap. 1992 ($)	Total exports 1992 ($bn)	World export market share[a] 1992 (%)
The FSU				48,836	1.7
Belarus	10,346	30.1	2,912	n.a.	n.a.
Estonia	1,554	4.3	2,765	n.a.	n.a.
Latvia	2,617	5.1	1,941	n.a.	n.a.
Lithuania	3,754	4.9	1,311	n.a.	n.a.
Moldova	4,359	5.5	1,258	n.a.	n.a.
Russia	148,920	397.8	2,671	n.a.	n.a.
Ukraine	51,900	87.0	1,677	n.a.	n.a.
Total	223,450	534.7[d]			
Grand total	759,577	8,592.2[d]			

Sources: OECD, *Main Economic Indicators*, December 1993; OECD, *Monthly Statistics of Foreign Trade*, December 1993; IMF International Financial Statistics, December 1993; IMF Direction of Trade Statistics, 1993 Yearbook; EBRD, *Current Economic Issues*, July 1993; *World Bank Atlas*, 1994.
Notes:
[a]World exports excludes intra-EC trade.
[b]Belgium and Luxembourg trade figures are combined.
[c]Czech and Slovak trade figures combined.
[d]1991 GNP figures; 1992 GNP will be significantly lower.

it encourages both defections from and intensification of relations with other trading blocs. Thus Britain, Ireland, Denmark and Portugal defected from EFTA to the EC; the European Economic Area (EEA) offered the remaining EFTAns more intense relationships with the EC after the Single European Act ushered in a new era of intra-EC integration; and Austria, Finland, Norway and Sweden will consult their electorates on membership of the European Union during 1994.

The fall of the Berlin Wall and the opening up of Central Europe and the Balkans in 1989 led to a new opportunity for further European integration, a trend intensified by the collapse of the Soviet Union in 1991. By the end of 1993 the European Community had signed first trade agreements and then full association agreements with the four Central European and two of the Balkan countries, and Slovenia and the Baltic states in the former Soviet Union (FSU) are likely to be offered association agreements in the future. Russia, Ukraine and Belarus are beginning to negotiate partnership and cooperation agreements (PCAs) in 1994. The conclusion of the Copenhagen European summit of June 1993 offered the Central European and Balkan associates (the Czech Republic, Hungary, Poland and Slovakia – sometimes known as the Visegrad Four – plus Bulgaria and Romania) the prospect of eventual EU membership. It is difficult to see how this offer could be withheld from any other East European states which sign association agreements. Hungary and Poland lodged applications for full membership of the EU in April 1994. The Czech Republic and Slovakia may follow in 1995 or 1996.

Beyond Eastern Europe there are three Mediterranean countries with association agreements with the EU – Turkey, Cyprus and Malta – which also wish to become full members. The Turkish association agreement, signed in 1968, includes a commitment to a full customs union (promised for 1995), as does the Cypriot agreement. Even if membership is long delayed, therefore, large elements of trade policy in these countries will be subservient to EU policy.

What emerges from this survey is that there are up to thirty-five countries in an area stretching from the Atlantic to the Urals (and beyond), and from the Arctic Circle to the northern Mediterranean littoral, which will have more or less intensive, preferential, commercial and political relations with the European Community and the European Union (which includes the second pillar of common foreign and security policy and the third pillar of justice policy cooperation as well as the EC). The purpose of this chapter is, first, to examine the status of these countries, their level of development, their level of integration with the EC and their existing trade and commercial policies; secondly, to examine the nature of existing and potential institutional links with the EC and EU; and thirdly, to discuss the potential impact of the different forms of integration on the rest of the world. The final analytical section will then draw on earlier sections to explore the implications for the behaviour of the EC/EU towards the rest of the world in the WTO and other fora and how the rest of the world might react.

2 The size of the new European economy

The European Community is building (or has built) preferential trade and commercial policy agreements with the countries in Table 3.1. The arrangements follow four main forms:

1   full membership;
2   the European Economic Area (EEA);
3   association agreements;
4   industrial free trade areas (FTAs).

2.1 Enlargement

The Community has undergone two enlargements and is now contemplating a third, with a fourth and fifth already beginning to take shape. Enlargement under current arrangements involves new members in adopting the full *acquis communautaire* – that is, all of the rules and regulations of the European Community and the European Union. In economic terms the *acquis* includes a full common market with internal freedom of movement of goods, services, people and capital; a degree of regulatory integration (minimum standards, home country control, common competition policy); social policy harmonization (the social chapter); the Common Agricultural Policy; the structural and cohesion funds; aid policies and the resulting budgetary obligations; and, since Maastricht, commitment to monetary integration. The immediate candidates for membership are Austria, Finland, Norway and Sweden. If their electorates and legislatures agree (which is by no means certain) they will be members by 1995. Even if these countries reject full membership (as Norway did once before), they are all members of the EEA (see below).

The other countries in the membership stakes fall into two groups – the Central and East Europeans and the Mediterranean group. These two groups also have association agreements (albeit of different types) with the EC and it is these which put them in the membership queue. There is no guarantee, however, that membership will be achieved soon – or, indeed, at all. Turkey, Malta and Cyprus have all lodged applications and the Commission of the EU has given opinions which see reason for delay. Turkey is blocked by Greece; Cyprus in its divided state provides special problems but is actively pushing; and Malta is also pursuing membership, but with as yet no timetable for negotiations let alone a date for joining.

The Visegrad Four (the Czech Republic, Hungary, Poland and Slovakia) had the objective of membership from the beginning of negotiations on the association agreement. They attempted to have eventual membership written into the terms of the association agreement, mainly as a guarantee against the then Soviet Union. The EC was unwilling to give the commitment (as they had done in the Turkey Association Agreement) to eventual membership, but the preamble to the agreements recognized the Central Europeans' aspiration to be members. At the 1993 Copenhagen European summit that recognition was advanced into an offer to consider the Central Europeans and Balkans for membership once the terms of the association agreement were fulfilled. By implication this is the year 2001 for the Visegrad Four. The Central Europeans in particular continue to push for earlier membership. Hungary and Poland lodged an application in 1994, and others will no doubt follow as there is competition among them to be the first to achieve EU membership. It is unlikely, however, that the Community will be willing to take any of them ahead of the others or very soon – not least because of the need to absorb the changes arising from the Maastricht Treaty and the planned accession of the four new EFTA members. The EU will have to consider very carefully how far and how fast its institutional obligations can be extended.

2.2 The European Economic Area

The EEA is a child of the single market programme. The EFTA countries became aware in the late 1980s, when EC growth and the rhetoric of the single market were both at a peak, that increased integration within the EC might lead to trade diversion away from them through lower transaction costs; that EFTA firms were already investing in the EC to take advantage of the single market; that EC investment in EFTA might be directed to other EC countries to take advantage of the new integrated market; and, above all, that EFTA was a small market for the EC while the EC was a giant market for EFTA, and they needed to be part of it. Their response was to ask for access to the single market.

On the EC side the late 1980s were a time of institutional innovation. The Single European Act had established qualified majority voting (QMV) and competition among rules, not unanimity and harmonization, as the way forward; it had also put economic and monetary union (EMU) on the agenda. The Delors Committee considered how EMU might be taken forward. The Maastricht project was under way. At the same time there was an implicit argument about a single *acquis communautaire* and the role of variable geometry in taking forward the European construction. Part of that debate emerged as a question of deepening versus widening. Thus, while the EFTAns were interested in access to the single market, there were those within the Community who wanted to extend the single market as a model for the new Europe and those who wanted to deepen integration among the EC of twelve but not beyond. That complex of motives met in the EEA.

The EEA was negotiated between 1989 and 1991. It built on the existing free trade agreement with EFTA in industrial goods and extended it to fish but not agriculture. It extended the four freedoms to the EFTAns (in goods, service, labour and capital). It also placed obligations on the EFTAns: they had to adopt economic regulation that was consistent with EC norms, notably competition policy. These regulations would be subject to EFTAn courts, except where the *acquis communautaire* itself was involved, when the European Court of Justice (ECJ) would be responsible. The EEA members also made a contribution of 500 million ecus per annum to the Community cohesion funds.

The EEA differs from full membership of the EC in three important operational respects: there is no customs union; agriculture is excluded; and there are no budgetary obligations or benefits (that is, EEA members are not party to the structural funds or aid effort), beyond the contribution to the cohesion funds. Most important of all, however, the members of the EEA, while subject to important parts of the *acquis communautaire* and directly in some instances to the ECJ, had no means of influencing the evolution of the *acquis*. Thus members of the EEA had not chosen to share sovereignty; rather, they had decided to give it up to an outside power.

It is not surprising, therefore, that as the EEA negotiations went on, the implications of this loss of sovereignty became clear. At the same time the Maastricht Treaty was taking shape and the EEA applicants saw the Community about to take another quantum jump in integration without them. Moreover, this inward integration would have important implications for them. Thus, before the EEA negotiations were complete, Austria applied for full membership, shortly followed by Finland, Norway and Sweden. In essence, they decided that there should be no regulation without representation.

The Swiss electorate took the same decision but in the opposite direction, and refused to ratify membership of the EEA. The EEA thus came into operation on 1 January 1994 with Austria, Finland, Iceland, Norway and Sweden as members. Liechtenstein will join as soon as it can dissolve its customs union with Switzerland. The irony is that if the applicants ratify EU membership by 1 January 1995, only Iceland and Liechtenstein (and perhaps Switzerland in the longer term) will remain as members of the EEA. This suggests that whatever the economic benefits of the EEA – and they are manifold – the political costs are high. Notably, it imposes most of the obligations of the EC but, while conferring economic rights on individuals and firms, gives no rights to governments and electorates.

2.3 The association process

There have been two distinct phases of association with the Community. The first was essentially Mediterranean, the second (and very recent) Central and East European. The Mediterranean association process is almost as old as the Community. Turkey, Yugoslavia, Greece, Cyprus and Malta are all beneficiaries. Turkey and Greece were the first associates. Their agreements included eventual customs union with the EC, freedom of movement of labour and a firm promise of membership. They also included financial protocols. The later Mediterranean association agreements also included customs unions and financial protocols but were not so specific about factor movements or EC membership. Since these agreements were signed, of course, Greece has become a full EC member (as have Spain and Portugal without the benefit of association) and Yugoslavia has broken up (although Slovenia, a republic of the former Yugoslavia, is likely to benefit from the eastern association process).

The remaining Mediterranean associates, despite lower levels of development and the likely competitive pressures they will face from full integration, are pressing to become members. The Community has not responded energetically to these applications. Greek political animus towards Turkey is one major obstacle. The potential budgetary cost via the CAP and structural and cohesion funds is another (House of Lords, 1992). Fears of the implications of freedom of movement of labour, particularly in post-Cold War circumstances, also contribute to EU reluctance to admit these countries to full membership.

The eastern association process dates from 1990. It followed a slow opening to the east before the fall of the Berlin Wall (Pinder, 1991). The precursors to the association agreements were a series of bilateral trade agreements, first with Hungary, then with Poland and what was then Czechoslovakia, which in essence extended MFN and GSP benefits to the Central Europeans. This, however, was perceived not to be enough (Rollo, 1991). The need for a relationship which encompassed trade but also contributed to embedding democracy and the market economy in Central Europe was widely felt. Thus emerged the so-called Europe Agreements, signed with Czechoslovakia, Hungary and Poland at the end of 1991 and with Bulgaria and Romania in 1993. These agreements include:

- the EC to remove barriers over five years, while the Visegrad Four have up to ten years in which to liberalize;
- freedom of movement of services, capital and labour;
- approximation of laws, including those governing competition policy;
- economic cooperation;
- political cooperation;
- aid provisions.

The points to note are:

- agriculture is largely excluded from trade liberalization;
- there are significant exceptions to industrial trade liberalization, notably textiles but above all contingent protection (Rollo, 1991; Winters, 1992; Rollo, 1993; Rollo and Smith, 1993);
- freedom of movement of labour is severely constrained, and rights of establishment might encourage a brain drain (Winters, 1992).

With these caveats in mind it is still fair to say that the association agreements offer the East Europeans significant opportunities for access to and integration with the countries of the EC. However, they do suffer from many of the drawbacks identified in discussion of the EEA above. Indeed, the nature of the relationship between the Europe Agreements and the EEA is not entirely clear. They both offer an FTA, the four freedoms and regulatory approximation. More widely, the aid relationship with Eastern Europe is not as generous as the cohesion funds, freedom of movement of labour is much less under the Europe Agreements and the role of the ECJ and rule-making in the EC generally for Eastern Europe is also unclear.

The analogies between the political economy of the Europe Agreements and the EEA are reason enough for expecting the East Europeans to press for early membership of the EC – an urgency intensified by the security situation in Eastern Europe and the FSU. The EC responded to this desire for membership by its declaration at the Copenhagen summit noted in section 1 above. In essence, completing the Europe Agreements becomes a necessary but not a sufficient condition for membership of the EU.

The uncertainty over the timing of eventual membership, however, brings the focus back to the application of the Europe Agreements. The Copenhagen summit also responded to criticism of the terms of the agreements by accelerating liberalization of access to EC markets, particularly in respect of the less sensitive products. It referred for further consideration the question of cross-cumulation of rules of origin among the Visegrad Four, the two Balkan countries and EFTA/EEA members. The important point here is that there are FTAs pairwise between the EC and EFTA, EFTA and the Visegrad Four, the EC and the Visegrad Four, the EC and the Balkan countries, the Balkans and the Visegrad Four and the Balkans and EFTA. They have been negotiated bilaterally and are essentially hub-and-spoke arrangements with the EC because (apart from among the Visegrad Four and between the Balkan countries) rules of origin treat goods sent from one group through any other group to the EC as having third-country origin and hence not qualifying for preferential treatment (see Rollo, 1991; Rollo, 1993; and Baldwin, 1994 for a fuller discussion). Cumulation would allow a much more integrated market across Europe, a matter to which we return below.

Finally in this section it is necessary to consider the likely other candidates for Europe Agreements. There are no rules of qualification for candidate status. The Baltic states and Slovenia are the most likely candidates. Other parts of the former Yugoslavia may also be potential members if a stable and acceptable peace is negotiated.

2.4 Free trade arrangements and the former Soviet Union

The EU is in the process of negotiating partnership and cooperation agreements (PCAs) with a number of the countries of the FSU. Russia signed agreements at the Corfu European Council; Belarus and Kyrgyzstan are some way behind. The agreements will contain provisions on trade in goods and services, establishment of companies, and movement of capital. In general they will follow MFN principles for trade in goods and, in the case of Russia, specific services. MFN principles will also apply for the establishment of companies and national treatment for their operation. Ultimately, national treatment is expected for establishment and operation as well as general liberalization of cross-border services. The provisions are not to be preferential and will be in conformity with GATT. In negotiation with Russia it has been agreed that the two parties will in 1998 examine the possibility of moving to a free trade area. Ukraine and Belarus have proposed similar provisions for their agreements.

3 The new European economy

Table 3.1 summarizes the basic economic statistics on post-Cold War Europe. Taking all the groups of countries discussed above, total GDP in 1991 was $8.6 trillion and population was three-quarters of a billion. Thus Europe accounts for 30 per cent of the world's income and under one-eighth of its population, with income per capita at market exchange rates varying from $300 in Albania to $35,000 in Switzerland. As a group these countries are responsible for over 30 per cent of world merchandise exports (excluding intra-EC trade). If this were a single market it would be pre-eminent in the world. It is not a single market yet: the EEA and EC enlargement are the main routes that would lead to the reality of a single market. The cumulation of rules of origin across both the existing and soon to be concluded hub-and-spoke arrangements between the EC and the other countries of the new Europe would do much to integrate the market in goods. However, even with cumulation of rules of origin the focus of integration might not be open trade. The use of contingent protection (safeguard clauses and anti-dumping procedures) against the Central European countries and the FSU in the early 1990s has suggested to some others (for details see Rollo and Smith, 1993; Wang and Winters, 1993) that *de facto* cartelization might be an important form of market integration towards the east. This has important implications for how such a Europe-wide grouping might react to the rest of the world. Before turning to that set of issues the next section will examine such data as there are on the degree of integration among the countries of Europe.

3.1 How much integration?

Table 3.2 explores differences in real living standards, comparing GDP per head at PPP exchange rates (where the data exist) as well as other measures of actual consumption (e.g. vehicles, telephones), education levels and other human capital indicators. A much lower degree of dispersion is evident here than in GDP per capita at market exchange rates. This is not surprising, as low-income countries tend to have market exchange rates which are undervalued relative to PPP. Furthermore, the shock of transition in the east will tend to cause exchange rates to fall below equilibrium levels.

Table 3.3 shows how European exports are distributed among the EC, EFTA, FSU and and developing countries. The data here underline the judgment

Table 3.2 European living standards

	GDP per capita 1992 PPP	Tertiary education enrolment ratio[a]	Commercial vehicles in use (1,000s)	Radio receivers per 1,000 pop.	Pop. per physician	Telephone lines per 1,000 pop.
EC						
Belgium	18,170	37	396	778	321	
Denmark	17,768	32	306	1,030	448	
France	18,665	40	3,810	896	421	50
Germany	16,310	33	1,895	952	710	
Greece	8,417	29	784	423	340	28
Ireland	12,427	26	150	583	410	
Italy	17,521	31	2,504	797	552	
Luxembourg	24,771	3	32	630	496	
Netherlands	17,023	34	557	906	444	
Portugal	9,736	18	813	218	575	24
Spain	14,731	34	2,379	306	360	
United Kingdom	16,300	25	2,908	1,146	870	
EFTAns						
Austria	18,005	33	648	624	333	
Finland	15,025	47	274	998	322	
Iceland	17,067	25	15	787	960	
Norway	17,785	43	331	798	503	
Sweden	16,496	33	658	155	355	68
Switzerland	22,159	28	304	888	1,441	
Mediterranean						
Cyprus		15	77	292	754	
Malta		11	21	527	500	
Turkey	3,800	14	453	161	242	12
Central Europe						
Czech Republic	6,923	18[b]	462[b]	587[b]	389[b]	16[b]
Hungary	5,297	15	289	595	740	11
Poland	4,081	22	1,138	429	416	9
Slovakia	5,224	Cz[b]	Cz[b]	Cz[b]	Cz[b]	Cz[b]
The Balkans						
Albania		7	3	176	2,070	
Bulgaria	4,770	31	145	259	340	23
Romania	2,370	9	53	198	n.a.	11
Slovenia	8,098	n.a.	n.a.	n.a.	n.a.	
The FSU		26	8,700	686	480	14
Belarus		n.a.	n.a.	306	n.a.	
Estonia		n.a.	n.a.	n.a.	n.a.	
Latvia		n.a.	n.a.	n.a.	n.a.	
Lithuania		n.a.	n.a.	n.a.	n.a.	
Moldova		n.a.	n.a.	n.a.	n.a.	
Russia		n.a.	n.a.	n.a.	n.a.	
Ukraine		n.a.	n.a.	794	n.a.	

[a]Tertiary education ratio is the number of pupils as a percentage of the population aged 20–24.
[b]Czech and Slovak figures combined.
n.a. not available
Source: PPP figures OECD and Planecon.

Table 3.3 Direction of exports 1992 (%)

	EC	EFTA	Other OECD	FSU	Developing countries	Gravity Model[a] Share EC	EFTA
EC							
Belgium	74.9	5.9	5.5	0.9	12.6		
Denmark	54.4	21.6	9.5	0.9	14.0		
France	62.7	6.2	9.7	1.4	20.7		
Germany	54.4	15.2	9.8	1.9	19.5		
Greece	64.1	5.4	6.0	1.7	22.2		
Ireland	74.3	5.2	12.8	0.2	6.8		
Italy	57.8	8.2	10.2	2.3	22.3		
Luxembourg							
Netherlands	76.1	6.2	5.7	1.7	10.8		
Portugal	75.1	8.8	5.3	0.4	9.8		
Spain	71.2	4.3	6.5	0.9	17.0		
United Kingdom	56.0	7.0	16.5	0.5	19.0		
EFTAns							
Austria	66.1	8.6	5.2	1.4	19.5		
Finland	53.2	19.5	9.2	7.2	17.6		
Iceland	68.8	7.3	19.3	1.5	4.7		
Norway	66.5	13.6	9.9	1.5	9.6		
Sweden	55.8	17.4	12.9	1.1	13.5		
Switzerland	58.9	6.3	13.9	0.4	20.1		
Mediterranean							
Cyprus	40.8	2.4	2.0	2.6	40.2		
Malta	74.4	2.4	6.5	1.0	12.4		
Turkey	51.7	4.3	7.6	5.4	35.9		
Central Europe							
Czech Republic	49.5[b]	10.6[b]	3.2[b]	10.3[b]	25.3[b]	65.3	9.4
Hungary	49.5	14.7	4.8	13.1	15.7	64.4	8.9
Poland	55.6	8.7	4.1	12.8	0.0	54.7	11.2
Slovakia	Cz[b]	Cz[b]	Cz[b]	Cz[b]	Cz[b]	n.a.	n.a.
The Balkans							
Albania	n.a.	n.a.	n.a.	n.a.	n.a.	n.a.	n.a.
Bulgaria	40.8	3.9	5.0	0.0	50.2	45.6	10.7
Romania	32.5	5.5	4.1	13.0	40.3	47.7	11.8
Slovenia	n.a.	n.a.	n.a.	n.a.	n.a.	n.a.	n.a.
The FSU	43.6	7.6	6.9	0.0	42.0	50.4	11.5
Belarus	n.a.	n.a.	n.a.	n.a.	n.a.	n.a.	n.a.
Estonia	n.a.	n.a.	n.a.	n.a.	n.a.	n.a.	n.a.
Latvia	n.a.	n.a.	n.a.	n.a.	n.a.	n.a.	n.a.
Lithuania	n.a.	n.a.	n.a.	n.a.	n.a.	n.a.	n.a.
Moldova	n.a.	n.a.	n.a.	n.a.	n.a.	n.a.	n.a.
Russia	n.a.	n.a.	n.a.	n.a.	n.a.	n.a.	n.a.
Ukraine	n.a.	n.a.	n.a.	n.a.	n.a.	n.a.	n.a.

Sources: OECD, *Monthly Statistics of Foreign Trade*, December 1993; IMF Direction of Trade Statistics, 1993 Yearbook.
Notes:
Belgium and Luxembourg trade figures are combined.
[a]Hamilton and Winters, 1992.
[b]Czech and Slovak trade figures combined.
n.a. not available

of the GATT Secretariat, noted above, that EFTA is already highly integrated into the EC. The Mediterranean countries and the Central Europeans are also highly dependent for trade on the EC: indeed, the Central Europeans are already close to the EC trade shares predicted by gravity models (Hamilton and Winters, 1992). The trade figures for the FSU countries are not available in the required form.

3.2 Commercial policy integration

Difficult as it is to gather data on trade and other aspects of market integration, it is even more difficult in the context of commercial policy. This is important because the sum of current policies may give some preliminary ideas on how the future commercial policy of a wider EC grouping might evolve.

The obvious point to begin with is that commercial policy in the EC is relatively homogeneous – but not completely so. Only in 1993 did national measures finally fade, as, for example, national quotas on Japanese cars were converted to EC-wide quotas. Even here, however, exceptions remain. Under the Treaty of Paris establishing the European Coal and Steel Community, national measures are still allowed, and were invoked by the Benelux countries in January 1994 when EC quotas on steel imports from Russia, Belarus and Ukraine were suspended as the result of a British veto. Even for members of the EEA, where regulatory integration is scheduled to intensify, the FTA gives them control over their own external protection (i.e. they could if they wished unilaterally liberalize to the rest of the world) and agriculture is still excluded.

The overall picture that emerges – given the uncertainty about how policy might evolve over the next few years, particularly in the FSU (the Europe Agreements exert some control over the Visegrad Four and the Balkans) – is that:

- tariffs in the CEE are generally higher, but not beyond the highest EC levels;
- agriculture in EFTA is more heavily protected than in the EC;
- EFTA and the Central Europeans are less likely to resort to contingent protection, but NTBs are in use in the CEE;
- there are few restrictions on foreign ownership of property and firms.

Thus, to take the extreme case, it seems unlikely that simply adding up policies would lead to a more restrictive Europe than the current EC. Any customs union is likely to be at existing EC tariff levels. On agriculture, new members have to adopt the CAP which on current policies would reduce protection in EFTA but increase it in Central Europe.

Thus the static picture does not suggest that a more integrated, cohesive Europe-wide economy would necessarily be more protectionist than that which exists now. But, as noted above, Winters and others see in the Europe Agreements potential for the cartelization of Europe through contingent protection. The institutional form of future European integration is therefore important in considering the potential impact of the new Europe on the rest of the world. Is a Europe-wide bloc in the making?

4 Institutional options for the new Europe

The European Union is already reacting to the demands of the new Europe, with enlargement towards EFTA, the EEA, Association Agreements and PCAs in the economic dimension alongside the nascent cooperation on migration and drugs in the third pillar of Maastricht plus the British-Italian proposal for cooperation with the Central Europeans on the Common Foreign and Security Policy (CFSP), the second pillar. The key word, however, is 'reacting'. Each of these actions has a logic of its own, but the overall logic is not clear. Can or should the EU differentiate among the new states to the east? If so, on what criteria? Is it enough to use existing EU instruments? Can the EU balloon simply be blown up? There is no obvious grand design to apply, let alone being applied. The needs of the countries in the east are changing, mainly in reaction to trends in Russia – the regional superpower – and the EU is reacting in turn. The difficulty in considering the implications for the world economy is that economic instruments may be brought into play to respond to political problems. This is not new – indeed, it is precisely the history of the current EU from Monnet and Schuman onwards. But the rest of the world may pay an economic price for desirable political ends. The most obvious system cost of the existing EU is the CAP, which has been brought inside multilateral rules after the three rounds of GATT negotiations.

The EU's approach to those outside it is far from uniform. The EFTA countries are favoured partners. They are offered membership or EEA status. But, as noted above, even attitudes towards EFTA change. In 1989 the EEA was considered an alternative to membership; now it is a second best to be taken only if domestic electorates will not approve full membership. Equally, association for the East Europeans was formerly seen as an end in itself; now it is considered an essential qualification for membership. The question now is who will qualify first. Do they enter in batches, with the Visegrad Four coming first (but Slovakia may lag), then the Balkans (but where does Slovenia fit in?), then the Baltics (and Croatia and Albania?)? Can the Mediterranean countries possibly be left out? Is it impossible to conceive of Ukraine or Belarus or Moldova being members? Much will depend on how the EU itself develops.

4.1 An ever greater union?

The Maastricht Treaty has created a European Union with three different pillars: economics; security and foreign policy; and migration and justice. The latter two of these are purely intergovernmental in nature. The EC, however, encompasses the Commission with a right of proposal, the Council of Ministers with a right of disposal and QMV on the large majority of issues, and the European Parliament with limited rights of oversight and amendment. It is thus the EC which provides the most immediate and difficult problems for integration with the rest of Europe, since in the other two pillars national vetoes apply.

There are already problems associated with intensifying integration within the existing Twelve. The British, German and Danish opt-outs on EMU and the British opt-out on the social chapter are the most obvious. Laying aside political/ ideological differences, the Maastricht Treaty lays down qualifying criteria for EMU: even those who want to join may not be allowed to. Maastricht thus embodies the principle of variable geometry in the *acquis communautaire*. However, new members will not be allowed to exempt themselves from the *acquis* even where existing members have derogations. There is therefore a strong incentive to be inside the EU when any extension of the *acquis* is being considered. Hence the EFTA rush to join, if at all, before the 1996 intergovernmental conference considers whether the Maastricht Treaty needs further amendment.

Already an EU of twelve finds it difficult to make decisions because of the divergent interests of its member states. These differences arise from levels of development, the varying importance of different sectors and specific geographical problems, as well as legal and regulatory incompatibilities and ideological factors; they show up in internal disagreement over such issues as trade policy, policy towards industry, regulation of financial services, free movement of people or goods inside the EU, spending on the structural funds, and the future of the CAP. Adding the EFTAns will create sufficient additional difficulties, even though they are rich and rather similar to the northern European bloc. They all nonetheless desire special treatment for their poorer regions, even though they hardly face the problems of the poorest regions of the Twelve. They demand higher environmental standards. They wish to have special treatment for their agriculture for as long as possible. How much more difficult will the problems be as we look beyond the EFTAns?

On the institutional side, how will the Community deal with an influx of small states? Malta and Cyprus have populations of well under 1 million; the Baltic states, Albania, Slovenia and Moldova, of between 1.5 and 4 million; the Slovaks 5 million; the Czechs, Hungarians and Bulgarians around 10 million. Together they do not add up to Germany in terms of population or France in terms of wealth, yet they will comfortably outvote either in the Council of

Ministers. This is even before the impact of larger countries such as Romania (bigger than the Netherlands), Poland (the same as Spain) and Turkey (the same as France, Italy or Britain and growing fast) is considered. Admittedly this is a maximalist vision of the EU with thirty-one members. But even if all potential members had similar economic structures and levels of development, a Council of Ministers of that size would be unwieldy. The practical policy problems with which such a cumbersome structure would have to deal would add to the likelihood of policy stagnation. The most obvious fall under five heads: agriculture, structural funds, EMU, the social chapter and freedom of movement of labour.

Agriculture provides an immediate problem in integrating Eastern Europe in particular into a wider Europe. Even the small, rich EFTAns are having difficulty with the implications of enlargement for agriculture. Turkey could cost the budget 4 billion ecus (House of Lords, 1992) and the Visegrad Four 5 billion ecus (CEPR, 1992), to take just two examples. (Baldwin, 1994, drawing on Andersen and Tyers, 1993, suggests that the Visegrad Four could cost 40 billion ecus. This is almost certainly too high, and Tyers, 1994, reduces these estimates to nearer 30 billion ecus – which in the author's view is still too high.)

Agricultural policies will not be constant, however. The current reform of the CAP will reduce prices and increase compensation payments to existing EC farmers. The GATT texts will lead to the tariffication of EC variable levies. This will not by itself reduce prices below the levels agreed in the CAP reform. Future GATT rounds will bring pressure for reduced EC protection, but not before the EU will have to confront East European enlargement. The potential accession of Poland, Hungary, Romania and Bulgaria in particular will put significant pressure on markets for livestock products, grains and oilseeds, fruit and vegetables, and wine. Current EC agricultural producers will face competition and support mechanisms will become even more expensive. After the CAP reform this expense will fall on taxpayers and is likely to be unacceptable as other budgetary pressures increase (see below).

How is this impasse to be broken? A root-and-branch reform of the CAP, reducing market prices to world levels, plus production-neutral direct subsidies mainly aimed at small/low-income farmers, is one option. A return to national financing under competition policy/state aid rules is another possible approach. The first option leaves a significant potential EC budget cost for low-income farmers in Eastern Europe and the Mediterranean areas. Depending on the degree of compensation, the cost of such a policy is unlikely to be lower than the estimates already quoted. One response is simply to say that new members, since they have not had the benefit of high EC prices, do not qualify for Community-financed compensation. This would be difficult to run on equity grounds, because poor taxpayers in Eastern Europe and elsewhere would be funding compensation to (relatively) rich farmers in Western Europe. National financing seems a more equitable approach. Whether the current Community members will live with this is, however, an open question. The Germans in particular seem likely to demand compensation for lower prices. Domestic politics and resentment at their net budget contribution may make them reluctant to give up any source of receipts, especially when enlargement is likely to increase budgetary costs in other directions.

Structural funds represent a problem of similar dimensions. These take three different forms: regional, social and cohesion funds. Low-income countries such as those in CEE and the Mediterranean will qualify in totality for regional aid on the basic objective 1 criterion of GDP per capita of 75 per cent of the EC average (even when they themselves reduce the average). The social fund is there to provide resources for retraining workers made redundant by structural change. The economies in transition are likely by their nature to qualify for this. The cost of cohesion and structural funds for the CEE and Turkey could be at least 20 billion ecus (CEPR, 1992). This is a very significant extra burden of around 25–30 per cent of the current budget, to which the main contributors will find it hard to agree.

The falling average GDP per capita of the Community might put many regions which currently receive objective 1 regional aid above the 75 per cent cut-off. Such graduation would reduce the cost of enlargement to the current net contributors to the EC budget but is unlikely to be politically acceptable. All member states receive some regional funds under other objectives. The EFTAn applicants will receive regional aid. Against this background it is difficult to see how new members could be excluded from the structural funds or existing members be graduated from them.

The Maastricht Treaty raises a further set of problems in the form of EMU. Countries which meet the criteria set out in the Treaty after 1998 must join EMU. This will be difficult for some existing member states. The low levels of productivity in the Mediterranean and the CEE (as represented by GDP per capita) suggest that the cost of EMU could be structural unemployment. The relatively poor labour mobility within the Community may lead to further demands for significant budgetary transfers to compensate. The alternative – likely to be politically unpalatable in Western Europe, despite the undoubted economic benefits – will be migration.

The consequences of EMU in respect of structural unemployment and migration are likely to be exacerbated if new members in the CEE and the Mediterranean are required to apply the social chapter. This will raise the costs of employment beyond levels commensurate with productivity. The result, again, will be structural unemployment and increased migration pressures.

The Maastricht agenda, if it results in overvalued exchange rates and increased regulatory costs, will also reduce CEE and Mediterranean competitiveness on EC and world markets. This in turn will force deflationary policies which will set back the growth process and the recovery in the CEE in particular. The political consequences of this in Eastern Europe may result in the Union creating the political instability it had hoped to prevent by offering membership.

Freedom of movement of labour represents a political problem for existing EU members. As noted above, to the extent that EMU and the social chapter reduce CEE and Mediterranean competitiveness, migration will be the result. Equally, trade restrictions or the effective cartelization of European markets will increase structural unemployment and hence migration pressures. To the extent that the existing members wish to keep low-wage competition out of their labour markets (and goods markets), they may need to offer financial compensation to buy the derogation: not a palatable choice.

4.2 Alternatives to membership

If the full *acquis* presents so many problems for existing and potential members, are there alternatives to full membership and do they offer more than relationships currently available through association agreements, the EEA, customs unions or PCAs? Perhaps this is the wrong question. It is entirely possible for the EU to come up with a selection of policies to offer to non-members which deal with at least some of the perceived problems of existing arrangements and avoid those of applying the full *acquis*. Are they politically acceptable?

The potential applicants fall into two groups: the Mediterraneans, who have trade and trade policy integration but no single market access, and the CEE and EEA members, who have trade policy autonomy but actual or potential single market access. For the first group inclusion in the EEA would significantly increase their integration but still leave them without any input into the decision-making process which determines their trade policy and the regulation of domestic markets. As with the EFTA contries, there would be an increase in obligations with no increase in participation. Even here existing member states are unlikely to extend freedom of movement of labour to Turkey in particular. Membership still looks preferable on political grounds. The extension of the EEA to the CEE countries would not increase single market obligations very significantly but would render domestic regulation subject to EC rule-making in some areas. Again the incentives that drove the EFTAns to go directly to membership would apply.

It is possible that the CEE might find the customs union option attractive. It would offer two distinct advantages. First, it would abolish the rules-of-origin problem intrinsic in the existing FTA. Secondly, it would make anti-dumping and safeguard actions very difficult, if not impossible, to prosecute – particularly if EC competition policy norms, including those on state aids, applied as the association agreements demand. It would nonetheless reduce policy sovereignty even further and open the CEE up to more competition from the rest of the world as tariffs fall. The question then comes back to how much policy sovereignty a country must give up before the benefits of going all the way to membership outweigh the perceived costs. Furthermore, even if customs union, as distinct from full membership, has some economic advantages for the CEE, it misses their political objectives. The need for recognition as 'West European' and for implicit, if (for non-NATO members) soft, security guarantees against Russia would not be met.

The broad conclusion of this section is that the Mediterraneans and in particular the CEE countries will find it difficult to identify resting places between association and full membership which are sustainable. The EFTAns have pointed the way. The EEA only represents a final destination if domestic electorates demand it. Otherwise it gives insufficient political benefits for the incremental economic integration.

4.3 Variable geometry

If there are no stable outcomes short of full membership, are there variants of full membership which would be acceptable to potential applicants and existing members? For existing members, the main problems are likely to be the budgetary cost of agriculture, the structural funds, and the political problem of free movement of labour. On the applicants' side, the problems are likely to be the social chapter, the potential costs of EMU (largely voluntary) and the higher consumer prices for food implied by the current CAP regime (but perhaps not by future regimes), while the advantages are that the applicants are likely to want full participation in CFSP and will benefit from untrammelled access to all EC markets.

There are two approaches to this set of policy difficulties. The first is some form of long-term derogations for the applicants. EMU is in any case voluntary in the sense that macro policy could be manipulated so as to avoid meeting the Maastricht criteria. More directly, application of the social chapter could be under derogation as long as migration was restricted for new members. CAP derogations are more difficult because they require trade barriers to insulate older members from new. This was not acceptable in the EFTA negotiations (unlike earlier enlargements, when up to seven years was allowed for agricultural transition). The concept of digressive derogation may make more sense in the context of structural and cohesion funds. The CEE countries and others face absorption problems. If Baldwin's estimates, quoted above, are correct they suggest that the transfers to the Visegrad Four will amount to over 20 billion ecus a year. This represents about 15 per cent of those countries' 1991 GDP – twice as big a proportion as the flows to any of the current recipients. A slow build-up, perhaps beginning before membership, would help this absorption problem. This, however, only postpones the costs for the existing members; thus this staged approach does not deal with the real underlying issues.

A deliberate variable geometry strategy might work better. On the CAP, for example, Community prices might apply for the new entrants but they might not qualify for compensation payments, since they did not have previously high prices. This would cut some budget costs, but would still leave original members facing stiff competition in domestic markets with consequent costs for export subsidies (although the outcome of the Uruguay Round will discipline export subsidies and push adjustment back onto the EC farmers). Adoption of this strategy would require a Treaty amendment. On structural and cohesion funds, it might be sensible in the light of both the budgetary burden and the absorption problem in the recipient countries to create a new fund for members in transition and in the process of economic development. The level of this would be a matter for negotiation, but for the Visegrad Four it might be no more than 10 billion ecus (7 per cent of GNP). If free movement of labour were denied then EMU and the social chapter provisions of the Maastricht Treaty might be applied with less vigour.

This deal looks more persuasive for the CEE than for countries such as Turkey, but that observation itself raises a question of timing, to which I turn next. Suffice it to say at this point that it is possible to retain a vision of a core Community of twelve or sixteen with other countries joining with derogations on one side and reduced financial commitment on the other but retaining the essential open market. This seems a more likely outcome than a continental EEA or the existing patchwork of customs unions and FTAs.

4.4 Timetable

On the above analysis the rest of the world is likely to confront a Community of around 30 (the present Twelve, plus the four EFTAn and three Mediterranean countries, plus six CEE countries, three Baltic states, Slovenia and perhaps Croatia and other former Yugoslav republics) – but over an uncertain horizon.

A Community of sixteen, including the EFTAns, is already likely by 1 January 1995. The Hungarian and Polish applications are likely to be followed by applications from the Czech Republic, Slovakia and (more speculatively) Slovenia, which on general economic criteria may already be in a position to accept EC disciplines. Negotiations on these could not begin before 1997, always assuming a positive opinion from the Commission, and the earliest date for membership would be around 2000. Malta and Cyprus, which already have opinions on their membership and are making the requested adjustments to their regulatory structures, may also join at that time. That suggests a post-EFTA enlargement wave of between three and seven countries by the end of the century. The Baltic states will by then be running the two Balkan countries close on readiness for membership, which may point to another five members by 2005–10. That leaves only Turkey (which has now in any event negotiated a customs union agreement with the EU) and the successor states of the former Yugoslavia. In other words a Community of twenty-five or more may be achieved in the next fifteen years.

A final word of warning is advisable. A more aggressive attitude by Russia could accelerate the CEE integration very significantly.

5 Implications for the rest of the world

The lengthy discussion above suggests that there is not likely to be much to choose between existing arrangements (basically Europe Agreements, customs union for Turkey and PCAs for the CIS) and full membership at least for the CEE, Baltics and Mediterranean countries. For the moment the remainder of the FSU is likely to remain at the PCA stage and thus evolve over time towards an industrial FTA with the Community. The barriers to membership are likely to be domestic politics (as for the EFTAn applicants) and resistance from inside the Community. Even if the EU expands to sixteen in 1995, itself far from certain, no further enlargement is likely in the rest of this century (Russia permitting).

Institutionally, therefore, the Community will join the WTO with up to sixteen members. That will not have much immediate impact on the rest of the world. Average tariffs will not increase; there is unlikely to be any additional trade diversion as a result of EFTA membership; agricultural support will fall in the EFTAns; and NTBs are unlikely to become more widespread, although the former EFTA members may, via the EU, increase the frequency with which they resort to anti-dumping actions. At the same time competition among rules, mutual recognition and single passport provisions should make for cheaper transaction costs to third-country exporters to the former EFTAns.

The main negative prospect is the possibility of more complex and hence slower decision-making on the part of the EU in negotiation. Even this may be counteracted by – on manufactured trade at least – a more liberal stance by the EFTAns, though even here Austrian attitudes to CEE imports are no more and perhaps less liberal than the sum of current EU members' attitudes. On agriculture the EFTAns start from a generally more protectionist stance than the EC and may turn out to be defenders of the CAP in the face of the adjustment costs that membership will already have forced upon them.

Further enlargement eastwards will not, on current economic performance, add much to the Community market. The CEE will add $200 billion to GNP (or 2.5 per cent of the combined EU and EFTA total) and $35 billion to total exports

(1992 levels). The Mediterranean countries, including Turkey, add a further 1.5 per cent to GNP and $17 billion to exports. The 1992 trade shares (Table 3.3) show that CEE exports to EC and EFTA are already close to the shares predicted by one gravity model (Hamilton and Winters, 1992). This is not enough to suggest that membership is unlikely to lead to further trade diversion. The uncertainty over agricultural policy and the potential impact of preferential trade liberalization under the Europe Agreements may increase the scope for trade diversion. As the export shares for the existing EC and EFTA countries show, small member states can have intra-EC shares as high as 75 per cent. Certainly the combination of preferential trade liberalization and the cartelization effect of contingent protection and rules of origin points to the possibility of substantial trade and investment diversion among the CEE and FSU countries before, and the CEE after, any enlargement of the Community.

The losses implied for the rest of the world are not large at current volumes of trade. Hamilton and Winters (1992), however, suggest a potential fivefold increase in potential trade for the CEE and FSU at 1985 levels of output. It is to be hoped that this level of output and trade will be attained again by the end of the century. At these predicted levels one per cent of trade diversion is worth $2 billion (Hamilton and Winters, 1992, Table 3). Projections of imports on optimistic assumptions (Rollo and Stern, 1992) show a fivefold increase in CEE and FSU imports between 1991 and 2010 to a total of $600 billion, giving a rather higher cost of any trade diversion to the rest of the world. Any such losses will, however, need to be set against a fall in the external tariff as a result of EC membership and a fall in transactions costs implied in the extension of the single market.

The one unambiguous increase in costs is once again that imposed by having to deal with an organization of twenty-five or more members, each with a view and a vote in trade policy-making. That will make the EU a more difficult negotiating partner. The main danger is that an enlarged EU may become more inward-looking. The continuing transition in the CEE, and economic development generally among the poorer member states, especially if Turkey joins, will also require special effort. Equally, there may be particular sectoral problems arising from enlargement which make the richer member states less inclined to face up to more competitive pressures from non-members. To the extent that the EU has time for member countries beyond its borders it is more likely to favour those with preferential arrangements. Thus difficulties in attracting the EU's attention, added to the difficulties that the EU will have in decision-making, plus the sheer size of the EU in world trade, will confront the rest of the world with hard choices. As we have seen, in Europe increasing size and deepening integration have made the EU magnetic to non-members. It might be reasonable to expect increased incentives for outsiders to look for their own preferential agreements with the EU. That may be difficult. Historically the EU has avoided significant preferential trade agreements with non-European countries, except where there has been a long-term relationship, as with, for example, the ACP or Maghreb. There might be some reluctance on the part of the EU to extend the existing set of extra-regional preferential agreements.

The alternative for outsiders is to form competing trade blocs. NAFTA and APEC are in part obvious reactions to the EC/EU and problems in GATT. As noted at the beginning of the chapter, these are not trade blocs in the sense of having common external policies. They may therefore suffer from the same problems as EFTA in being unable to deploy whatever theoretical negotiating strength they have. The result in EFTA's case was defection and practical absorption. This is unlikely to occur in the same way with NAFTA and APEC because of their size. The danger here is that they too will retreat inwards. Whether that retreat, given common membership of the two groups, will result in a transpacific trade bloc is difficult to predict. Current transpacific trade disputes give some grounds for scepticism.

Trade blocs are not the only choice. The new trade agenda – trade and the environment, trade and social policy, trade and competition policy – shows more of a tendency towards cooperation across potential trade-bloc boundaries. These coalitions – US/EU on social policy and competition policy, US/Japan/EU on environment policy – are not all necessarily benign for the world trading system. They may nonetheless retard any tendency to growing blocs. The strengthened WTO may also make a significant difference. In the past, scrutinies of preferential agreements under Article XX1V of GATT have not always been stringent. Under the new dispute settlement system it will be difficult for even a large bloc like the EC to block an adverse finding. Thus non-members may be encouraged more readily to question extensions to or intensifications of even the most powerful trade blocs.

6 Conclusion

It is not easy to judge the likely outcome of this constellation of forces. The pressures to further enlargement of the EU seem very strong, at least among policy elites in other European countries. This will put severe strains on existing EU institutions and may lead to more extensive use of variable geometry. As far as the rest of the world is concerned, however, the core Community is certain to encompass trade policy and all the major aspects of economic regulation. As a result the EU may expand to over twenty-five members and will present the world with a common policy front – perhaps after long internal negotiations – which will be difficult to change in bilateral or multilateral negotiation. This much seems more likely than not. Combined with free trade agreements with the remaining European countries, notably the FSU but also any residual EFTA countries, Europe will represent a preferential trading area amounting to a 30 per cent share of world output and trade. If the FSU and CEE enjoy catch-up growth, as has happened in China, this could impose a cost on the rest of the world in trade diversion, although there is likely also to be considerable trade creation, in particular from regulatory integration.

The application of strengthened WTO rules will interact with the formation and buttressing of competing trade blocs. If rules win then it may be possible to ensure that Article XXIV of GATT is more stringently applied, thus disciplining blocs. The history of EFTA suggests, however, that a combination of competition between blocs and increased integration among them may result. The first move in this latter direction might be a US/EU preferential agreement. Such a move might be encouraged by common interests in the trade and environment, social policy and competition policy agendas. Such a combination might not augur well for the rest of the world – but that is another story.

References

Andersen, Kym and Tyers, Rod, 1993, *EC Enlargement and East European Agriculture*, CEPR Working Paper 792.

Baldwin, Richard, 1994, *Towards an Integrated Europe*, CEPR, London.

CEPR, 1992, *Is Bigger Better? The Economics of EC Enlargement*, London.

GATT, 1990, *Trade Policy Review, Sweden, August 1990*, Geneva.

GATT, 1991, *Trade Policy Review, Norway, December 1991*, Geneva.

Hamilton, Carl and Winters, L.A., 1992, 'Opening up trade with Eastern Europe', *Economic Policy*, 14.

House of Lords, 1992, *Report of the Select Committee on the European Communities on EC Enlargement*, HMSO, London.

Pinder, John, 1991, *The EC and Eastern Europe*, Pinter for RIIA, London.

Rollo, J.M.C., 1993, 'Economic transition and European integration', mimeo, RIIA, London.

Rollo, J.M.C., 1991, 'Integrating Eastern Europe with a wider Europe', in Richard O'Brien, ed., *Finance and the International Economy*, Oxford University Press, Oxford, pp. 80–91.

Rollo, Jim and Smith, Alasdair, 1993, 'The political economy of EC trade with Eastern Europe: why so sensitive?', *Economic Policy*, 16, April, pp. 140–81.

Rollo, J.M.C. and Stern, Jon, 1992, 'Growth and trade prospects for Central and Eastern Europe', *World Economy*, 15, 5, September, pp. 645–68.

Tyers, Rod, 1994 (forthcoming), *Economic Reforms in Europe and the Former Soviet Union: Implications for International Food Markets*, IFPRI, Washington.

Wang, Z.K. and Winters, L.A., 1993, *EC Imports from Eastern Europe: Iron and Steel*, EBRD Discussion Paper, London.

Winters, L. Alan, 1992, 'The Europe Agreements: with a little help from our friends', in CEPR Occasional Paper 11, London.

4 REGIONAL ECONOMIC INTEGRATION IN EAST ASIA: SPECIAL FEATURES AND POLICY IMPLICATIONS

Masami Yoshida, Ichiro Akimune, Masayuki Nohara and Kimitoshi Sato*

1 INTRODUCTION

Three major regions in the world economy, the EC, North America and East Asia, have made progress in regional economic integration (REI) since the second half of the 1980s.[†] We define regional economic integration as deepening intra-regional economic interdependence in a given region, through intra-regional trade and foreign direct investment (FDI), thereby differentiating it from regional trade agreements (RTAs) and institutional integration.[‡] The two types of integration are not, however, completely independent from each other. For instance, progress in REI could induce RTA, while RTA could bring about further REI. We also define 'regionalism' as political movement towards the creation or expansion of regional trade agreements.[**]

Regional economic integration in the EC and North America since the second half of the 1980s has been associated with the formation of regional trade agreements: the European single market in 1992 and the US-Canada Free Trade

* The authors wish to thank Dr Masaru Yoshitomi, Noriki Hirose and Kunio Miyamoto for giving many valuable comments; also Todd Zaun and Petra Ludwig for assistance in proofreading; and Takashi Seita for research assistance. Any remaining errors are the authors' responsibility.

† We use the abbreviation EC rather than EU because this chapter deals mainly with a period before the Union came into being. We define Europe as the twelve member countries of the European Community (now the EU); North America as the three member countries of NAFTA. Defining the region of East Asia is is more complicated because of a lack of regional identity of the same kind that prevails to a greater or lesser degree in Europe and North America. In this chapter we use the term East Asia to mean the ten Asian economies with relatively high GDP growth: Japan, the NIEs (including Singapore), ASEAN and China.

‡ In this chapter we use the term RTA (regional trade agreements) for convenience, although the literal meaning does not fully cover the actual integration process now under way. 'Regional institutional integration' would better express what we mean, including the harmonization of working conditions, taxes and so on.

** In the second half of the 1980s an accelerating trend towards the conclusion of RTAs was evident. Lloyd (1992) remarks that developed countries extended their involvement in already existing RTAs through so-called 'second generation agreements'. Torre and

Agreement (CUSFTA) in 1989, followed by NAFTA, effective from 1994. In contrast, since the ASEAN Free Trade Area (AFTA) came into effect in 1993, the process of REI in East Asia has not seen the formation of any regional trade agreements involving all the nations of the region. Furthermore, Japan is the only advanced country that has not joined any RTAs. Although, as mentioned above, each of the three regions has advanced in REI, they are different in nature: in case of the EC and North America integration has taken place *de jure*, while in the East Asian case it is occurring *de facto*.

The respective background circumstances of the European and North American RTAs differ, however. The EC, threatened by Japan moving far ahead in the field of high-technology production and menaced by the advance of the Asian newly industrializing economies (NIEs) in other areas, launched its 1992 single market programme in order to regain competitiveness. In addition, the 1992 programme can be regarded as one stage in the movement towards a European political union, as set out in the Maastricht Treaty. In North America, motivation for NAFTA varies among the participants. The United States hopes to lock in Mexican economic reforms, to move beyond the Uruguay Round of GATT, and to prevent illegal immigration from Mexico. Mexico wishes to lend internal and external credibility to its economic reforms, while Canada is trying to avoid FDI diversion to Mexico. Both Canada and Mexico are motivated by a desire to secure access to the US market.

Considering the weakness of GATT, it is only natural that its members should be inclined to adopt a wait and see approach to discover whether these moves towards REI will complement or weaken the world free trade system.[*] It should be kept in mind, however, that even if they conform to Article XXIV of GATT, all RTAs discriminate between member countries and non-member countries, at least in relative terms. Further, the discriminatory nature of RTAs could be heightened in some circumstances: for example, in the case of an economic slump in a member country or when the motivation for the RTA

Kelly (1992) point out that the RTAs of the 1980s have new features not present in the RTA boom of the 1960s, including the US conversion to regionalism, the forming of RTAs between developed and less developed countries, and a shift in attitude on the part of the less developed countries away from inward- towards outward-oriented RTAs.

[*] The professionals' opinions concerning the benefit of RTAs are divided: a warning note is sounded by Bhagwati (1991) and Torre and Kelly (1992); optimistic views are expressed by Krugman (1991), Lawrence (1991) and Dornbusch (1991). Krugman (1991) argues that the effect of trade diversion in case of a 'natural block' poses only a negligible danger to world trade; Lawrence (1991) argues that the increase in inter-dependence of the world economy would prevent any exclusive RTAs; Dornbusch (1991) points out that RTAs would be able to open and connect more markets faster and further than GATT would be able to do.

becomes inward-looking (this argument is advanced in Drysdale and Garnaut, 1993). Such circumstances may even lead to mutual retaliation among RTAs, resulting in the worst possible scenario not only for those concerned but also for the rest of the world.*

How, then, should East Asian countries, in particular Japan, respond to the present state of affairs: a weakened GATT, *de jure* integration in the EC and North America, *de facto* integration in East Asia, and institutional movement, initiated by the United States, in APEC? In order to answer this question it is important to clarify what *de facto* integration in East Asia actually involves and what kind of economic interests the region's countries have.

To arrive at a better understanding of the special case of Asian REI – an integration process without a formal trade agreement – we compare it with REI in the EC and North America. In sections 2 and 3 below we look at inter- and intra-regional trade and intra-regional FDI in the three regions. Section 4 examines the integration process in each of the three regions since 1985. While section 2 centres on a comparison of intra- and inter-regional trade, section 4 concentrates on intra-regional trade itself, and the influence on it exercised by FDI and RTAs. In section 5 we inquire what role Japanese multinational companies (MNCs) play in REI in East Asia. In section 6 we draw our analysis together and consider what kind of political implications are connected with REI in East Asia, especially from the point of view of Japan.

2 INTRA- AND INTER-REGIONAL TRADE IN EAST ASIA, NORTH AMERICA AND THE EC

In this section we focus mainly on intra-regional trade ratios in the three regions. Intra-regional trade is taken to cover intra-regional exports, imports and their totals; the ratios relate those data to total trade and to GDP.

As a result of recession in the industrialized countries and the serious debt burden of developing countries, the growth of world trade declined in the first half of the 1980s compared with the second half of the 1970s. However, in the second half of the 1980s the growth of world trade accelerated again. The growth of East Asian trade in this period was particularly remarkable, with the region's share of world trade, in both exports and imports, increasing dramatically. Between 1985 and 1992 East Asia's share of total world exports increased from 20.1 per cent to 23.6 per cent, and of world imports from 16.8 per cent to 20.6 per

---

* Using a three-bloc model, Stoeckel et al. (1990) calculate that under conditions of enhanced protection in the EC and America (taking the year 1988 as a base) the world would have had a US$214 billion lower GDP in 1988, with the EC down by US$132 billion, the Asia-Pacific region down by US$18 billion and North America down by US$64 billion.

Table 4.1 Intra-regional trade ratios (%)

(a) Exports and imports

		With: East Asia	N. America	EC	Others	World
East Asia	1975	30.6	22.6	11.5	35.3	100.0
	80	33.6	22.2	11.8	32.4	100.0
	85	36.5	28.6	10.8	24.1	100.0
	90	41.3	25.0	15.1	18.7	100.0
	92	45.0	22.9	14.3	17.8	100.0
N. America	75	15.7	34.8	18.8	30.8	100.0
	80	18.9	32.8	19.2	29.0	100.0
	85	25.0	38.0	17.9	19.1	100.0
	90	27.0	36.9	18.6	17.5	100.0
	92	27.4	38.9	17.0	16.7	100.0
EC	75	3.7	8.7	51.2	36.3	100.0
	80	4.5	8.5	52.4	34.6	100.0
	85	5.5	10.5	53.3	30.7	100.0
	90	7.3	8.4	59.2	25.1	100.0
	92	8.0	8.0	59.8	24.2	100.0

(b) Exports

		To: East Asia	N. America	EC	Others	World
East Asia	1975	32.5	23.0	13.3	31.1	100.0
	80	34.5	24.3	14.5	26.7	100.0
	85	33.9	35.7	11.4	19.1	100.0
	90	39.6	29.0	16.5	14.9	100.0
	92	42.3	26.8	16.1	14.8	100.0
N. America	75	14.1	34.4	20.9	30.5	100.0
	80	17.2	33.6	24.9	24.3	100.0
	85	17.4	43.9	17.8	20.9	100.0
	90	21.8	41.4	20.4	16.4	100.0
	92	21.1	43.3	18.5	17.1	100.0
EC	75	3.2	7.1	52.3	37.5	100.0
	80	3.3	6.8	55.7	34.2	100.0
	85	4.4	11.6	54.4	29.7	100.0
	90	5.7	8.3	60.6	25.5	100.0
	92	5.9	7.8	61.4	24.9	100.0

cent. These results reflect the high growth rates of East Asian economies and the success of industrialization.

Table 4.1 illustrates the development of intra- and inter-regional trade in the three regions. A comparison of the figures for 1985 and 1992 reveals that the

(c) Imports

		From: East Asia	N. America	EC	Others	World
East Asia	1975	28.7	22.1	9.9	39.2	100.0
	80	32.8	20.3	9.2	37.7	100.0
	85	39.5	20.5	10.1	29.9	100.0
	90	43.1	20.6	13.6	22.8	100.0
	92	48.0	18.7	12.3	20.9	100.0
N. America	75	17.3	35.1	16.6	31.0	100.0
	80	20.5	32.0	14.2	33.3	100.0
	85	30.5	33.7	17.9	17.8	100.0
	90	31.3	33.3	17.0	18.4	100.0
	92	32.7	35.2	15.8	16.3	100.0
EC	75	4.3	10.3	50.2	35.2	100.0
	80	5.6	10.1	49.4	35.0	100.0
	85	6.6	9.5	52.7	31.3	100.0
	90	8.8	8.6	57.8	24.8	100.0
	92	9.9	8.3	58.3	23.5	100.0

Source: IMF, *Direction of Trade*, 1991 and 1992.

ratio of intra-regional trade increased in each region.* The ratio of intra-regional trade in the EC in 1992 was nearly 60 per cent, higher than in the other two regions (about 40 per cent in both North America and East Asia), where the ratios of inter-regional trade were higher than the ratios of intra-regional trade. However, the ratio of intra-regional trade is rising fastest in East Asia. Intra-regional trade in both the EC and East Asia has grown faster than world trade; but only in East Asia did inter-regional trade also grow faster than world trade.

A high percentage of intra-regional trade does not necessarily mean that there is a high regional bias. To take two extreme cases, where one country represents one region, the intra-regional trade level shrinks to zero while if the whole world is seen as one region then the intra-regional trade share would be 100 per cent. It is thus clear that the bigger the share a given region holds of world trade, the greater a proportion of its total trade will be intra-regional trade. If we look at the intra-regional trade percentages of the three regions in 1992, normalized in respect of share of world trade,† we see that Asia and North America had

---

* The ratio of intra-regional trade is calculated thus: (intra-regional exports + intra-regional imports)/(total exports of each region + total imports of each region).
† This method can be observed in Frankel (1991). A further refined method is the gravity model. Frankel and Wei (1993) found that for the 1980s East Asia's regional bias was shrinking, while that of the Atlantic region, especially the EC, increased. Further, Saxonhouse (1993) points out that the gravity model, which also incorporates factor endowments, is able to explain East Asia's trade pattern.

Table 4.2 Intra-regional bias

Region	Year	Bias
East Asia	1975	2.48
	1980	2.32
	1985	1.98
	1990	2.06
	1992	2.04
N. America	1975	2.01
	1980	1.98
	1985	1.80
	1990	2.06
	1992	2.15
EC	1975	1.35
	1980	1.38
	1985	1.50
	1990	1.44
	1992	1.51

Note: Intra-regional bias is obtained by dividing the intra-regional trade ratio within each region by that region's share in the world.
Source: IMF, *Direction of Trade*, 1991 and 1992.

a relatively high regional bias of approximately 2.0, compared with the EC at 1.5 (Table 4.2). If we further compare the figures for 1980 and 1992 we find that the EC's bias was almost unchanged, while North America's increased and East Asia's declined.

By examining past trade patterns and the features of both exports and imports we can identify the unique features of each of the three regions up to 1992. In East Asia, the ratio of intra-regional imports has been rising since 1975, and the ratio of intra-regional trade, both imports and exports, has been rising from the second half of the 1980s. This is a new feature in the East Asian trade pattern: increases in the intra-regional export ratio had previously been absent. More detailed examination of the East Asian intra-regional pattern reveals that exports from Japan to the Asian NIEs and to ASEAN, as well as exports from China to the Asian NIEs (especially Hong Kong), have contributed to the increase in the ratio of intra-regional exports in East Asia. In the EC, too, the intra-regional trade ratios for both exports and imports have been increasing since the second half of the 1980s. Although the intra-regional trade ratio was very high between 1975 and 1985 in the EC, change during that period was small. Compared with East Asia and the EC, the increase in the North American intra-regional trade ratio since the second half of the 1980s has been moderate.

Notably, the ratio of intra-regional exports is lower in 1992 than it was in 1985. This seems to be a result of the fact that the United States' intra-regional exports began to increase only after 1987.

If we turn next to look at inter-regional trade among these three regions, we see that while there was little change, during the 1980s, in the ratio of North American trade with the EC to total North American trade, and in the share of total EC trade accounted for by trade with North America, the growth of trade with East Asia is higher than intra-regional trade growth in both the EC and North America. As a result, East Asia's share of total North American exports increased from 17.2 per cent in 1980 to 21.8 per cent in 1990; and its share of total North American imports increased from 20.5 per cent in 1980 to 31.3 per cent in 1990. Figures for the EC are similar: East Asia's share of the EC's total exports increased from 3.3 per cent in 1980 to 5.7 per cent in 1990, and its share of imports from 5.6 per cent to 9.9 per cent.

In the period between 1980 and 1990 there was a significant change in trade patterns in North America (US and Canada), the EC and Asia (Asia-Pacific countries) (GATT, 1992), with a sharp drop in raw material imports from East Asia as a proportion of total North American and EC imports. By 1990 US raw material imports from East Asia had declined to 7 per cent of total imports from a level of 20 per cent in 1980. The EC saw a similar decline, with raw material imports from East Asia falling from 29 per cent of total imports in 1980 to 13 per cent in 1990. At the same time the share of total imports accounted for by machinery and transport equipment increased, from 42 per cent in 1980 to 53 per cent in 1990 for the United States and from 30 per cent to 48 per cent in the EC. In particular, the share of office and telecommunications equipment imports increased remarkably, as did the share of consumer goods such as textiles and clothing imported from Asia (excluding Japan) during the same period (from 33 per cent to 43 per cent for the United States and from 33 per cent to 40 per cent for the EC).

The ratio of intra- and inter-regional trade to GDP is a more exact indicator of a region's dependence on intra- and inter-regional trade than the ratio of such trade to total trade (Lawrence, 1991). Even when the ratio of intra-regional trade is at the same level in two or more regions, the meaning of this ratio differs according to the degree of dependence of each region on foreign trade. For example, an intra-regional trade ratio of 40 per cent has a different meaning for a region whose degree of dependence on foreign trade is 10 per cent than for a region with 80 per cent dependence on foreign trade. In addition, in the case of trade between regions an increase in the ratio of intra-regional trade accompanies a decrease in the ratio of inter-regional trade. However, seen in relation to GDP an increase in the degree of dependence on intra-regional trade is not necessarily accompanied by a decrease in the degree of dependence on inter-regional trade.

Table 4.3 Ratios of intra- and inter-regional trade to GDP in the three regions

(a) Exports

		Intra-regional	Inter-regional
East Asia	1980	5.8	11.1
	1985	6.8	13.3
	1992	7.2	9.9
North America	1980	3.2	6.4
	1985	3.1	4.0
	1992	3.9	5.1
EC	1980	12.6	9.9
	1985	10.6	8.9
	1992	13.1	8.2

(b) Imports

		Intra-regional	Inter-regional
East Asia	1980	5.9	12.0
	1985	6.9	10.6
	1992	7.5	8.1
North America	1980	3.4	7.2
	1985	3.3	6.6
	1992	3.7	6.9
EC	1980	12.5	12.8
	1985	10.5	9.4
	1992	13.0	9.2

Sources: IMF, *International Financial Statistics Yearbook*, 1993; IMF, *Direction of Trade Statistics Yearbook*, 1993; Asian Development Bank, *Key Indicators of Developing Asian and Pacific Countries*, 1993.

We have therefore compared the degree of dependence on intra- and inter-regional trade in each of the three regions in relation to GDP in 1985 and 1992 (see Table 4.3). The following differences were found when these data were compared with each region's ratio of intra-regional trade to its total trade. First, in East Asia and in the EC, the degree of dependence on intra-regional trade, both imports and exports, increased while the degree of dependence on inter-regional trade decreased. In North America, dependence on both inter- and intra-regional trade increased. Second, the EC's degree of dependence on intra-regional trade increased more than in the other regions, by twice as much as in East Asia and three times as much as in North America. Third, although the differences in the level of inter-regional trade between these regions are less than the difference in the level of intra-regional trade, East Asia's degree of dependence on inter-regional exports is the highest of all the regions.*

To sum up, it is apparent that East Asia has been making progress in REI, and strengthening its role as a supplier of manufactured goods vis-à-vis North America and the EC; also that East Asia has driven world trade, for although the ratio of intra-regional trade has increased, the degree of dependence on inter-regional trade means that the external market is still important for East Asian economies.

3 FOREIGN DIRECT INVESTMENT IN THE EC, NORTH AMERICA AND EAST ASIA

Since the second half of the 1980s, each region's intra-regional FDI has increased more rapidly than its inter-regional trade. In this section we look at the trend of both intra- and inter-regional FDI in the three regions.

FDI in the EC

The total amount of FDI within the EC in the period from 1982 to 1985 (hereafter, the first half of the 1980s) was $57.3 billion, and from 1986 to 1989 (hereafter, the second half of the 1980s) $231.1 billion – a fourfold increase.

Between 60 per cent and 70 per cent of total FDI in the EC in this period was accounted for by the United States and intra-regional economies. Japan was the source of only 3 per cent of the total, even in the second half of the 1980s, when Japanese FDI in the EC increased rapidly. During the 1980s FDI in the United Kingdom accounted for almost 50 per cent of total FDI inside the EC, and FDI to Spain and France combined for about 10 per cent of it. In 1990 and 1991, while FDI inflows to the United Kingdom and France decreased, FDI to Spain increased hugely to 29.8 per cent of total FDI to the EC ($21.8 billion), turning Spain into the largest FDI host country inside the EC, ahead of even the United Kingdom with 21.8 per cent ($16 billion).

When we break down the investors in each EC country, we find that US FDI in the EC accounted for more than 30 per cent of total FDI inflows to the EC during the 1980s (31.2 per cent in the first half and 32.9 per cent in the second). Seventy per cent of total US FDI in the EC during the first half of the 1980s was concentrated in the United Kingdom, a figure which increased to 90 per cent in the second half of the decade.

* If the EC is replaced by the EC plus EFTA, East Asia is also highest in the degree of dependence on inter-regional imports.

The share of intra-regional FDI in total FDI to the EC increased from 30.6 per cent in the first half of the 1980s to 42.2 per cent in the second, when the amount of intra-regional FDI exceeded the amount of US FDI in the EC. In the first half of the 1980s France's share of intra-EC FDI was the largest at 21.0 per cent, followed by Spain, the United Kingdom, Belgium-Luxembourg and Germany, at around 13 per cent. In the second half of the 1980s the United Kingdom, after the deregulation of financial markets known as the Big Bang, became the biggest absorber of intra-regional FDI with 26.5 per cent of the total. France's share of intra-regional FDI slipped to 16.3 per cent in the second half of the 1980s as did the shares of Germany and Belgium-Luxembourg, while Spain and the Netherlands increased their shares of intra-regional FDI in the same period.

FDI in North America

Total FDI inflows in the NAFTA region increased from $70.5 billion (on a flow basis) in 1982-5 to $239.6 billion in 1986–9. FDI in the United States accounted for 90 per cent of FDI in North America in this period; however, it has been decreasing since 1989, when it stood at $69 billion, to $12.6 billion in 1991. In contrast, FDI in Mexico increased from $0.6 billion in 1988 to $4.7 billion in 1991 and reached almost the same level in Canada ($5.14 billion in 1991).

The EC countries (Germany, the United Kingdom, France, Spain and Italy) together constituted the biggest investor in North America. Although its share of FDI in North America decreased from 59.7 per cent in the first half of the 1980s to 55.8 per cent in the second half, it remained high; with Japanese FDI in the NAFTA region expanding from 16.7 per cent in the first half of the 1980s to 22.7 per cent in the second, about 80 per cent of FDI flows into North America came from the EC and Japan. Intra-regional FDI was therefore very low. However, it must be pointed out that a slightly different result is obtained if stock-basis data are used. These data still point to the EC as the biggest investor in North America; but its share as calculated on this basis is only about 46 per cent for 1991, with Japan's share only 16.7 per cent. Conversely, the level of intra-regional FDI, decreasing from 30.5 per cent in 1982 to 22.6 per cent in 1991, is higher than that derived from FDI data on a flow basis. As before, we can see that intra-North American FDI stock was already formulated to some extent before the 1980s.

In addition, the stock data show that 60 per cent of FDI stock in the United States came from the EC. Japanese FDI stock was the second largest contributor, increasing to 20 per cent of total FDI in the United States in 1991. However, intra-regional FDI was low in the United States at less than 10 per cent of total FDI, while in Canada and Mexico it accounted for 60 per cent of total FDI stock (most of this was from the United States). Intra-regional FDI in North America is dominated by the United States.

FDI in East Asia

Total FDI inflow in East Asia increased from $26.5 billion in 1980–85 (hereafter, in this section and with regard to East Asian figures generally, the first half of the 1980s) to more than twice this figure, $64.6 billion, in 1986–90 (hereafter the second half of the 1980s).

From the middle of the 1980s, FDI flows into East Asia increased dramatically, coming first to Asian NIEs. During the first half of the 1980s the amount of FDI inflows into Asian NIEs, on flow-based data, was $13.1 billion, increasing to $33.4 billion during the second half of the 1980s. FDI inflows to the Asian NIEs continued to increase until 1988, decreasing slowly thereafter as ASEAN took over as the major absorber of FDI in the region. FDI inflows to the ASEAN nations increased steadily and overtook FDI in the Asian NIEs in 1991. FDI flows to China also increased during the same period, from $4 billion in the first half of the 1980s to $14.3 billion in the second half of the decade, a threefold increase.

Among the sources of FDI in East Asia, in the second half of the 1980s Japan accounted for the highest proportion of FDI to the NIEs with 38.0 per cent, followed by the United States with 27.9 per cent, and the EC with 16.5 per cent. Other Asian countries contributed only about 10 per cent. Between the first half of the 1980s and the second, Japanese FDI inflows to the NIEs increased by $50 billion, while corresponding US inflows increased by only $10 billion in the same period. Accordingly, the US share of total FDI inflows to the NIEs declined from 44.1 per cent in the first half of the 1980s to 27.9 per cent in the second half, with the Japanese share overtaking the US share in the second half of the decade.

The highest proportion of ASEAN's FDI inflows in the second half of the 1980s, 35.7 per cent, came from other Asian countries (essentially Asian NIEs), followed by Japan with 25.8 per cent, and the EC with 15.2 per cent. The share of the total FDI inflow to ASEAN contributed by the United States in the same period was only 7.5 per cent. With China, too, the proportion of FDI inflows that came from other Asian countries (again, almost equal to Asian NIEs) was the highest at 64.9 per cent, while FDI from the United States and Japan accounted in each case for only about 10 per cent.

Overall, FDI inflows to Asian NIEs have been dominated by developed countries; nevertheless, inflows to both ASEAN and China were primarily from Asian NIEs. Especially from 1986 to 1989, the proportion of Chinese FDI inflows that emanated from Asian NIEs was extremely high at 60 per cent. (Even on a stock basis, 50 per cent of Chinese inward FDI stocks came from Hong Kong.)

Figures showing the relative prominence of investors in the individual NIEs also reveal interesting trends. In Taiwan, where the FDI inflow increased to $8.1 billion in the second half of the 1980s from $2.9 billion in the first half of the decade, the largest share of total FDI inflows in the first half of the 1980s came from the United States, with 40.2 per cent. In the same period Japanese FDI accounted for 26.4 per cent and intra-regional FDI for 16.6 per cent. But in the second half of the 1980s, the relative positions of Japan and the United States as sources of Taiwanese FDI were reversed, with the Japanese share of 32.6 per cent overtaking the US share of 21.2 per cent. FDI inflows into Singapore (excluding the petrochemical and oil industries) increased to $4.1 billion in the second half of the 1980s from $3.3 billion in the first half. Although the rate of increase here is relatively low (25 per cent), FDI from Japan and from the EC increased rapidly, so that in the second half of the 1980s the Japanese share of Singapore's total FDI inflows was 40 per cent; the EC's was 20 per cent and the US share was 40 per cent, a 10 per cent decline from the 50 per cent in the first half of the 1980s. In Korea, where FDI inflows increased by 500 per cent from $0.70 billion in the first half of the 1980s to $3.6 billion in the second half of the decade, the US share of these inflows fell from 48.5 per cent in the first half of the decade to 31 per cent in the second, while Japanese FDI's share increased from 30.4 per cent to 47.9 per cent in the same period. In Hong Kong, too, we can see the Japanese FDI share increasing and the US share decreasing with total inflows to Hong Kong falling from $1.6 billion in the first half of the 1980s to $1.4 billion in the second. Hong Kong is alone in the region in showing a decrease in FDI inflows during the 1980s.

Hong Kong's and Taiwan's FDI inflows showed a relatively high ratio of intra-regional FDI to total FDI compared with the other two Asian NIEs. In the second half of the 1980s, Hong Kong's ratio of intra-East Asian FDI to total FDI inflows was 11.9 per cent, and Taiwan's 16.2 per cent. Korea's ratio was only 4 per cent, and Singapore's negligibly low.

The ASEAN countries showed a much higher ratio of East Asian FDI to total FDI inflows than the Asian NIEs. In the second half of the 1980s, this ratio was 46.6 per cent for Malaysia, 41.4 per cent for the Philippines, 31.1 per cent for Thailand, and 29.6 per cent for Indonesia. Only in Thailand was Japanese FDI larger than East Asian FDI. (The Japanese share of Thailand's total FDI inflows increased to 44.0 per cent in the second half of the 1980s from 26.6 per cent in the first half, while the US share decreased dramatically from 85.5 per cent to 11.4 per cent during the same period.)

On the stock data basis, Singapore and Hong Kong were important contributors to FDI in ASEAN. During the 1980s, in Malaysia, FDI from Singapore and Hong Kong accounted for more than 90 per cent of the East Asian FDI. Singapore's FDI in Malaysia was particularly striking at 70 per cent of the East Asian FDI in this country. In the Philippines, FDI accounted for 70 per cent of East Asian FDI during the 1980s. Hong Kong's share of total East Asian FDI in Thailand was 50 per cent during the 1980s; Singapore's was 20 per cent in the same period. The Taiwanese share increased to 20 per cent in 1988 from only one per cent in 1980. In Indonesia, Hong Kong contributed the highest share of all East Asian FDI during the 1980s, but this proportion decreased from 70 per cent in 1980 to 40 per cent in 1991. FDI in Indonesia from Korea and Taiwan increased in the 1980s, with Korea contributing 20 per cent of East Asian FDI in Indonesia in 1991 and Taiwan 30 per cent.

Quantitative evaluation of FDI in the three regions

The value of FDI inflows in each of the three regions may be assessed by comparing the ratio of FDI inflows to GDP. 'FDI-intensive countries' are defined here as countries whose recorded FDI inflows/GDP ratio exceeded one per cent during the period 1971–91. As Table 4.4 indicates, there are six FDI-intensive countries in Europe (i.e. Belgium-Luxembourg, Greece, the Netherlands, Portugal, Spain and the United Kingdom). In North America, only Mexico is an FDI-intensive country, while in East Asia Hong Kong, Singapore, Malaysia and Thailand fall into this category. Four countries – Portugal, Spain, Mexico and Thailand – became FDI-intensive countries during the 1980s, while Singapore was the most FDI-intensive economy throughout the whole period. The FDI/GDP ratios in the FDI-intensive countries ranged between one and three per cent, apart from Singapore, where they ranged between 6 and 11 per cent.

The FDI/GDP ratio may be divided into two parts: FDI/GDCF (gross domestic capital formation) and GDCF/GDP. The GDCF/GDP ratios of North American and EC countries were lower than those of East Asian countries, which all recorded a GDCF/GDP ratio in excess of 30 per cent. In the other two regions, only the Netherlands reached this level, in 1971–5. But the FDI/GDCF ratios of FDI-intensive countries in North America and the EC were higher than in some of the East Asian countries.

Overall, though FDI was less important for capital formation in some East Asian FDI-intensive countries than in North America and the EC, the greater significance of capital formation in East Asia generally meant that FDI was relatively important for each economy in that region. Over the whole of East Asia the FDI/GDP ratio in the second half of the 1980s was 1.53 per cent – higher than that of either the EC as a whole (1.32 per cent) or of North America as a whole (1.13 per cent). See Table 4.5.

Summary

The above review of East Asian inward FDI in the second half of the 1980s gives rise to three main points.

First, East Asian FDI inflow in the second half of the 1980s was $72.8 billion

Table 4.4 Ratios of FDI inflows to gross domestic capital formation, and of GDCF to GDP (%)

(a) FDI/GDCF

	1971–75	1976–80	1981–85	1986–91
USA	0.9	2.0	3.0	**5.6**
Canada	3.6	1.7	–0.7	3.7
Mexico	3.5	3.6	2.7	**7.0**
Belgium-Lux.	**7.1**	**5.8**	**7.6**	**16.0**
Denmark	3.0	0.3	0.9	3.7
Germany	2.1	0.8	0.6	1.8
France	1.8	1.9	2.0	4.4
Greece	1.0	**5.4**	**6.0**	**8.0**
Italy	1.8	0.8	1.1	2.0
Netherlands	**6.1**	4.5	**6.1**	**12.3**
Portugal	3.1	1.5	3.0	**10.7**
Spain	1.9	2.8	**5.3**	**9.2**
UK	**7.3**	**8.4**	5.4	**14.4**
Korea	1.9	0.4	0.5	1.1
Taiwan	1.4	1.2	1.5	3.5
Hongkong	**5.9**	4.2	**6.9**	**12.1**
Singapore	**15.0**	**16.6**	**17.4**	**29.4**
Indonesia	4.6	2.4	1.0	2.4
Malaysia	**15.2**	**11.9**	**10.8**	**9.7**
Thailand	3.0	1.5	3.1	**6.3**
Philippines	1.0	0.9	0.7	5.7
Japan	0.1	0.1	0.1	0.1
China	0.0	0.1	0.9	2.3

Bold figures = above 5%

(b) GDCF/GDP

	1971–75	1976–80	1981–85	1986–91
USA	19.0	20.0	18.4	16.7
Canada	24.4	24.2	20.6	21.5
Mexico	21.2	24.3	22.8	21.6
Belgium-Lux.	22.9	21.8	16.3	18.4
Denmark	24.1	21.4	17.1	18.3
Germany	23.4	22.4	20.3	21.0
France	26.1	24.1	20.6	21.1
Greece	**30.0**	28.0	21.8	19.0
Italy	22.6	23.2	23.1	20.9
Netherlands	**30.2**	21.5	18.7	20.5
Portugal	25.7	29.6	28.4	27.8
Spain	27.8	23.8	20.1	23.6

	1971–75	1976–80	1981–85	1986–91
UK	19.0	20.1	19.0	18.4
Korea	26.5	**31.3**	29.2	**34.2**
Taiwan	**30.5**	**31.2**	23.5	22.0
Hongkong	24.7	**31.9**	28.0	26.8
Singapore	**41.4**	**42.0**	**46.8**	**37.7**
Indonesia	18.3	20.7	27.8	**33.4**
Malaysia	24.0	27.2	**34.1**	29.3
Thailand	24.7	27.3	23.5	**32.1**
Philippines	25.3	**30.1**	24.0	17.9
Japan	**35.8**	**31.9**	29.2	**31.0**
China	**33.6**	**32.0**	**32.5**	**38.3**

Bold figures = above 30%

(c) FDI/GDP

	1971–75	1976–80	1981–85	1986–91
USA	0.2	0.4	0.6	0.9
Canada	0.9	0.4	–0.1	0.8
Mexico	0.7	0.9	0.6	**1.5**
Belgium-Lux.	**1.6**	**1.3**	**1.2**	**2.9**
Denmark	0.7	0.1	0.2	0.7
Germany	0.5	0.2	0.1	0.4
France	0.5	0.5	0.4	0.9
Greece	0.3	**1.5**	**1.3**	**1.5**
Italy	0.4	0.2	0.3	0.4
Netherlands	**1.8**	**1.0**	**1.1**	**2.5**
Portugal	0.8	0.4	0.9	**3.0**
Spain	0.5	0.7	**1.1**	**2.2**
UK	**1.4**	**1.7**	**1.0**	**2.6**
Korea	0.5	0.1	0.1	0.4
Taiwan	0.4	0.4	0.4	0.8
Hongkong	**1.5**	**1.3**	**1.9**	**3.2**
Singapore	**6.2**	**7.0**	**8.1**	**11.1**
Indonesia	0.8	0.5	0.3	0.8
Malaysia	**3.6**	**3.2**	**3.7**	**2.8**
Thailand	0.7	0.4	0.7	2.0
Philippines	0.3	0.3	0.2	**1.0**
Japan	0.0	0.0	0.0	0.0
China	0.0	0.0	0.3	0.9

Bold figures = above 1%

Source: UN, *World Investment Report 1993*, Annex table 3.

Table 4.5 FDI inflows in the three regions in the second half of the 1980s (US$ billion)

	EC 1986–9	North America 1986–9	East Asia 1986–90
Total inward FDI	231.1	239.6	72.8
Intra-regional FDI	97.6	11.3	44.6
Intra-regional FDI's share	(42.2)	(5.7)	(61.3)
Ratio of FDI in second half of 1980s to FDI in first half	4.0[a]	3.4[a]	2.5[b]
FDI/GDP (%)	1.32	1.13	1.53

Note: In this table the East Asia data excludes Japan.
[a]Ratio of 1986–9 to 1982–5.
[b]Ratio of 1986–90 to 1980–85.

Sources: UN, *World Investment Report*, 1992 and 1993; UN, *World Investment Directory Volume I*, 1992; IMF, *International Financial Statistics*, 1992; ADB, *Key Indicators of Developing Asian and Pacific Countries*, 1992; OECD, *National Accounts 1960–1992, Volume I*, 1994.

($64.6 billion on the IMF basis), much smaller than EC and US inflows (both were about $230 billion). The increase of East Asian FDI inflow was also smaller than those of the EC and United States. In the case of East Asia, FDI inflows in the second half of the 1980s were two and a half times those of the first half of the decade, while in the EC they grew four times, and in North America 3.3 times.

Secondly, intra-East Asian FDI in the second half of the 1980s accounted for 60 per cent of total East Asian FDI inflow in the same period. This is much higher than intra-EC FDI, which was 40 per cent of total FDI, while intra-North American FDI was only 5.7 per cent of the total FDI inflow.

Thirdly, the East Asian ratio of FDI to GDP in the second half of the 1980s was higher than that of both the EC and North America. This reflects the fact that the contribution of FDI in East Asia to the growth of local economies is larger than in the other two regions.

Further, the pattern of FDI may be summarized in terms of the relationship between investor countries and host countries in the three regions.

In the EC, intra-regional FDI accounted for 30 per cent of all FDI during the first half of the 1980s and 40 per cent during the second. During the whole decade, US FDI accounted for 30 per cent of the EC total, while FDI from other regions, including Japan, accounted for only a small proportion. When we examine the composition of FDI flows into the EC in more detail, we see that the share of total FDI that came from within the region constituted a majority of the investment inflows for each of the EC member countries, with the exception of the United Kingdom and Denmark (the United States had the highest share of UK FDI, while Denmark's largest contribution was from non-EC West European countries).

In North America, FDI from the EC accounted for half of the total inward FDI stock in the region. Intra-regional FDI stock accounted for 20 per cent, making it the second largest component of total FDI in North America, although declining. On the other hand, Japanese FDI in North America accounted for about 10 per cent of the total and was increasing. Examining the composition of inward FDI among the members of NAFTA we see that the EC countries accounted for half of total inward FDI to the United States while investment from the United States to Canada and Mexico accounted for 70 per cent of those countries' intra-regional FDI. Conversely, Canadian and Mexican investment in the United States made up less than 10 per cent of UD FDI inflows. It is thus clear that the structure of NAFTA is deeply dependent on the United States.

In East Asia, Japan, Europe and North America together account for 80 per cent of total FDI in Asian NIEs. East Asia's share of total FDI was high in ASEAN, where the Asian NIEs accounted for most of the investment. The level of investment from within the region was especially high for China, where 60 per cent of total FDI inflows in the second half of the 1980s came from within the region, with 90 per cent of this intra-regional FDI coming from Hong Kong.

4 THE DRIVING FORCES OF REGIONAL INTEGRATION IN THE THREE AREAS

In this section, we will discuss why intra-regional trade has been active and why it has been growing fast. We will break down intra-regional trade into bilateral or sub-intraregional trade, thereby pointing out those sub-regions which have grown at a faster pace than total intra-regional trade since 1985, and will then consider what factors have contributed to those developments. Before assessing the driving forces, we will examine intra-regional trade patterns in the three regions.

REI in the EC

The trade pattern of the EC

Variations in national income per capita among the members of the EC are less than in the other regions because most of the EC member states are economically advanced. Geographically and culturally, too, relations among the EC members are deep; and member countries are similar in the extent to which they rely on the intra-regional market. The ratio of intra-regional trade to total exports and imports in all member countries was 50–60 per cent in 1992, except in Belgium-Luxembourg and Portugal, where the figure was 74 per cent. The intra-regional trade ratio for the EC as a whole was below 40 per cent in 1958 when intra-regional customs tax was first reduced; in the early 1970s, after completion of a customs union in 1968, the intra-regional trade ratio rose above 50 per cent. This was due not only to high economic growth in the region but also to trade creation and trade diversion caused by the customs union.* It was not until 1985 that the ratio went up again.

Manufactured goods accounted for 77 per cent of total intra-regional trade in the EC in 1992, 16 per cent of which was in motor vehicles. Intra-industry trade is highly developed in the EC, reflecting the small difference in per capita income of member countries. It is not possible to determine precisely how much intra-industry trade based on differentiated products occurs there; as far as passenger cars are concerned, however, it can be inferred that they are well differentiated among major European companies. It is also difficult to measure how much intra-regional trade in the EC is accounted for by trade associated with MNCs. Judging from the fact that intra-regional exports of affiliates of US MNCs (72 per cent of which was intra-firm trade) account for as much as 18 per cent of total intra-regional manufactured goods trade, it could be said that a large proportion of intra-regional trade is conducted by MNCs within their own region.

The driving forces of EC REI in the second half of the 1980s

During the second half of the 1980s all EC member countries saw increases in intra-regional imports relative to extra-regional imports. Particularly striking are the cases of relatively low-income countries such as Spain, Portugal and Greece: the ratios of imports from member countries to total imports in 1985 and 1992 respectively are 52 per cent and 64 per cent for Spain, 63 per cent and 75 per cent for Portugal, and 52 per cent and 71 per cent for Greece. Between 1985 and 1992 imports into Spain and Portugal from other member countries increased by 434 per cent and 534 per cent respectively, compared with an increase in total intra-regional EC trade of 154 per cent. Imports into other member countries from Spain and Portugal also increased noticeably. With regard to the increase in the intra-regional imports of Spain and Portugal, both of which joined the EC in 1986, trade creation and trade diversion might well have taken place. More important, however, is the fact that the two countries have received large

---

* Most of the empirical studies on this point show that trade creation was larger than trade diversion (Balassa, 1975).

amounts of FDI from both inside and outside the Community since 1985. In particular, Spain became the largest host country in the EC in 1991. The ratio of inward FDI in the EC to GDCF increased from 3.8 per cent in 1981–5 to 7.6 per cent in 1986–91, implying that the inward FDI contributed to a fixed investment boom in the region in the second half of the 1980s. In particular, the inward FDI ratios of Spain and Portugal jumped to 10 per cent from 4.2 per cent in the first half of the 1980s. MNCs both inside and outside the region selected those countries as production bases from which to serve the region-wide market, taking advantage of their low labour costs. This explains the two-way increase in trade between those countries and the rest of the Community.

It is, however, too much to say that intra-regional trade involving Spain and Portugal was a dominant force in advancing REI in the EC, in the light of its contribution to total intra-regional trade since 1985. In the first place, the recent development of REI in the EC is attributable to the higher economic growth of the region, rising from an annual average of 1.2 per cent in the first half of the 1980s to 3.1 per cent in the second half of the 1980s, mainly as the result of a boom in fixed investment targeting the prospective single market after 1992. We should also stress the role of inward FDI in intra-regional trade, which contributed to fixed investment in the region. There are two forces behind this inward FDI: first, both member and non-member countries expected higher growth in the EC to result from the movement towards institutional integration in 1992; second, non-members like Japan and the NIEs promoted intra-regional FDI out of fear of 'fortress Europe' and protectionism on the part of several member countries.

REI in North America

The trade pattern of North America

The structure of intra-regional trade in North America is characterized by a situation in which Canada and Mexico are highly dependent on the US market. The United States accounted for more than 60 per cent of their exports and more than three-quarters of their imports in 1992. Although the two countries are important trading partners for the United States, the USA is far more dependent on extra-regional trade. This tendency has been strengthening. The share of extra-regional trade in total US trade was more than 70 per cent in 1992, for both exports and imports. Trade between the United States and Canada dominates intra-regional trade at about a 70 per cent share of the total in 1992. Trade between the United States and Mexico is the next largest share, while Canada-Mexico trade is very small in comparison.

Trade between the United States and Canada   Manufactured goods accounted for 82 per cent of US exports to Canada and 66 per cent of US imports from

Canada in 1990 (GATT, 1992). Both figures had increased from 1980. In manufactured goods trade, automobiles and automobile parts constituted the largest item, with a 29 per cent share of exports and a 45 per cent share of imports. Auto trade between the US and Canada increased faster than total bilateral trade over 1980–92; in particular, US auto imports from Canada increased faster than total US imports of manufactured goods from Canada.

The auto trade between the US and Canada has been facilitated by the bilateral auto agreement of 1965 and the US-Canada Free Trade Agreement of 1989. All car makers in Canada are foreign-owned. The 'Big Three' US firms, the Japanese car makers and the Europeans all manufacture there with the aim of serving the North American market, particularly the US segment. A large part of the auto trade is accounted for by such transactions as importing engines and parts and then exporting completed cars from Canada to the United States. Recently it has been reported that Chrysler's LH series is produced almost entirely in Canadian plants. There are also two-way transactions in engines and parts and a high level of car exports from the United States to Canada. This evidence suggests that the intra-industry trade of autos between the two countries consists of not only division of labour but also trade in differentiated products. In 1989 intra-firm trade involving the US auto MNCs in Canada accounted for as much as 86 per cent of total US auto exports to Canada and 76 per cent of those imports from Canada.

Roughly speaking, intra-industry and intra-firm trade by and among the Big Three is a major force driving REI between the United States and Canada. In this sense, integration between them is FDI-led. It should be noted, however, that the regional trade agreements between the two countries which facilitated such FDI are somewhat discriminatory. In effect, eligibility for the US-Canada auto agreement is limited to the Big Three; Japanese car makers in Canada have no way of enjoying the benefits of the Auto Pact such as the freedom to import auto parts freely from third countries. The local contents rules for the auto industry are stricter in NAFTA than they were previously. Specifically, the minimum proportion of local contents, which is now 50 per cent, will be raised to 56 per cent in 1998 and to 62.5 per cent in 2002.

Trade between the United States and Mexico   Relations between the United States and Mexico have long been close, as a result of both geographical proximity and US national security policy. In the past their trade pattern was a typical north-south vertical trade, with the United States exporting manufactured goods and importing crude petroleum. Even in 1980 manufactured goods accounted for 72 per cent of total US exports to Mexico and crude oil accounted for 52 per cent of total US imports from Mexico, while US imports of manufactured goods made up only 28 per cent. The shares of manufactured goods in total trade increased dramatically in 1990, to 78 per cent on the export side and to 64 per cent on the import side. Major items of manufactured goods imported from Mexico are transportation equipment, electric machinery, telecommunication equipment and consumer goods. Consequently, the intra-industry trade index between the United States and Mexico has risen as high as that among the industrialized countries (Hosen, 1991).

About 60 per cent of US manufactured goods imports from Mexico in 1987 came from the Mexican *maquiladoras* (production facilities engaged in processing or secondary assembly of imported components for re-export) (Hufbauer and Schott, 1992). Imports from US MNCs in Mexico, most of which were from the US parent companies, accounted for 35 per cent of all manufactured goods imports from Mexico. By the same token, about 30 per cent of US manufactured goods exported to Mexico involved US MNCs. It follows, therefore, that US MNCs, as well as MNCs from outside the region, contribute to the level of US manufactured goods imports from Mexico. In addition, the GSP accorded to Mexico by the United States and the US Harmonized Tariff System also facilitate the trade of manufactured goods between the two countries (Hufbauer and Schott, 1992). Under the HTS, if a company imports components or capital goods from the United States for later export to the United States, only the value added locally is taxable.

In summary, in addition to REI resulting from geographical proximity, inward FDI, both intra- and extra-regional, aimed at serving the regional market, has contributed to economic integration in North America. Specifically, division of labour by the Big Three plays an important role. Although US inward FDI is the largest in the region, it does not seem to have contributed a great deal to the increase in intra-regional trade in North America. This is because intra-regional transactions, such as sales and procurements by foreign MNCs in the United States, are mainly limited to the domestic area. Some FDI in the United States, such as that from Japanese car makers may, however, reduce US dependency on extra-regional trade and hence raise the intra-regional trade ratio, since it substitutes for exports from the source countries to the United States.* The Japanese and EC shares of total US imports have been declining since the second half of the 1980s, partly reflecting the depreciation of the dollar against their currencies.

---

* Japanese exports of passenger cars to the United States decreased from 2.35 million units in 1986 to 1.45 million units in 1993, while production in the US transplants increased from 0.62 million units to 1.61 million units during the same period.

The driving forces of North American regional integration in the second half of the 1980s

As mentioned earlier, the intra-regional trade ratio in North America rose slightly from 1985 to 1992. More precisely, it has been going up since 1987. Which transactions, then, have been growing faster than total intra-regional trade? The answer is trade involving Mexico. Particularly striking was the growth rate of Mexican imports from the United States which is 353 per cent, much higher than the 70 per cent growth in total intra-regional trade. US imports from Mexico have also been growing faster than intra-regional trade as a whole. Bilateral trade between the United States and Mexico is the engine for intra-regional trade in North America, since its growth accounts for about half of the growth in total intra-regional trade from 1985 to 1992.

Recovery in the Mexican economy may well be a major cause of the increase in US-Mexico trade. Economic reforms that President Salinas's administration inherited from its predecessor, going beyond debt relief, have begun to bloom. These reforms include such outward-oriented measures as trade liberalization, liberalization of foreign ownership and privatization of public-owned firms. Furthermore, the prospect of NAFTA helped to raise expectations of Mexican economic growth and improve the investment environment there, encouraging FDI from both inside and outside the region, since 1989 in particular. The United States is the largest foreign investor in Mexico, on both a flow and a stock basis, with a share of more than 60 per cent of the total. US FDI in Mexico, whether oriented towards the local market or towards export to the home market, may well accelerate US imports from Mexico. There are some concerns, particularly among East Asian countries, that FDI in less developed countries (LDCs) could be diverted to Mexico. So far, Japan does not seem to have diverted its FDI from Asia to Mexico; however, the US firm Zenith announced the closing of a factory in Taiwan in order to move back to Mexico. This movement can be interpreted as diverting future FDI in ASEAN countries. FDI is determined not only by labour costs, but also by other factors in the host countries, including economic and political stability, the quality of labour, infrastructure and the level of technology.

From the investor's point of view, East Asian countries have the advantage over Mexico in terms of infrastructure and quality of labour, suggesting that a large amount of FDI diversion from Asia to Mexico will not be seen in the near future. However, a considerable proportion of intra-regional FDI in East Asia (specifically, FDI from NIEs and Japan into ASEAN and China) aims at exporting to the United States by taking advantage of cheaper labour and/or GSP status in the host countries. Some such investment projects were triggered by the appreciation of their currencies in relation to the dollar; others were caused by trade friction with the United States. Since NAFTA increased the attractiveness of Mexico, at least in relative terms, some FDI in East Asia, such as that aimed at establishing export bases to the United States, could be diverted to Mexico.

Regional integration in East Asia

The trade pattern of East Asia

Reflecting the differences in the national income of member countries and in their traditional factor endowments, inter-industry or vertical trade was formerly dominant in intra-regional trade in East Asia. This trade pattern has seen drastic change with the industrial development of the East Asian LDCs.

It can be said that intra-regional trade in East Asia had been one-way: the NIEs, ASEAN and China imported manufactured goods from Japan. The share of Japan in their intra-regional imports was about 60 per cent on average in 1975. If Hong Kong, Singapore (both of which were active in intermediary trade) and Malaysia are excluded, the figure rises to nearly 80 per cent. At the same time Indonesia, a major oil exporter, accounted for 33 per cent of total Japanese imports from East Asia.

After the mid-1970s the NIEs succeeded in achieving industrialization, followed by ASEAN in the middle of the 1980s and China in the late 1980s. The trade structure in those countries, in particular that of exports, has consequently been changing dynamically. The shares of manufactured goods (defined as SITC 5-8) in total exports in 1980, 1986 and 1989 are 78 per cent, 86 per cent and 89 per cent for the NIEs; 17 per cent, 33 per cent and 48 per cent for ASEAN countries; and 49 per cent, 44 per cent and 55 per cent for China. On an aggregate basis, the figures are 52 per cent, 67 per cent and 74 per cent.

Although the increase in the share of manufactured goods in total exports is common to the whole region, there are some differences in the details. In the case of the NIEs, although there is a small increase in the total share of manufactured goods during the second half of the 1980s, the importance of basic and other manufactured goods declined, while that of machinery rose. For ASEAN countries, the shares of both basic manufactured goods and machinery increased, with the latter overtaking the former in 1989. The share of total manufactured goods in Chinese exports changed little between 1980 and 1989, but the export of machinery and other manufactured goods increased. China's machinery exports remained at less than half the level of those in the ASEAN countries, while its share of other manufactured goods exports was high in comparison.

Japan has also seen a dynamic change in its trade structure since 1985 as its exports have been concentrated in more technology-intensive goods. Even more striking is the change in Japanese imports: manufactured goods imports have increased beyond 50 per cent of the total. In particular, Japanese manufactured goods imports from East Asia have not lost momentum, even since 1990,

Figure 4.1 Japanese manufactured goods imports

Source: Ministry of finance, *Gaikoku Boueki Gaikyo* (foreign trade statistics)

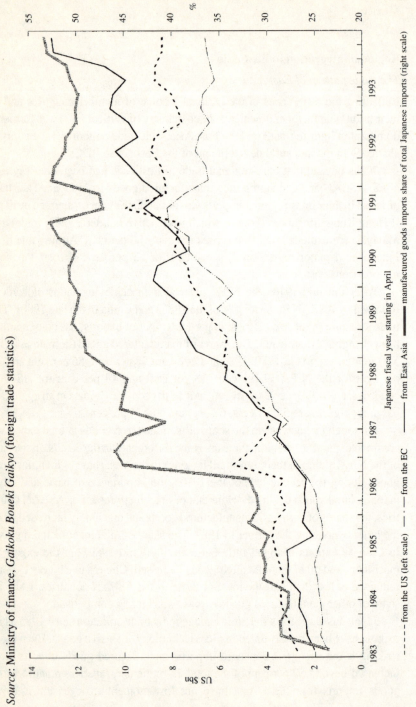

Japanese fiscal year, starting in April

----- from the US (left scale) ——— from East Asia ----- from the EC ——— manufactured goods imports share of total Japanese imports (right scale)

Table 4.6 Aggregate IIT index of manufactures in East Asian economies

	1979	1988
Hong Kong	52.3	74.6
Singapore	65.6	71.7
Malaysia	33.4	54.8
Korea	35.4	41.0
Taiwan	34.1	40.7
Thailand	18.9	34.9
Japan	28.2	30.2
Philippines	14.5	27.7
Indonesia	9.1	17.3

Note: Each IIT Index is calculated on trade weighted average (SITC 3-digit level).
Source: Fukasaku (1992).

surpassing those from the United States and the EC (see Figure 4.1). From this, combined with the fact that the East Asian share of Japanese exports has also increased, it can be inferred that there has been a substantial increase in intra-industry trade between Japan and other East Asian countries. We will now examine this point more closely.

Within East Asia, Hong Kong and Singapore are much higher on the intra-industry trade (IIT) index than other countries. This reflects their character-istics as places of high intermediary trade. The index level of Malaysia, Korea and Taiwan has increased rapidly, and, although they remain low, that of the Philippines and Indonesia has also increased (see Table 4.6). If the intra-industry trade index for East Asian countries is examined by trading partner, it can be seen that Japan's IIT index level for trade with North America and OECD Europe changed little from 1979 to 1989, rising from 25.9 per cent to 26.7 per cent with North America, and from 36.2 per cent to 34.1 per cent in OECD Europe. In contrast, during the corresponding period Japan's IIT index for other East Asian countries rose substantially, from 19.5 per cent to 27 per cent for the NIEs,* from 5.6 per cent to 11.4 per cent for ASEAN and from 6.6 per cent to 14.5 per cent for China. The IIT of each of the East Asian countries other than Japan is in most cases highest for a certain country or area within the region: Japan for Taiwan and Korea, China for Hong Kong, and ASEAN for Singapore. The IIT index for ASEAN, except Indonesia, was highest for North America, reflecting the fact

* With regard to Japan's IIT index position with the NIEs, both the level and the amount of increase of the IIT for textiles, apparel, steel, non-ferrous metals, other metals, office and computer equipment, communication equipment and other manufactured goods were high.

that intra-firm trade among US MNCs was active between ASEAN and the United States.

Economic theory distinguishes two types of intra-industry trade. Horizontal intra-industry trade is the trade of differentiated goods, while vertical trade is trade based on the division of labour. The former is based on differences in national income and in tastes. It can be exemplified by such activity as Japan decreasing exports (and/or increasing imports) of fans, tape recorders and car stereos: products in which it lost competitiveness. Another example is when, in a certain product category, Japan specializes in the production of high-tech models, while it imports medium- and low-tech ones from the NIEs and ASEAN countries. For instance, in pursuit of an international division of labour NEC has completely transplanted the production of colour televisions under 21 inches to Siam NEC in Thailand and specializes in the production of those larger than 25 inches at its Nagano plant in Japan.

Vertical trade is based on the national comparative advantages which MNCs exploit to realize the most efficient production. This type of trade can be seen mainly in the electrical/electronics industry where there are a lot of components and many processing stages. A typical example can been seen in the semiconductor industry, where Japanese MNCs locally concentrate on technology-intensive forward processes such as designing and wiring, and transfer to ASEAN countries standardized and labour-intensive backward processes such as assembling and inspection. For example, Oki Electronics built a semiconductor factory in Thailand in 1990, where it started to assemble and inspect 1 M DRAM and logic ICs. Another example is the production of electric ovens by a Japanese MNC. The company produces the high-tech components locally and the other components in Singapore, then assembles them in Malaysia for export to the United States.

As illustrated above, intra-firm trade by Japanese MNCs has greatly contributed to the recent development of intra-industry trade, both horizontal and vertical, between Japan and other East Asian countries.

The driving forces of East Asian FDI in the second half of the 1980s

Intra-regional trade in East Asia increased by 204 per cent as a whole from 1985 to 1992. Among this group, rapid growth was recorded in the NIEs' imports from China (426 per cent), the NIEs' imports from other NIEs (384 per cent), China's imports from the NIEs (387 per cent), ASEAN imports from the NIEs (297 per cent) and ASEAN imports from Japan (272 per cent).

Trade between the NIEs and China was dominated by the exchange of goods between Hong Kong and China. In 1992 Hong Kong accounted for $20.5 billion (84 per cent) of the $24.4 billion of total Chinese imports from the NIEs and for $45.8 billion (89 per cent) of the $51.7 billion of the NIEs' imports from China.

According to its own trade statistics, Hong Kong exports to China totalled HK$270.5 billion in 1992. From this total, domestic exports came to HK$59.6 billion, of which HK$44.3 billion (74 per cent) was destined for outward-processing zones in China. A further HK$210.9 billion consisted of re-exports, of which HK$97.4 billion (46 per cent) was for the purpose of creating outward-processing zones in China. Similarly, HK$254.0 billion (72 per cent) of the HK$352.1 billion total imports from China came from outward-processing zones in China. Bilateral trade between Hong Kong and China increased by more than 500 per cent from 1985 to 1992 and accounted for almost 20 per cent of the increase in total intra-regional trade in East Asia during the same period. Of a total of HK$35.8 billion of trade within the NIEs, Hong Kong's imports from other NIEs amounted to HK$22.0 billion, of which HK$11.2 billion came from Taiwan, while other NIEs' imports from Hong Kong amounted to HK$8.8 billion. Trade involving Hong Kong accounted for about 70 per cent of intra-regional trade among the NIEs.

Among ASEAN imports from Japan, Thailand's and Malaysia's were large in both volume and growth, while among ASEAN imports from the NIEs, Indonesia's, Thailand's and Taiwan's imports from Korea and Taiwan are large in both volume and growth. The largest in volume is Malaysian imports from Singapore, accounting for 23 per cent of that country's total imports in 1992. Singapore's imports from Malaysia were also large, accounting for 11 per cent of its total imports. Interdependence between Singapore and Malaysia is far-reaching.

Not only Hong Kong firms but also firms from other NIEs invested in outward-processing zones in China. This FDI was triggered by a rise in domestic labour costs in the NIEs in the late 1980s, which made their labour-intensive exporting industries less competitive. They tried to restore their competitiveness by taking advantage of outward-oriented policies and low-cost labour in China. Trade related to the NIEs' FDI in China, investment which was aimed at exporting outside the region, plays an important role in trade between Hong Kong and China and within the NIEs. Hong Kong and Taiwanese firms in China concentrate in Guandong and Fujian respectively. Hong Kong's firms in the Shenzhen Special Economic Zones (SEZ) employ two to three million local workers. Four thousand foreign companies are located in the SEZ, of which 80 per cent are owned by Hong Kong (Jones et al., 1993). Most Hong Kong and Taiwanese firms are medium or small in size, and engage in producing light industrial products. Recently it was reported that Japanese electronics affiliates in Hong Kong had transplanted into the SEZ (JETRO, 1992). Major products in Hong Kong's outward-processing exports to China are textiles, machinery, mechanical appliances, electrical equipment and plastic articles. Also important are re-exports from Hong Kong to China. All this implies that intra- and extra-regional exports serving the rapidly growing Chinese market have been increasing remarkably.

Both as an attractive market and as a production base, activity in China acceler-
ates the flow of goods in East Asia.

The ASEAN economy has witnessed high growth since the second half of
the 1980s. ASEAN inward FDI from Japan and the NIEs has increased significantly during the same period, encouraging imports of intermediate and capital
goods from the home countries. The NIEs' FDI in ASEAN is concentrated in
labour-intensive industries such as textiles, basic metal products, and electronics. Singapore has a special role as a regional and international procurement base
for semiconductors and other electronic components, partly due to advantages in
financial and communications infrastructure and to favourable tax treatment. As
a result, quite a few MNCs have built regional operational headquarters (ROHs)
there, facilitating trade by way of Singapore.*

An evaluation of East Asia's FDI promotion policy

Through trade and FDI, interdependence between East Asian countries has
significantly increased. An understanding of the primary causes of FDI in both
home and the host countries will enable policies to be formed for attracting
foreign capital through favourable host country conditions.

Since the 1960s or 1970s, each of the Asian NIEs and ASEAN countries has
created some kind of policies for the introduction of foreign capital. These
included such measures as expanding the areas open to foreign investment,
loosening restrictions on foreign investment, loosening or abolishing taxation on
foreign capital, and simplifying many procedures. (As an aside it is worth noting
that in Hong Kong there is no discrimination between domestic and foreign
companies in terms of trade and investment; the corporate tax rate is only 17.5
per cent; and there is a tax exemption for capital gains, so that Hong Kong's
taxation system itself is very attractive to foreign capital.)

According to research by JETRO conducted in the Japanese fiscal year 1990
on the situation of Japanese MNCs in the Asian NIEs and ASEAN, these MNCs
generally evaluate such points as 'political and social stability' and 'low wages'
as the superior features of both regions. Both factors, as well as 'special treatment for foreign capital' and 'policies for enhancing exports', were appreciated
more in the Asian NIEs than in ASEAN. However, regarding 'taxation',
Japanese MNCs were unimpressed by the special provisions for foreign capital
existing in both regions, except in the case of Hong Kong.

The same JETRO revealed the Japanese MNCs' specific evaluation of each
East Asian country's policies for the introduction of foreign capital. The number
in parentheses signifies the ratio of local Japanese affiliates responding affirma-

* Data General, Hewlett-Packard, Nixdorf Computers, Philips, Sony, and Matsushita
established ROHs in Singapore (Lim and Fong, 1991).

tively. For special treatment for foreign capital, Malaysia (56.3 per cent), Thailand (31 per cent) and Singapore (24.5 per cent) got relatively high evaluations. Regarding policies for enhancing exports, the evaluations are generally low, at levels of only about 10 per cent, with the exception of both Malaysia and Thailand (about 30 per cent). Lastly, regarding tariffs on parts and materials and East Asian import policy, Singapore (50.9 per cent) and Hong Kong (40 per cent) got relatively high marks, but the evaluations of the other countries are all very low at about 10 per cent.

Japanese MNCs' evaluations of the East Asian countries' policies for introduction of foreign capital (as they stood in 1990) are clearly diverse, reflecting differences in the countries' policies.

In Korea, whose policies for foreign capital are unpopular on all points, while the possible fields for foreign capital investment have been expanded since the second half of 1980s, as a rule all special treatment on taxation for foreign capital has been abolished. In Indonesia, which was also evaluated poorly, policies for the introduction of foreign capital were abolished between the second half of the 1970s and the first half of the 1980s; instead, Indonesia planned to industrialize by using only those domestic companies with huge revenues from petroleum. (The plan failed.) In Malaysia, on the other hand, a country whose policies for foreign capital are much appreciated on all points, particularly its special treatment for foreign capital and the policy for enhancing exports, all kinds of deregulation have been pursued aggressively since 1988. This is because the old 'Bumiputra policy', which had aimed to expand Malaysia's power in its own market by means of Malaysian government interventions, had weakened the economy. As a result of this deregulation, 40 per cent of capital investment projects in Malaysia are between half and wholly owned by foreign companies, and FDI in Malaysia became diversified with regard to host countries, industry and location. Recently, however, Malaysians have begun to think that this deregulation has become excessive.

This analysis shows that the policies for the introduction of foreign capital in the Asian NIEs and ASEAN are effective to some extent in increasing the FDI of Japanese manufacturers in these regions.

Summary

High economic growth in the region, particularly in China and ASEAN, and FDI from Japan and the NIEs are major driving forces for REI in East Asia. This FDI has taken advantage of the benefits offered by the host countries and has facilitated intra-regional trade. Outward-oriented policies pursued in the region have contributed to REI in East Asia, as has the unique location of Hong Kong and Singapore as ports of entry.

Figure 4.2 Trend of Japanese FDI in each region

Source: Ministry of finance

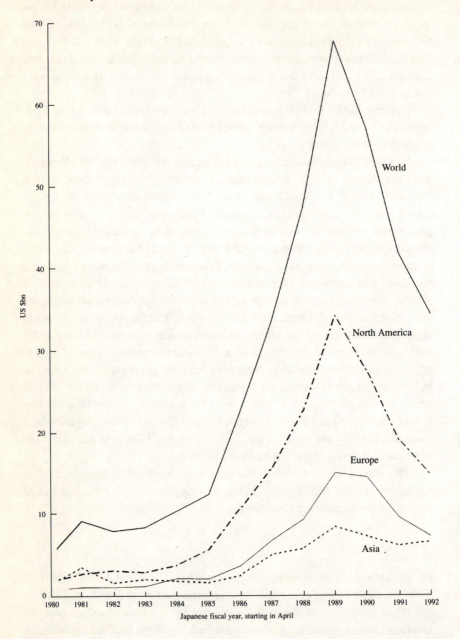

Also of interest in this context is the relationship of East Asia to areas outside the region. Japan's share of US imports decreased from 20 per cent in 1985 to 18 per cent in 1992, while the NIEs' share remained unchanged. ASEAN and China, however, increased their share of US imports from 3 per cent to 5 per cent and from 1 per cent to 5 per cent respectively during the same period. Those increases more than offset the Japanese and NIE decrease, resulting in an overall increase in the East Asian share of US imports from 36 per cent to 39 per cent. This shift in individual East Asian groups' share of US imports partly reflects the fact that Japanese and NIE investment in ASEAN was for the purpose of exporting to the US market. On the other hand, the strength of intra-regional trade relative to extra-regional trade in East Asia since the second half of the 1980s does not imply that the region became more self-sufficient, but rather that it was still dependent on extra-regional advanced countries.

5 THE ROLE OF THE JAPANESE MNCs IN THE REI OF EAST ASIA

In this section, we first provide an overview of Japanese FDI in East Asia. Then we examine the differences in Japanese FDI between the first half of the 1980s and the second, and between Japanese FDI in the developed countries and in the developing countries of East Asia. We then go on to compare Japanese FDI in East Asia with US FDI there, using data from US MNCs. (On the presence of Japanese FDI in East Asian countries, see Section 3 above.) We then evaluate the contribution of Japanese FDI to the growth of intra-Asian trade. Finally we offer some insights, from the viewpoint of regional economic integration, into the importance of technology transfer through Japanese MNCs.

The special characteristics of Japanese FDI in East Asia

Japanese FDI outflows increased dramatically from 1985 onwards, in terms of both the number and the value of projects, and involving small as well as big companies. However, since 1990 the Japanese FDI outflow (on a notification basis, that is, subject to reporting to the Ministry of Finance) has, as a whole, decreased, so that the outflow in 1992 at $34.1 billion was only half of the figure at its peak ($67.6 billion in 1989: see Figure 4.2). Three points in particular characterize the difference in Japanese FDI before and after 1985.

First, the share of Japanese FDI in developed countries increased from 1985 to 1989. While Japanese FDI in East Asia increased, at the same time Japanese FDI in the United States and in Europe increased even more dramatically. Equally, since 1990 the outflow of Japanese FDI to developed countries has decreased more dramatically than that to less developed countries.

Secondly, the proportion of total Japanese FDI outflow accounted for by non-manufacturing industry (especially finance and real estate) increased in the second half of the 1980s. This pattern is apparent in outflows to Europe, the United States and East Asia. On the other hand, among Japanese manufacturers, the proportions of FDI emanating from the electrical/electronics industry and the transportation equipment industry were relatively high. While Japanese non-manufacturing FDI has been declining since 1990, Japanese manufacturing FDI has been relatively stable in East Asia.

Thirdly, the Japanese FDI outflow for East Asia has also changed in terms of destination and industrial mix. Until 1985, Japanese FDI in East Asia was fairly strongly concentrated in textiles and went mainly to the Asian NIEs, with the exception of resource-developing investment in ASEAN countries. Since the late 1980s, however, Japanese FDI in East Asia has shifted away from ASEAN countries, and over the same period FDI in China has begun to increase.*

We turn next to the differences between Japanese FDI in East Asia and Japanese FDI in Europe and the United States. The proportion of Japanese FDI in manufacturing industry in East Asia is larger than in Europe and the United States. The proportions of total FDI taken up by manufacturing from 1951 to 1992 (on an accumulated flow basis) are approximately 40 per cent, 30 per cent and 20 per cent, respectively, in these three regions. To gain a clearer view of the situation in practice, we have examined the motivation and behaviour of Japanese MNCs in sales and procurement. (In the following paragraphs we refer only to Japanese manufacturing MNCs.)

At the outset, the Japanese MNCs' motivation to expand was fourfold. First, Japanese MNCs in Europe and the United States think more of dealing in the local (or intra-regional) market than those in East Asia. The dominant tendency for Japanese MNCs in East Asia was to be interested in a cheap and abundant labour force more than in the local market. Secondly, the Japanese MNCs in Europe and the United States think more of avoiding protectionism and trade friction with local companies (especially with the machinery industries in the United States, and the electrical machine industries in Europe); and the Japanese MNCs in the United States also think more of avoiding exchange rate risk. Thirdly, few of the Japanese MNCs in East Asia think of avoiding friction with local companies or exchange rate risk; instead they think more of selling to third countries. Japanese MNCs in Europe as well as in East Asia think much of selling to third countries also, but in the case of Europe, 'third countries' means 'other intra-EC countries', while in the case of East Asia it means mainly extra-regional countries (specifically, Europe and the United States). Fourthly, Japanese MNCs in East Asia export to the home country more than those in the

---

* According to a survey of the Japan Export-Import Bank (1993), Japanese FDI in China will become more and more important in the future.

United States do, and the Japanese MNCs in Europe export to the home country very little.

Selling and procurement behaviour depends on these differing motivations. Comparing the features of Japanese MNCs' behaviour in selling with those of US MNCs, using data from 1989, we see that in Europe and the United States, about 95 per cent of Japanese MNCs' sales depend on the intra-regional market, that is, the local area and other countries within the region. However, in the case of East Asia, only about 70 per cent depends on the intra-regional market, while 15 per cent is exported to the home country, and 11 per cent is exported to the extra-regional market (mainly North America and Europe). Sales of US MNCs in Europe show a similarly heavy reliance on the intra-regional market, which accounts for 90 per cent; but in East Asia 50 per cent of US MNC sales depend on the intra-regional market, and 40 per cent on exports to the home country. In other words, US MNCs in East Asia are more apt to export to the home country than are Japanese MNCs.

The pattern of sales by the Japanese MNCs has changed in Europe and in East Asia since 1986. In Europe, the dependency on the intra-regional market has not changed as a whole, but within that market dependency on the local market has declined while that on intra-regional third countries has increased. A similar pattern is seen in East Asia, too. When we separate East Asia into the Asian NIEs and ASEAN (data are available only since 1987), we see that in 1987 Japanese MNCs in the Asian NIEs had a higher tendency to export to the home country than the MNCs in ASEAN. The latter group, however, subsequently began to increase this tendency steadily, and eventually in 1990 and 1991 it overtook the former group.

There are fewer differences in the pattern of Japanese MNCs' procurement in North America, Europe and East Asia than in their selling patterns. Everywhere, about 50 per cent of their procurement is from within the region, while another 40 per cent is from the home country. Even though corresponding data from the US MNCs are not available, we can use data on US exports to foreign affiliates of the US MNCs, which may be regarded as imports of the affiliates from the home country. The ratio of affiliates' imports from their home country to their total sales in all areas is 32 per cent for Japanese manufacturing MNCs, of which 83 per cent comes from their parent companies, and 13 per cent for the US manufacturing MNCs, of which 87 per cent comes from the parent companies.* In the case of affiliates in East Asia, the corresponding figures are 22 per cent (63 per cent) for Japan and 18 per cent (82 per cent) for the United States. As

---

* US affiliates of Japanese manufacturing companies imported $48,000 per worker in 1987, which is three times as high as the average of all US affiliates of foreign manufacturers (Graham and Krugman, 1991).

Table 4.7 Changing procurement pattern of a Japanese affiliate in East Asia (%)

	1977	1980	1991
Local procurement	5	20	72
from other Japanese affiliates	0	10	13
	(0)	(2)	(22)
from domestic companies	5	10	59
	(0)	(10)	(60)
Imports	95	80	28
from Japan	95	75	21
from NIEs or ASEAN countries		5[a]	7[b]

Note: The affiliate was established in 1973 in Malaysia to produce room air conditioners. Figures are shares of total procurement in each year; Figures in parentheses are numbers of companies.
[a]Singapore
[b]Singapore and Thailand
Source: Sunada et al. (1993).

import data of affiliates of Japanese MNCs cover only intermediary goods, the gap between the US and Japan would actually be wider than they suggest.

Over time, the pattern of Japanese MNCs' procurement has changed. First, both in North America and in Europe, the ratio of procurement from the home country has declined. In the case of North America, it fell from 62 per cent in 1986 to 47 per cent in 1991; in Europe from 51 per cent to 41 per cent. On the other hand, in the case of East Asia, there is little change in the ratio of procurement from the home country. Second, the ratio of procurement from within the region has risen for Japanese MNCs. In North America, procurement from within the region is almost the same as that from the local market. In Europe and East Asia, there is some change in the procurement from the local market, while the ratio of procurement from intra-regional third countries has increased from 13 per cent to 23 per cent and from 6 per cent to 12 per cent, respectively. However, when we break down the ratio of intra-regional procurement in East Asia into that in the Asian NIEs and that in ASEAN, there is little change in the ratio for the Asian NIEs, but, in the case of ASEAN, the ratio of procurement from intra-regional third countries has increased. In the case of a Malaysian affiliate of a Japanese electric company shown in Table 4.7, intra-regional procurement increased through business with local firms – both domestic firms and other Japanese firms – and with companies in Singapore, which is the international procurement centre of electrical parts.

Why has there been an increase in procurement from intra-regional third countries? We can approach this question by using data on the reasons why Japanese MNCs procure from local markets. The data are given below; figures are based on MITI (1992). Note that each company was allowed to choose multiple answers. In addition, we must recognize that the increase of endogenous supply contributes to the increase of the ratio of local procurement by decreasing procurement from outside the company and thus decreasing the denominator of the ratio.

In North America the reasons for procuring locally were as follows (the number in parentheses is the proportion of companies responding affirmatively):

- price advantage (48 per cent);
- a set policy of endogenous supply (30 per cent);
- the rising ability of local companies (29 per cent);
- to deal with local affiliates of a Japanese company (17 per cent);
- to avoid strengthened restrictions in the local market (6 per cent).

In Europe the reasons for procuring locally were slightly different:

- to avoid strengthened restrictions in the local market (31 per cent);
- price advantage (26 per cent);
- to deal with local affiliates of a Japanese company (24 per cent);
- a policy of endogenous supply (21 per cent);
- the rising ability of local companies (19 per cent).

The reasons in East Asia were as follows:

- price advantage (44 per cent);
- the rising ability of local companies (38 per cent);
- to deal with the local affiliates of a Japanese company (27 per cent);
- a policy of endogenous supply (23 per cent);
- to avoid strengthened restrictions in the local market (14 per cent).

Regarding the Japanese MNCs in East Asia, the tendency to deal with local affiliates is more evident in ASEAN than in the Asian NIEs. Also, efforts to avoid restrictions are seen mainly in the automobile industry in ASEAN, while this tendency is not seen in the Asian NIEs. Among Japanese MNCs in East Asia, a higher proportion of companies give the local companies' rising ability and dealing with local affiliates as reasons for procuring locally compared with MNCs in the other two areas. Further, according to research by JETRO many Japanese companies in East Asia have extended, or are going to extend, their horizontal division of labour within the region. This movement will contribute to

Table 4.8 Comparison between Japanese and US manufacturing affiliates in East Asia in 1989

	Japanese	US
FDI (stock base) ($m)	15,591	8,280
Number of companies	1,351	(N/A: total industry 1,848)
Total assets ($m)	27,584	28,749
Total wages ($m) [A]	1,306	3,539
Number of employees (000s) [B]	417.1	464.5
Wage per employee ($000s) [A/B]	3.13	7.62
Investment for equipment ($m)	2,328	2,827
Investment in R&D ($m)	3.2	52
Number of researchers (000s)	2.1	1.6
Total sales ($m)	32,244	36,535
Return to sales (%)	3.8	7.9
Sales pattern (%)		
Total	100	100
Local sales	73	36
Exports to home country	10	40
Exports to third countries	16	23

Sources: Ministry of International Trade and Industry, *Kaigai toshi tokei soran* (A comprehensive survey of foreign investment statistics), No. 3, 4 (Tokyo: MITI, 1987, 1990); US Department of Commerce, *US Direct Investment Abroad 1989, Benchmark Survey, Final Results*, 1992.

an increase in their intra-regional procurement. Also, BBC (Brand-to-Brand Complementation in the automotive industries) in ASEAN will facilitate intra-regional procurement.

A comparison between Japanese MNCs and US MNCs

In this section we compare the Japanese MNCs in East Asia with the US MNCs in the region (see Table 4.8). To align the time of comparison, we used the fourth basic research of the 1989 fiscal year in Japan and the 1989 *Benchmark Survey* in the United States. However, it must be noted that the former is far less comprehensive than the latter and therefore tells only a part of the story.

In the first half of the 1980s, the size of Japanese MNCs' FDI outflow was almost the same as that of US MNCs. However, in the second half of the 1980s, it overtook that of the latter, and so in 1989 the stock of the Japanese MNCs' FDI was larger than that of US MNCs, while the gross assets of each amounted to $28 billion. The Japanese MNCs had just under 420,000 employees, while the US

MNCs had slightly more than 460,000. However, in 1991 the Japanese MNCs had 660,000 employees: many more than the US MNCs' 500,000. In respect of wages, both the total wages and wage per employee, those of US MNCs are higher than those of the Japanese MNCs. On investment for equipment in 1989, the US MNCs' figure was a little larger than that of their Japanese counterparts. On investment in R&D, the US MNCs' figure was again higher than the Japanese; however, the number of researchers in the Japanese MNCs was greater than that in the US MNCs.

The Japanese MNCs' total sales were $32.2 billion, while the US MNCs' total sales were $36.5 billion. However, the return to sales of the US MNCs was more than twice that of the Japanese MNCs. Regarding the pattern of sales, as noted above, both Japanese and US MNCs in East Asia have a higher propensity to export than the MNCs in developed countries. The proportion of the Japanese MNCs' local sales to their total sales is larger than that of the US MNCs; on the other hand, the US MNCs' propensity to export to the home country is greater than that of the Japanese MNCs (in the case of the US MNCs in Mexico, the ratio of local sales is as much as 66 per cent, while exports to the home country are only 29 per cent).

Why is the US MNC's propensity to export to the home country so much higher than that of the Japanese MNCs? To address this question we will examine both sales and the pattern of sales. According to the US MNCs' pattern of sales, a relatively high propensity to export to the home country can be seen in the machinery industry (excluding electronic machines), at 67 per cent, and the electronic machine industry (45 per cent). In the case of the Japanese MNCs, a relatively high propensity to export to the home country can be seen in the lumber and pulp industry (36 per cent), the electronic machine industry (27 per cent), and the precision instrument industry (22 per cent). In both countries the machinery industry, excluding transportation machines, has a relatively high propensity to export to the home country. However, in the electronic machine industry, the US MNCs' propensity to export to the home country is much higher than the Japanese MNCs'. Regarding the pattern of sales, in US MNCs the electronic machine industry (35 per cent) and the machinery industry, excluding electronic machines (25 per cent), are the dominant sectors. In the case of the Japanese MNCs, it is the electronic machine industry (39 per cent) and the transportation machine industry (19 per cent) that are the major sectors.

It can thus be seen that the electronic machine industry, which has a relatively high propensity to export to the home country, has almost the same importance in both Japanese and US MNCs' total sales. There are two points that determine the sales pattern of the Japanese MNCs. One is their electronic machine industry's lower propensity to export to the home country. The other is the larger share of the total (by more than 10 per cent) taken by its transportation machine industry, which has a 90 per cent propensity to sell in local markets, for both countries, because of local regulations.

Why, then, does the US electronic machine industry export more to the home country than Japanese MNCs? And why does the Japanese transportation machine industry sell to local markets more than that of the United States? Total sales by the US MNC electronic machine industry in East Asia amounted to $9.7 billion in 1989. Of this sum, $8.2 billion arises from sales of parts and attachments; finished goods sales are very small by comparison. In the case of Japanese MNCs in East Asia, by contrast, of a sales total of $7 billion, parts accounted for only $3.1 billion, with sales of finished goods relatively high. This difference reflects the fact that the nature of the US MNCs is as a supplier of parts for the home country's electronics industry, while the nature of the Japanese MNCs is as the sales department in the local market as well as a supplier of parts.

The automobile industry is one which most East Asian countries want to make their main domestic industry because of the number of related industries. It is therefore difficult for foreign companies to export automobiles to these countries; the only way to access these markets is by establishing affiliations with domestic firms. However, because of the strict criteria for local contents as well as for financing, and because of widespread protectionism, the MNCs in East Asia cannot hope to realize the economies of scale necessary to generate sufficient return on investment, at least in the short term. Therefore the US MNCs, for which immediate returns are a high priority, are not convinced of the need to invest in East Asian markets, while the Japanese automobile MNCs have invested in East Asia with a view towards future returns and towards capturing markets.* In addition, the fact that the Japanese automobile industry is relatively good at producing small cars contributes to the increase in their investment in East Asia.

Japanese MNCs in East Asia are sometimes regarded as unique because of their particular sales and procurement patterns: first, their high dependence on the home country in procurement, possibly reflecting the fact that they are extensions of domestic *keiretsu* or business groups (see Yoshitomi, 1990, for a detailed explanation of the economic functions of the *keiretsu*); and secondly, their relatively high dependence on third country markets for sales. One of the reasons for the first aspect is that a large amount of Japanese FDI in East Asia has taken place since 1985, so a high propensity to import from the home country may be considered natural. It is also the case that the proportion of intra-regional procurement by Japanese MNCs in East Asia appears to be increasing. Given that FDI involves the transfer of intangible assets such as high technology and management know-how (Caves, 1982), this might imply that the Japanese lean

---

*This difference in attitude between the US and Japanese companies may underlie the higher profitability of foreign affiliates of the US MNCs.

production system represented by just-in-time supply management and *keiretsu*, which is acknowledged worldwide, has been planted in East Asian countries. Also, firms can transfer their comparative advantages through FDI. This implies, however, that their home country loses comparative advantage, while the host country gains it. This shift of comparative advantage results in increases in imports from the host country into the home country. Indeed, Japanese manufactured goods imports from East Asia have been increasing since the second half of the 1980s.

The share of Japanese MNCs in inter-regional trade creation within East Asia

Before thinking about the effect Japanese MNCs have on increasing intra-regional trade in East Asia, we analyse the general relation between FDI and intra-regional trade, considering the source countries of MNCs (whether they are intra-regional or extra-regional), and the pattern of their sales and procurement in a partial equilibrium framework.

When an MNC's FDI is in the same region as the home country, the ratio of intra-regional trade increases, whether its sales depend mainly on the intra-regional market or the home market. Also, trade with extra-regional third countries generated by that MNC's FDI has a neutral effect on the ratio of intra-regional trade because such trade is simply a substitution for the home country's. In this way, we can say that intra-regional FDI contributes to the increase in the ratio of intra-regional trade.

When an MNC's FDI is in a different region from the home country, where the MNCs head office is located, then sales within the region that are generated by that investment also increase the ratio of intra-regional trade, as do sales to the local market for the purpose of avoiding trade friction (called a substitute for exports), by decreasing the region's imports from the home country. However, the MNCs dealings (sales and procurements) with the home country or with an extra-regional third country decrease the ratio of intra-regional trade.

From such relations, we can estimate the effects on East Asian intra-regional trade of FDI in East Asia by Japan, the United States and the Asian NIEs. In the case of the US semiconductor industry's FDI in East Asia, as the affiliates import semi-manufactured goods from their home country and export assembled goods to the home country, the ratio of East Asian intra-regional trade decreases. As for Japan and the Asian NIEs, since they are intra-regional countries, their FDI in East Asia generally increases the ratio of intra-regional trade. However, as the Asian NIEs' FDI produces more exports to the extra-regional third countries than Japanese FDI does, Japanese FDI in East Asia contributes more to an increase in the ratio of East Asian intra-regional trade than the Asian NIEs' FDI does.

Table 4.9 Exports and imports by affiliates of Japanese manufacturing MNCs in NIEs and ASEAN ($bn)

(A) Exports and imports by Japanese MNCs' affiliates
(Exports)

	1983	1986	1989	1990	1991
World (a)	139.9	175.0	321.4	354.0	406.4
Japan (b)	23.2	25.6	49.1	51.4	55.1
NIEs+ASEAN (c)	31.6	30.3	65.3	76.2	97.3
Intra-region (b+c)	54.8	55.8	114.5	127.6	152.4

(Imports)

	1983	1986	1989	1990	1991
World (a)	146.4	152.6	311.1	364.5	423.5
Japan (b)	33.7	40.1	75.2	85.9	99.9
NIEs+ASEAN (c)	29.5	27.6	60.5	71.5	87.7
Intra-region (b+c)	63.2	67.7	135.7	157.4	187.6

(B) Exports and imports of NIEs and ASEAN
(Exports)

	1983	1986	1989	1990	1991
World (d)	4.8	9.1	12.9	20.6	27.1
Japan (e)	1.2	3.2	5.6	6.0	9.3
NIEs+ASEAN (f)	0.9	2.6	3.5	6.5	9.3
Intra-region (e+f)	2.1	5.7	9.1	12.5	18.6

(Imports)

	1983	1986	1989	1990	1991
World (d)	5.2	5.8	23.9	26.5	27.5
Japan (e)	2.9	3.3	12.0	13.7	15.2
NIEs+ASEAN (f)	0.2	0.3	1.5	2.0	3.2
Intra-region (e+f)	2.2	2.9	13.3	14.9	15.4

(C) Japanese affiliates' share
(Exports)

	1983	1986	1989	1990	1991
(a/d)	3.4	5.2	4.0	5.8	6.7
(b/e)	5.2	12.4	11.5	11.7	16.8
(c/f)	2.9	8.5	5.3	8.5	9.6
(b+c)/(e+f)	3.8	10.3	7.9	9.8	12.2

(Imports)

	1983	1986	1989	1990	1991
(a/d)	2.0	2.2	3.9	3.8	3.6
(b/e)	5.9	6.5	15.8	15.0	12.2
(c/f)	0.7	1.2	2.4	2.9	3.6
(b+c)/(e+f)	3.5	4.3	9.8	9.5	8.2

Note: Exports by affiliates are authors' estimate.
Sources: Ministry of International Trade and Industry, *Wagakuni kigyo no kaigai jigyo katsudo* (Survey of the overseas activities of Japanese companies), 21, 22 (Tokyo: MITI, 1991, 1992); *Kaigai toshi tokei soran* (A comprehensive survey of foreign investment statistics), 2, 3, 4 (Tokyo: MITI, 1986, 1987, 1990).

The trade of Japanese MNCs in East Asia may be classified as follows. Total exports (the sum of exports to Japan and exports to third countries) are classified as exports to Japan and exports within the region. Similarly, total imports (imports from Japan plus imports from third countries) are classified into imports from Japan and imports from within the region. Table 4.9 shows time series data for each item's share in total East Asian trade, East Asian trade with Japan, East Asian trade within the region (excluding Japan) and East Asian trade within the region including Japan. We refer to the Japanese manufacturing affiliates as the Japanese MNCs. From the data in the table the following points are evident. First, the proportion of Japanese MNCs' exports to total East Asian exports is larger than the proportion of their imports to total East Asian imports. The tendency of the proportion of exports to increase has become stronger and stronger, while the proportion of imports remains almost at the same level. Secondly, both in exports and in imports, the ratio of Japanese MNCs' trade to East Asian trade with Japan is relatively high, about 10 per cent. Also, in 1991, the ratio to East Asian exports increased, while the ratio to East Asian imports decreased slightly. Thirdly, the proportion of Japanese MNCs' trade within the region, *excluding* Japan, has increased slowly. Fourthly, the proportion of Japanese MNCs' trade to East Asian trade within the region, *including* Japan, has increased to about 10 per cent since the second half of the 1980s. It should be noted that the Japanese MNCs' imports given in this table are those of intermediate goods only. Imports as a whole are therefore undervalued because local imports of capital goods relating to their investment are excluded.

In 1989 US MNC exports in East Asia (manufacturing, majority-owned foreign affiliates or MOFA) totalled $23.5 billion, comprising $12.5 billion of exports to the home country, and $11 billion of exports to third countries (including exports to East Asia of $6.3 billion). On the total value of the exports, the US MNCs in East Asia ($23.5 billion) surpassed the Japanese MNCs in East Asia ($12.9 billion), but in exports to East Asian countries, the Japanese MNCs in East Asia ($9.1 billion) topped the US MNCs in East Asia ($6.3 billion). Therefore, the US MNCs' contribution to total East Asian exports is larger than that of the Japanese MNCs, while the Japanese MNCs' contribution to intra-East Asian exports is greater than that of the US MNCs.

It has been shown above that the Japanese MNCs' trade contributes to the growth of intra-East Asian trade more than the trade of US MNCs does. Further, since the MNCs' trade is usually intra-industry, they make intra-regional trade more valuable through technology transfers. In addition, dealing actively with such MNCs contributes to an increase in the productivity of local companies through technology transfer of both skills and management techniques. The contribution of Japanese companies to the growth of East Asian trade and technology transfer,* not only through their production in local markets but also through their original equipment manufacturing (OEM) style – mainly in the Asian NIEs – and through technological cooperation, mainly in China, is so large that we can say the total contribution of Japanese companies to East Asia is much larger than their share of East Asian intra-regional trade. However, we have also to recognize that the role of Japanese MNCs is limited to justify calling it the dominant factor in regional integration, and that FDI by both US and the Asian NIEs has also played an important part.

Technology transfer through Japanese MNCs

Transmission of technology and/or knowledge occurs through imitation, FDI and technology trade. While imitation (unintended technology transfer) does not bring originators of the used technology any benefits, FDI and technology trade do. Owners of technology can circumvent the difficulties associated with technology transfer through market transactions (see Yoshitomi, 1991). From the

---

* It is difficult to measure technology transfer quantitatively. One estimate has shown Japanese technology transfer embodied in capital goods to East Asia to be twice as large as that of the United States in 1987 (Hanasaki, 1990).

host countries' point of view, business with more highly developed countries' companies has the merit of increasing the knowledge of and challenging the technology used by the local firms.

Japanese FDI to East Asia consists to a large extent of investment in consumer electronics and transport equipment. This industrial mix of Japanese FDI has two particular implications for technology transfer. First, the share of assembled parts in both industries is very high, which creates the possibilities of high linkage effects between the local parts producers and the MNCs. Secondly, both industries have loosely integrated with parts industries. This loose vertical integration is characterized by features such as long-term/continuous transactions and joint product developments. Given such an industrial structure, new technology developed by either assembler or parts producer is easily and quickly disseminated. Recent increases in the local contents of the products of Japanese electrical/electronics industries suggest that technology transfer has been facilitated between Japanese MNCs and local parts industries.

6 POLICY IMPLICATIONS OF REI IN EAST ASIA

Free trade regimes and the high growth of East Asia

East Asian economies have had remarkable success in sustaining rapid growth for more than thirty years.* There are four main features of this development:

(1) Outward-looking policies on such issues as exports and promotion of inward FDI have played an important role in achieving rapid growth.
(2) Growth at this speed resulted in rapid change in industrial structure and comparative advantage, i.e. a shift from light industries to heavy industries, and eventually to high-tech industries.
(3) High growth occurred in sequence in countries of the region. Japan took the lead in the 1960s, followed by the Asian NIEs in the 1970s, and then by ASEAN and China in the 1980s. As a result, the region as a whole was able to sustain rapid growth for a long time.
(4) Technology that was invented in industrial countries enabled the East Asian economies to expand.

According to the World Bank (1993), there are significant commonalities among the outward-looking policies of East Asian economies. 'Each [policy] contributed to one or more of the four elements of a successful export push:

* Academics have recently paid more attention to the high growth of the Asian economies, partly because of the theoretical development of the endogenous growth model. See Young, 1993; Lucas, 1993.

Table 4.10 Preferential treatment to promote export activities in ASEAN countries

	Thailand	Malaysia	Indonesia	Philippines
Export financing scheme	Agricultural export financing Manufacturing export financing	Export credit refinancing Pre-shipment financing Post-shipment financing Preferential rate loan for exporter, commercial banks present this loan and central bank refinances for the commercial bank		Rediscount of export bill by the central bank at preferential rate
Preferential treatment to promote export activities	Exemption from corporate income tax Tax credit for duties and tax on imported capital equipment Exemption from tariffs on imports of materials to be assembled or processed for export	Deduction of corporate income tax rate (rate of deduction = 50% of export sales from total sales) Deduction of taxable income corresponding to half of exports Tariff exemption for imported materials to be assembled or processed for export	Refund of or exemption from tariffs on imports of materials to be assembled or processed for export Unrestricted and duty-free import access for exporters	Exemption from corporate income tax Exemption from duties and taxes on imported capital equipment Exemption from tariffs on imports of materials to be assembled or processed for export Utilization of bonded warehouse Deduction of taxable income corresponding to half of labour costs
Export processing zone or free trade zone	Exemption from corporate income tax Exemption from duties and tax on imported capital equipment Exemption from tariff on import of materials to be assembled or processed for export	Tariff exemption for imported materials to be assembled or processed for export Unrestricted and duty-free access to import for exporters Deduction of taxable income corresponding to half of exports	Refund of or exemption from tariff on import of materials to be assembled or processed for export Unrestricted and duty-free import access for exporters	Exemption from all taxes (except real estate tax) Utilization of bonded warehouse Unrestricted and duty-free import access for exporters

Sources: JETRO, *Sekai to Nihon no kaigai chokusetu-toshi* (World and Japanese foreign direct investment), 1993; Nihon Ajia Toshi Co. Ltd and consulting centre, *Ajia no toshi kankyo* (Investment environment in Asia), 1992.

access for exporters to imports at world prices; access for exporters to long- and short-term financing; government assistance in penetrating markets; and flexibility in policy implementation' (p. 143).

Among the four elements cited above, the second and third are relevant to the problem of consistency with GATT. GATT prohibits export subsidies on products other than certain primary products (Article XVI). More specifically, the Code on Subsidies (Agreement on Interpretation and Application of Articles VI, XVI and XXIII of the General Agreement on Tariffs and Trade) identifies the contents of subsidies (Annex: Illustrative List of Export Subsidies) and treats export credit with preferential interest rates as a subsidy (Annex (k)). With regard to the third element, the Code stipulates that the exemption, remission or deferral of direct taxes specifically related to exports and/or the allowance of special deductions directly related to exports or export performance constitutes an export subsidy (Annexes (e) and (f)). The Code also states that indirect taxes constitute export subsidies under certain conditions (Annexes (g) and (h)). Most of the NIEs and ASEAN have implemented such measures as export financing with preferential interest rates and/or special deductions for export-related income in order to promote export activities (see Table 4.10). Those NIEs and ASEAN countries that would violate the rules of the Code are not signatories, so they do not violate the GATT explicitly. However, they will have to curtail such export promotion policies in the near future. China, too, will have to change its preferential treatment for export activities of the firms located in SEZs once it signs up to GATT. It should also be acknowledged that the successes of the outward-looking policies of East Asian economies are based on the fact that those economies have access to large markets such as the US because of the multilateral liberalization under GATT.

With regard to the second and fourth features of rapid growth in East Asia, FDI from industrial countries, especially from Japan, precipitates technology transfer to East Asia. Overall, East Asian economies have been the greatest beneficiaries of the world free trade regime. It is therefore in the East Asian countries' interest that they do not let other countries tilt towards protectionism. We should recall that in the past those countries that have gained the largest benefits from free trade regimes have advocated multilateral trade liberalization. The United States took the initiative in the GATT rounds in response to EC integration.* Today, it is diverting its attention away from GATT towards regional initiatives and/or bilateral approaches to realizing freer trade. The EC, for its part, seems to accord first priority to the difficult task of establishing monetary and political union. In the face of these inward-looking stances taken

---

* Sapir (1992) states: 'European integration was the main driving force behind the Dillon and Kennedy rounds of the multilateral trade negotiations which produced substantial tariff reductions'.

by industrialized countries, Japan should promote multilateral trade liberalization to prevent the EC and the United States from moving towards protectionism.

Merits of regionalism and its implications for East Asian economies

Two merits of regionalism as a second best to multilateral trade liberalization may be identified, other than the Vinerian trade creation effect and terms of trade effect. First, economic integration enhances efficiency by increasing competition within the enlarged market. Here discrimination against non-member countries is required to protect and promote member countries' industries. Secondly, it is much easier for a smaller number of like-minded countries to come to an agreement on trade and investment liberalization, a problem with which GATT has not dealt successfully so far. In this sense, regionalism can become a vehicle for multilateral liberalization.

The first merit, stimulating competition within a regional market, is emphasized in the EC integration process. Though the EC has a north-south gap, it is a more homogeneous economic sphere than the East Asian economies. If the economies are homogeneous, then the integration of markets is easier. EC firms are in a better position to enjoy economies of scale within this enlarged market, even if they fail to expand extra-regional exports. We should note, however, that the EC has discriminatory trade policies, such as import restrictions aimed at Japan, in order to protect and encourage some industries within the region. The associations CUSFTA and NAFTA make a point of the second merit, showing that regionalism can become a vehicle for multilateral liberalization. Furthermore, NAFTA stipulates that membership is open-ended, which makes it easy to apply the intra-regional liberalization to other countries.

Are there any advantages for the East Asian economies in adopting a regionalism which discriminates against non-member countries? The answer to this question is 'no', for the following reason. Although economic integration has intensified among East Asian economies, as shown by the increase in the intra-regional trade ratio, East Asia is still highly dependent on extra-regional trade. In fact, its extra-regional export dependency ratio is higher than that of either the EC or North America. This reflects high ratios of extra-regional sales of MNCs located in East Asia compared with those of MNCs located in North America and the EC. As access to extra-regional markets (i.e. the US and EC markets) continues to be important, East Asia should not establish an institutional economic bloc which might make regionalism in other industrial countries more inward-looking.

In addition, if the East Asian economies were to form a new institutional bloc, all the industrial economies would belong to one of three blocs. The formation of these blocs could have an adverse effect on developing countries that are excluded from the blocs.

The need for an 'open' regionalism

That East Asian countries should not adopt a position of regionalism does not necessarily mean they should only follow the GATT multilateral trade liberalization process. Having reached agreement in the Uruguay Round in December 1993, GATT is likely to be strengthened by new rules, including the establishment of the World Trade Organization. Still, the tasks remain so enormous that the negotiation process among the large number of participants continues to be slow. Thus, East Asian economies must provide a negotiation framework consistent with and complementary to GATT to achieve a freer world trade regime, while deterring the EC and North America from protectionism.

Several conditions must be considered. First, the trade barriers of the East Asian developing economies are high. Trade liberalization is a far-reaching task for both domestic and international organizations. Second, East Asian economies have been gradually liberalizing trade. This strategy matched very well with export-led growth. From an international coordination point of view, high-growth economies should and can liberalize trade voluntarily and unilaterally. Third, it is more beneficial to freer trade if East Asia and North America cooperate in trade liberalization than if each region were to proceed individually. In stark contrast to the self-sufficient EC, neither North America nor East Asia is a self-contained region. This lack of self-sufficiency could be a foundation for cooperation between East Asia and North America. In this regard, we can make use of APEC, which is larger than East Asia and North America. Adjustment costs associated with trade liberalization within APEC could be more easily absorbed than those within East Asia to the extent that East Asian developing countries have access to the US market. It is of equal importance that Japan proceed with market-opening measures and sustain domestic demand-led growth. Japan could mitigate the adjustment costs of the developing countries by importing more goods and services from them. Fourth, if APEC member countries provided non-member countries with preferential treatment in trade liberalization (i.e. regional trade liberalization on an MFN basis), it would be a quick way to link APEC trade liberalization with global trade liberalization. Even though the trade liberalization negotiations are on a 'minilateral' basis, involving only a small number of countries, they would not trigger protectionist movements if the benefits were given on an MFN basis. For developing countries that are excluded from the EC or APEC, non-discriminatory APEC liberalization would not generate any harmful effects.

Overall, East Asian economies need an 'open' regionalism with two important facets. First, member countries proceed with intra-regional trade liberalization irrespective of RTA and extend the benefits of liberalization to third countries. Secondly, the extension of benefits to third countries is instant and is not restricted by imposing the condition on third countries that they offer reciprocal liberalization. This collective liberalization by members (membership should be open-ended) for third countries is an expanded version of unilateral liberalization by each country. Why, then, do we need such unilateral collective liberalization? One reason is that we need some enforcement mechanism for liberalization. Another reason is that trade liberalization is in reality a concession from a political point of view. Thus it is inevitable that each participant takes the stance 'we will not give a concession [i.e. trade liberalization], unless you give us an equivalent concession.'

East Asian economies should implement collective unilateral trade and investment liberalization with other APEC members as a complement of GATT. Each government within the region would need great political resources to complete the process. ASEAN countries have been promoting their industries by gradual import liberalization since the early 1980s; in order for 'open' regionalism to be accepted by ASEAN, it is necessary to strengthen the political power of groups in ASEAN that support trade liberalization. Japan, as the only industrialized country in East Asia, should take the initiative in promoting trade and investment liberalization within APEC, and should help to sustain the dynamic growth in the region. Japan faces a very demanding task of sustaining the region's economic vitality by coordinating the conflicts of interests of East Asia and the United States to get APEC working while at the same time putting more resources into the GATT process. That is the enormous but unavoidable task for Japan as a prominent country throughout the twenty-first century.

References

Balassa, Bela, 1975, 'Trade creation and diversion in the European Common Market', *European Economic Integration*, North-Holland, Amsterdam.

Bhagwati, Jagdish, 1991, *The World Trading System at Risk*, Princeton University Press, Princeton, NJ.

Caves, Richard E., 1982, *Multinational Enterprise and Economic Analysis*, Cambridge Surveys of Economic Literature.

Dornbusch, Rudiger, 1991, 'Dornbusch on trade', *The Economist*, 4 May, p. 65.

Drysdale, Peter and Garnaut, Ross, 1993, 'The Pacific: an application of a general theory of economic integration', in C.F. Bergsten and M. Noland, eds, *Pacific Dynamism and the International Economic System*, Institute for International Economics, Washington DC.

Export-Import Bank of Japan, 1993, *Questionnaire Survey of Japanese FDI (FY 1993)*, December.

Frankel, Jeffrey A., 1991, 'Is a yen bloc forming in Pacific Asia?', in Richard O'Brien, ed., *Finance and the International Economy, The Amex Bank Review Prize Essays*, Oxford University Press, Oxford.

Frankel, Jeffrey A. and Wei, Shang-Jin, 1993, *Trade Blocs and Currency Blocs*, NBER Working Paper, no. 4335.

Fukasaku, Kiichiro, 1992, *Economic Regionalisation and Intra-industry Trade: Pacific-Asian Perspectives*, Technical Papers No. 53, OECD Development Centre, February.

GATT, 1992, *International Trade 90–91*, Vol. II, Geneva.

Graham, E.M. and Krugman, Paul R., 1991, *Foreign Direct Investment in the United States*, Institute for International Economics, second edition, Washington DC.

Hanasaki, Masaharu, 1990, *Kinmitsuka suru kan-Taiheiyo no keizai rinkeiji (Intensified Economic Linkage in the Asian-Pacific Region)*, Chousa No. 138, Japanese Development Bank, February.

Hosen, Mitsuo, 1991, 'Wagakuni Boueki Kouyou no Suihei Bungyoka to Kigyo no in Gurobarizeishon' ('Development of horizontal division of labour between Japanese trade pattern and globalization of Japanese firms', *Kaigaitoushi kenkjujou*, 17, 11, Research Institute of Overseas Investment, The Export-Import Bank of Japan, November.

Hufbauer, G.C. and Schott, J.J., 1992, *North American Free Trade*, Institute for International Economics, Washington DC.

JETRO, 1992, 'Sekai to Nihon no Kaigai Chokusetu Toshi', *World and Japanese FDI*, May.

JETRO, 1993, *Unfair Trade Policies by Major Trading Partners*, Industrial Structure Council, Japan.

Jones, R.S., King, R.E. and Klein, M., 1993, *Economic Integration between Hong Kong, Taiwan and the Coastal Provinces of China*, OECD Economic Studies No. 20, Spring.

Komiya, Ryutaro, 1993, 'Japan's comparative advantages in the machinery industry', *MITI Research Review*, 2, December.

Krugman, Paul R., 1991, 'The move to free trade' (mimeo).

Lawrence, Robert Z., 1991, 'Emerging regional arrangements: building blocks or stumbling blocks?', in Richard O'Brien (ed.), *Finance and the International Economy, The Amex Bank Review Prize Essays*, Oxford University Press, Oxford.

Lim, Linda Y.C. and Fong, Pang Eng, 1991, *Foreign Direct Investment and Industrialisation in Malaysia, Singapore, Taiwan and Thailand*, Development Centre Studies, Paris.

Lloyd, Peter J., 1992, 'Regionalisation and world trade', *OECD Economic Studies*, 18, Spring.

Lucas, Robert, 1993, 'Making a miracle', *Econometrica*, 61 (2), pp. 251–72.

Ministry of International Trade and Industry (MITI), 1992, *Kaigai toshi tokei soran* ('A comprehensive survey of foreign investment statistics'), 4.

Sapir, André, 1992, 'Regional integration in Europe', *Economic Journal*, 102.

Saxonhouse, Gary R., 1993, 'Trading blocs in East Asia' in Arvind Panagariya, Arvind and Jaime de Melo, eds, *New Dimensions in Regional Integration*, Center for Economic Policy Research.

Stoeckel, A., Pearce, D. and Banks, G., 1990, *Western Trade Blocs – Game, Set or Match for Asia-Pacific and the World Economy?*, The Center for International Economics, Pirie Printer, Australia.

Sunada, T., Kiji, M. and Chigira, M., 1993, *Japanese Direct Investment in East Asia – Changing Division of Labour and Technology Transfer in the Household Electric Appliance Industry*, Kenkyu Series No. 13, Research Institute of International Trade and Industry.

Torre, A. de la and Kelly, M.R., 1992, *Regional Trade Arrangements*, Occasional Paper 93, International Monetary Fund, Washington DC, March.

Tran, Van Tho, 1993, 'Technology transfer in the Asian Pacific region: implication of trends since the mid-1980s', in T. Ito and A.O. Krueger, eds, *Trade and Protectionism*, NBER Vol. 2.

US Department of Commerce, 1992, *US Direct Investment Abroad 1989, Benchmark Survey, Final Results.*

World Bank, 1993, *The East Asian Miracle: Economic Growth and Public Policy*, Oxford University Press, Oxford.

Yoshitomi, Masaru, 1991, 'Foreign direct investment in Japan: What accounts for its low penetration?', in Sumitomo-Life Research Institute, *Japanese Direct Investment in Europe: Motives, Impact and Policy Implications*, Avebury, Aldershot.

Young, Alwyn, 1993, 'A tale of two cities: factor accumulation and technical change in Hong Kong and Singapore', *NBER Macroeconomics Annual.*

5 REGIONAL INTEGRATION AND MULTINATIONAL PRODUCTION

Stephen Thomsen

Preferential trading arrangements among neighbouring countries have prolifer-ated since the mid-1980s. Western Europe first began with the Single European Act, turning later to negotiate EC accession agreements with EFTA and Eastern Europe. The United States negotiated a free trade agreement with Canada and then promptly enlarged it to include Mexico. Debates still rage about the possibility of a regional bloc forming in Asia and whether this would include the United States and other industrialized countries bordering on the Pacific. Devel-oping countries have also been active in creating new agreements or reinvigorating old ones. By now, very few countries are not negotiating some sort of agreement with their neighbours, occasionally dusting off previous agreements that had not proved possible to implement in the inward-looking climate of import substitution in the 1970s.

At the same time, as described at length in this chapter, regional trade and investment are flourishing as never before. For many regions, intra-regional trade is growing faster than trade with partners outside the region. Direct investment appears to be following a similar path. The purpose of this chapter is to discuss the link between political moves towards liberalization on the one hand and shifts in the pattern of trade and investment on the other. The causality is assumed to move from politics to economics, and indeed government policies are a vital ingredient in this process. But, contrary to what is commonly asserted, evolving patterns of trade and investment are not simply the result of this move towards preferential agreements. In some cases, regional agreements result from pressures by producers within the region eager to take advantage of a regional division of labour. In others, the agreements merely seek to redress a former bias *away* from regional integration. Territorial disputes and historical animosities have always plagued relations among neighbours, particularly in the developing world. The present agreements merely allow exporters and investors to do what they have been unable to do freely in the past: trade and invest with neighbouring countries. In this sense, the growing regional integration that we observe, orchestrated in large part by multinational enterprises (MNEs), is a natural result of geographical and cultural proximity, not the outcome of political negotiations. Governments have played a role in this process, not by dictating where firms should sell their goods but by allowing firms to conduct business with their own natural partners.

The economics of geography

What do we mean by geography? It is admittedly a nebulous term, the economic implications of which are often difficult to measure. But its importance has been shown for all types of economic transactions across space, including both trade and direct investment. One possible explanation for this importance is that firms possess only imperfect information about profit opportunities abroad and that geographical distance can serve as a rough proxy for the impediments to goods and factor mobility. Distance imposes several costs on an exporter or investor. The first is the cost of transportation. While the costs to the exporter are clear, the investor will also be influenced if the affiliate is intended as an export platform for markets elsewhere. Similarly, there may be diminishing returns to management from trying to organize production on a global scale. But more important than these costs are information costs more generally. Both the exporter and the market-oriented investor have to acquire information about sales opportunities abroad, particularly if they produce a non-standardized product which might have to be adapted to local market conditions. It could be argued that many of the largest MNEs are already represented throughout the world, so that for them these information costs are no longer an obstacle. One of the biggest hurdles to global production strategies for such firms is likely to be the continued segmentation of markets due to differences in demand across different countries or regions. If demand does differ to reflect different needs and cultures, then it is possible that countries within the same region are likely to have the most similar types of demand. This could well account for regional trade in general and for regionally organized multinational production in particular.

The importance of geography is confirmed again and again in econometric tests applying gravity models. Most studies have concerned themselves with intra-European trade and investment. Looking at intra-European trade, Beckerman (1956, p. 31), argues that the costs of covering distance exist and are significant. His simple test noted a striking degree of concentration of each country's trade on a small range of other countries. Balassa and Bauwens (1988) apply a far more sophisticated test which distinguishes between intra- and inter-industry trade in Europe. Using a form of gravity model, they find that distance, or a common language or border, are all significant determinants of the pattern of trade in Europe, while membership in the European Community is not. Bergstrand (1985) finds similar results for a larger sample of all OECD member countries. Very few tests of foreign direct investment patterns have applied gravity models. Molle and Morsink (1991) and Thomsen and Woolcock (1993) both find distance factors to be relevant in the context of intra-European investment patterns. It is well known that when American firms first ventured abroad, they chose neighbouring Canada or English-speaking Britain and Australia as locations. For much the same reason, German firms prefer Austria in Europe over many other larger markets. German firms are also most active at present in Eastern and Central Europe. In none of these cases has preferential access played a prominent role. More often than not, governments prevent trade and investment among these 'natural' partners rather than encouraging them. The Berlin Wall kept German firms at bay in what was traditionally their *chasse gardée* in Central Europe.

Trends in regional integration

To demonstrate that regional integration is a natural consequence of what I refer to generically as geography, I will review the trend of economic integration in each of the world's major regions. I hope to show that intra-regional trade is growing in part because firms are increasingly orchestrating their production on a regional basis. While political changes are behind this ability to seek regional partners, it is not preferential treatment that is driving the trend: rather, it is geography.

The degree of integration among groups of countries is usually measured by trade flows. We will supplement this measure with an examination not only of the pattern of foreign direct investment (FDI) but also, more specifically, of the way in which MNEs organize their production on a global basis. This approach can be justified on the basis of the ubiquitous role that MNEs play in economic integration. Trade between parent firms and their affiliates represents the largest share of world trade, and other internal transfers of services, technology, patents, etc. are often the only way in which such factors are exported. MNEs are already responsible for the largest share of the world's technological patents. With such a prominent role in the production and trade of goods and services and in the generation and dissemination of technologies, MNEs are clearly powerful agents in the process of economic integration. With their global networks, they are also able to respond quickly to opportunities abroad and, as such, their foreign investments represent a leading indicator of changes under way in the world economy. An analysis of FDI into and within each region of the world can therefore provide clues to the degree of existing integration, to the future pattern of that integration and to the fundamental driving forces behind it.

It should be made clear at the outset that I am not arguing that regional agreements are preferable to multilateral solutions. Rather, I am simply suggesting that regardless of the liberalization process followed – whether unilateral, bilateral, regional or multilateral – the result in the 1990s is likely to be greater integration within regions relative to, but not at the expense of, global integration.

North America

North America is already fairly well integrated through trade. US-Canadian trade represents the largest bilateral trade flow in the world. Such intra-regional trade is dominated by MNEs, principally American ones which already account for one-half of American manufacturing imports from Mexico. One-fifth of US imports from Mexico come from only five companies (IBM, Ford, Chrysler, General Motors and Nissan), four of which are American (Hufbauer and Schott, 1992, p. 71). US firms also account for a large share of Canadian exports, principally in the automotive sector. American enterprises have long exploited the opportunities for a regional division of labour, with trade liberalization measures such as the US-Canada Automotive Pact and the offshore assembly provisions for *maquiladora* plants in Mexico pointing the way. US firms now employ almost 1 million Canadian workers out of a total population of only 26 million. Mexican affiliates of US MNEs employ one-quarter of all workers in American firms in developing countries, a share which has grown quickly in recent years. General Motors is the largest private employer in Mexico.

US firms are not the only active regional players in North America. Canadian firms are the fourth largest national group of direct investors in the United States, directing two-thirds of their foreign acquisitions to the US market between 1987 and 1991. During the same period, takeovers of Canadian companies by American investors represented almost one-half of total foreign takeovers. Canadian firms now employ 740,000 US workers.

Because Mexico is a developing country, it is not surprising to see that direct investment into the United States from that country has not been at very high levels, but there is clear anecdotal evidence to suggest that the trend is upward. In 1989, the Mexican glass company Vitro SA acquired interests in Anchor Glass Container Corporation and the Latchford Glass Company. Cemex, the largest cement company in Mexico, purchased US companies throughout the southern and western United States in the late 1980s.

Not all investment within North America is from firms headquartered within the region. Indeed, it is widely acknowledged that regional integration increases inward investment from firms on the outside eager to take advantage of improved growth prospects in an enlarged market and to avoid potential barriers to exports. The United States attracts the lion's share of investment into the region, but outside companies have shown some indication of a desire to use Mexico and Canada as platforms from which to serve the whole market. Such regionally oriented production plans are most prevalent in the automotive sector.

Mexico is clearly benefiting from an immense surge in confidence on the part of investors in its economy. German companies alone have recently pledged $3 billion in investment in Mexico, with $1 billion from Volkswagen to increase vehicle output, $800 million from Hoechst for a petrochemical plant, and $650 million for the tourism industry (*Financial Times*, 1991). Nissan has also announced a three-year investment programme totalling nearly $1.2 billion. Overall, vehicle-makers are expected to pour $5 billion into Mexico. While the projected capacity of the Mexican automotive industry well exceeds domestic demand, it would be inappropriate to consider this investment as predominantly export-oriented. By the year 2000, Mexico will be producing 2 million cars a year, of which 30 per cent will be exported to the United States. Some will also go to other countries such as Canada and Japan, but the majority will be sold to Mexicans. The Mexican car market has been growing at 20 per cent a year for five years and is expected to expand by 12–15 per cent in each of the next six years (Griffiths, 1992).

The same attraction of the growing Mexican market can be seen in other sectors. The British firm Cadbury Schweppes made one of the largest acquisitions of a Mexican business in 1992 by buying Mexico's leading bottler and distributor of mineral water for $325 million. Mexico is the world's second largest market for carbonated soft drinks and the market is growing by 9 per cent a year (Fuller and Fraser, 1992). The large American brewer, Anheuser-Busch, has recently invested almost half a million dollars in a Mexican brewery. These investments will improve production and distribution techniques of the local firms as well as providing an international network for exporting Mexican brands. But, at the same time, it must be remembered that the investments were largely made to gain access to the local market.

Not all investments in Mexico and Canada will be directed towards those relatively small markets. With lower costs of production than in the United States, these countries clearly offer the potential for a regional division of labour. The important question from our perspective is whether American firms, when looking for a lower-wage export platform to serve the US market, prefer a location within the region or whether they are truly global scanners. The evidence suggests a regional bias in export locations to serve the US market in almost all sectors, as can be seen in Table 5.1.

In addition to Canada and Mexico, two other countries appear again and again in US MNE imports to the parent firm: the United Kingdom and Singapore. The importance of Britain relates to the weight of that country in total FDI by American firms. It should not be seen as an export platform for the US market, *per se*. The importance of Singapore appears to constitute a direct contradiction of my hypothesis of a regional bias. As we shall see later, however, in spite of the role that Singapore plays as an export platform for the American market, a far higher share of sales of American affiliates in that country is sold within Asia itself. If we look at exports to the United States as a percentage of total sales then Mexican affiliates are the most strongly oriented towards the US market of affiliates in any major country. The evidence from Table 5.1 shows not only that

Table 5.1 Intra-firm trade by US-owned manufacturing affiliates abroad, 1990

Sector	Total affiliate exports to the US (US$m)	Share from Canada and Mexico (%)
Transportation equipment	29,840	92
Metals	1,913	69
Other manufacturing	8,408	60
Chemicals	3,862	34
Electronics	10,161	31
Food	1,233	29
Machinery	12,327	21
Total manufacturing	67,744	61

Source: US Department of Commerce.

MNEs are very selective in where they locate their export platforms, but also that they seem to prefer neighbouring countries.

The North American market is integrating rapidly, and MNEs are active in that process. Intra-regional investment is driven partly by the desire of states in the region to gain access to one another's markets, but also by the potential for a regional division of labour. NAFTA will enhance this potential, but its effect should not be exaggerated. A good deal of export-oriented production in Mexico already enjoys various tariff exemptions, for example through the Generalized System of Preferences (GSP) and the *maquiladora* programme, which levies duties only on the amount of value added in Mexico. These agreements arose because US MNEs wished to use Canada and Mexico as export platforms. To suggest that such intra-firm trade results from the agreements is of course true, but it confuses cause and effect. By and large, US MNEs seem to prefer to supply the parent company from these two countries. There are significant exceptions, such as Singapore, but even with that country we are likely to see affiliates in Singapore playing more of a role within the Asian region in the future rather than as a platform for exports to the US, as discussed in the section on East Asia below.

South America

Although much of this chapter focuses on Europe, North America and East Asia, it is instructive to glance quickly at the prospects for regional integration among relatively rich developing countries in other regions. Regional trade and investment in South America are still at very low levels, but they are increasing.

Chile's trade with Argentina has more than trebled since 1987. Furthermore, as governments remove regional barriers, albeit slowly, MNEs from other regions are responding by rationalizing production on a regional basis.

The recent history of renewed South American integration demonstrates that intra-regional direct investment is not limited to the industrialized world. Chilean firms have invested almost $3 billion in Argentina since 1990. In return for access to the much larger Argentine market, particularly in newly privatized sectors, Chilean firms offer expertise in how to run firms in an environment which is rapidly being liberalized, privatized and deregulated. Recent steps towards regional integration have also been accompanied by rationalization of the existing operations of MNEs from outside the region. The signing of a complementarity agreement between Argentina and Brazil in 1986 encouraged Ford and Volkswagen to rationalize their operations into a joint venture, Autolatina. Renault and Nestlé have also supposedly increased their investment in the region as a result of the agreement.

Europe

Western Europe is generally recognized as the most integrated region within the world economy, although still much less integrated than large national markets such as the United States. Almost three-quarters of its trade flows among the two dozen or so countries that comprise Western Europe, an intra-regional share more than double that in other regions. Much of this trade relates to the European Community. Intra-EC imports (for a constant sample of all twelve EC members) grew from 35 per cent of total imports into those countries in 1958 to 59 per cent by 1990. During the same period, the intra-Community share of exports grew from 37 per cent to 61 per cent. When one considers that another 10 per cent of Community exports go to neighbouring countries belonging to the European Free Trade Agreement (EFTA), then the regional bias of trade is uncontestable. Unlike in other regions, however, the intra-regional share is falling back slightly, as the degree of integration with the rest of the world catches up with that inside Europe.

Direct investment by European firms has tended to follow a different path from that of trade. Historically, European firms have invested in their former colonies or, more recently, in the fast-growing American market. European firms are by far the largest outside investors in the United States, in spite of the attention given to Japanese firms. This outward focus began to change only in the late 1980s, as documented in Thomsen and Woolcock (1993). For the first time in the history of the Community, intra-EC FDI in 1989 equalled external flows in both directions. For all member states with the exception of the United Kingdom, the stock of outward investment is now concentrated principally in Europe.

In terms of trade flows, the history of European integration provides some surprises to economists. After thirty-five years of gradual integration, the exports from individual countries to the rest of Europe are still highly concentrated in only a few markets, much more so than the relative market size of each importing country would suggest. The top three export markets within the Community for each member state take in anywhere from 56 to 77 per cent of total intra-EC exports from that country. Naturally the largest economies figure prominently in this list as export markets, but market proximity is also a factor. Balassa and Bauwens (1988) look at the determinants of the pattern of intra-European trade and find that market size, distance, common borders and similar languages are all more important than membership of the Community or EFTA in explaining both the importance of intra-industry trade and the pattern of overall trade in Europe. Geography, not politics, is the most important factor behind European trade.

The same point can be made for investment within Europe. German firms dominate investment in Austria, employing more Austrians than they do Spaniards or even British, and more Swiss than Greeks and Portuguese combined. Denmark has invested three times as much in Sweden since 1978 as it has in Belgium, an economy of roughly similar size. Almost two-thirds of German investment in Western Europe goes to the seven countries that border on Germany while much of the rest goes to the three remaining large markets of Britain, Spain and Italy. Dutch firms invest the most in Belgium and Luxembourg. Spanish firms prefer Portugal and then France. Thus, even within Europe, the ties of membership within one or the other integrated area seem to take second place to those of geography.

Wijkman (1990) has taken the analysis of geographical factors further by looking at what he calls webs of dependency. He finds that there are three sub-regional trading areas in Europe. The first is the North Periphery consisting of the British Isles and Scandinavia. The second is the South Periphery, comprising the Iberian peninsula, Greece and Turkey. The remaining countries are clustered around Germany; these he calls Core Europe. In comparing the trade pattern in 1958 with that in 1987, he finds that in many cases these clusters have become more, rather than less, clearly defined as integration has gone ahead. As Eastern Europe opens to the outside world, it is likely to find itself pulled into the region known as Core Europe. Germany has historically dominated the region to the east, and renascent trade and investment patterns seem to point to a re-establishment of that trend.

This trend in integration within a region is analogous to the one identified in integration across regions. The evidence from European integration suggests that, as the region has moved closer together, trade and investment have grown most quickly among neighbouring countries. I suggest that the same is likely to continue to be true at a global level. Multilateral liberalization or even unilateral moves may well promote integration within regions more than across them.

American firms in Europe

Jean-Jacques Servan-Schreiber wrote in 1967 that by 1982, 'it is quite possible that the world's third greatest industrial power, just after the United States and Russia, will not be Europe but American industry in Europe.' American firms first began to invest in Europe in the 1850s and are now often indistinguishable from local firms. In spite of almost four decades of integration, the European market still sometimes appears to be a series of national or sub-regional markets, as judged by the sales patterns of these affiliates. Sixty per cent of affiliate sales in manufacturing are to the national market in which the affiliate is located.

Unfortunately, we possess little information about where within Europe these affiliates sell when they export. The most recent information comes from a 1977 survey by the US Commerce Department. It found that affiliate exports in Belgium were fairly widely dispersed, given the central location of that country within Europe. Nevertheless, much of the exports went to Germany, France and the Netherlands in that order. Affiliates in Ireland were found to export primarily to the United Kingdom while those in Denmark focused on Sweden and Germany. Affiliates in the largest markets predominantly exported among themselves, though neighbouring countries were also targeted. Indeed, the main conclusion that emerges from these export patterns is that the behaviour of American firms in Europe is not much different from that of local firms. In almost all cases, the top four markets for affiliate exports within Europe were also the same as for total host country exports, though the exact ranking was often slightly different. This suggests that clustering is as much a phenomenon for US affiliate exports as it is for the total pattern of intra-European trade as described by Wijkman (1990).

How much do US majority-owned manufacturing affiliates in Europe sell back to the US parent? Out of total sales of $352 billion, only $13 billion are exported back to the United States, compared to exports to third countries of $135 billion. In other words, these affiliates are in Europe to supply the European market with American goods produced locally. Their exports to the US represent only 12 per cent of total European exports to that country. In spite of the endless discussion of global firms, it appears that American investment in Europe is doing more to integrate the European economy with itself than it is to tie the American and European markets more closely together through trade. Indeed, intra-regional exports by American-owned affiliates have grown faster than total intra-European trade.

American firms in Europe were already well integrated in their European operations considerably before the advent of the single market. Table 5.2 shows the destination of sales by manufacturing affiliates in the original six members of the Common Market at three points in time. It is clear that most of the change in the sales pattern to reflect the greater degree of European integration occurred

Table 5.2 Sales patterns of US MNEs in the original Common Market (local sales as % of total by manufacturing affiliates)

	1966	1977	1989
Belgium	49	29	30
France	82	68	67
Germany	75	65	57
Italy	83	73	73
Luxembourg	*	11	28
Netherlands	53	39	33
EC6 total	73	59	54

Source: US Department of Commerce.
*Luxembourg included in Belgium.

between 1966 and 1977. The behaviour of American-owned firms has changed very little since then, in spite of all the discussion of the single market. In other words, rather than being driven by political changes, these affiliates actually anticipated further regional liberalization.

East Asia

East Asia is the least inward-looking of the regions considered here. Only one-third of its trade is with itself, while one-half is with the rich markets of Western Europe and North America. Nevertheless, the Asian share of trade is growing quickly. In terms of East Asian trade flows, the growing importance of intra-regional trade is evident. Taking Japan, China, the newly industrializing economies (NIEs) – South Korea, Hong Kong, Taiwan and Singapore – and the ASEAN countries – the Philippines, Indonesia, Thailand, Malaysia, Singapore and Brunei – as a group, export growth was fastest towards the United States in the first half of the 1980s. By 1986, North America was their largest export market, accounting for 39 per cent of their global exports, compared with only 28 per cent for intra-regional trade. In the second half of the 1980s, intra-regional trade became the largest share of the total. The twelve East Asian countries now take in 37 per cent of the total, far ahead of either North America (31 per cent) or Europe (17 per cent). The regional share is below that achieved in the European Community, for example, but it is growing quickly. Because future trade patterns will depend on trends in FDI, it is on investment patterns that attention will be focused here.

Investment both within and into Asia is expanding more rapidly than in any other region. Japanese manufacturing investment in Asia has always exceeded that in Europe, in spite of the attention that the latter has received. The cumulative value of Japanese investment in manufacturing abroad amounted to $94 billion at March 1992. Of this amount, one-half was in North America, one-quarter in Asia and less than one-sixth in Europe. In terms of the number of affiliates, Asia is responsible for over one-half of the total in manufacturing. This discrepancy between number and value simply reflects the smaller size (i.e. relative labour intensity) of Japanese manufacturing affiliates in Asia.

The regional bias of Japanese manufacturing FDI is likely to grow in the future. A survey of investment intentions conducted by the Japanese Export-Import Bank (EXIM) reveals not only that Japanese firms will devote relatively more investment to Asia, but also that this investment will largely be oriented towards the local Asian market (Tejima, 1992, p. 26). This local market orientation applies across East Asia, including the NIEs and ASEAN, two groups commonly associated with MNE export platforms. Fully 90 per cent of the new projects in Asia are intended to target Asian markets, including Japan. This investment will be directed particularly to China and the ASEAN region. The further appreciation of the yen in 1993 will no doubt accelerate the exodus of component production from Japan to the rest of Asia.

The EXIM survey also provides evidence on the destination of sales of Japanese affiliates abroad. In each of the three main regions, roughly 94 per cent of output is at present destined for the regional market. The respondent Japanese firms expected this share to fall only slightly in the future. In electronics, virtually all production in Europe and North America is sold locally. In Asia, the electronics share is lower at 78 per cent for existing production bases but for future bases it is expected to grow to 82 per cent. Furthermore, for each Asian region (the NIEs, ASEAN and other Asia), the largest share of output is sold within the region itself, followed by Japan. Only for electronics production in ASEAN is the North American market in second place ahead of the Japanese one. In terms of future production bases in both the NIEs and ASEAN, the share of output remaining in the region is expected to grow.

The same appears to be true for American investment in Asia. In static terms, the share of American manufacturing investment going to Asia (including Japan, Australia and New Zealand) amounts to only 15 per cent of the total, less than that received by Canada alone. But it has nevertheless increased from only 12 per cent since 1986 at a time when the European single market supposedly captured the imagination of American investors. Even more important than the levels of investment is the behaviour of American firms in Asia. In 1990, American firms sold $75 billion worth of merchandise to Asia through their local manufacturing affiliates. Of this amount, almost two-thirds was sold in the national market in which the affiliate was located, while remaining affiliate sales were shared roughly evenly between the regional market and the home American market.

Table 5.3 Sales of US majority-owned affiliates in Singapore (manufacturing only)

Year	Total sales (US$m)	Local (%)	To US (%)	To other (%)
1985	3,073	10	64	26
1986	3,091	10	62	27
1987	3,996	11	60	29
1988	4,843	14	57	29
1989	7,579	13	55	33
1990	10,058	16	53	31

Source: US Department of Commerce.

If globalization is taken to mean a global factory, then we would expect a large share of the output of these affiliates to be exported either back home to the United States or to affiliates in other regions of the world. The fact that around three-quarters of the output was sold in Asia itself suggests that global strategies are far from the minds of most investors. Furthermore, the local and regional focus of sales is increasing at the expense of markets outside the region.

This point can best be seen by taking the most extreme case of an Asian country which fits into the global production strategy of American firms. American majority-owned affiliates in Singapore sold over $5 billion worth of goods and services back to the United States, mostly to their own parent companies. These sales constituted over one half of the total for these affiliates, suggesting that global strategies were the main reason for investing in Singapore. Table 5.3 shows the destination of sales since 1985, a period during which total sales have tripled. What is immediately clear is that within that growing total, both local and regional sales have outgrown traditional intra-firm sales back to America. (Of course, some of the sales to countries other than the United States go to Europe and thus are not intra-regional. It is estimated that the regional component of these 'other' sales amount to two-thirds of that total. This adjustment in no way alters my conclusions.)

Singapore is the quintessential export platform for MNEs interested in serving the global market, so it is not surprising that sales back to the United States are still the largest component of the exports of American-owned firms located there. The example of Singapore was provided because it indicates that even in this extreme case, the trend is towards greater regional integration on the part of what are supposedly globally oriented manufacturing firms. Affiliates in virtually all other Asian economies are more regionally oriented than are those in Singapore. In all of these countries except Malaysia, regional sales constitute over two-thirds of total affiliate sales, sometimes much more.

The discussion so far has concentrated on Japanese and American firms, the two largest global investors. However, an increasing share of investment in Asia comes from developing countries in Asia itself, particularly the NIEs. Firms from these four countries are becoming major regional investors, as well as starting to invest both in North America and Europe. Hong Kong business is responsible for one-half of all investment in China, though some of this no doubt represents investments by other countries, such as Taiwan, which are channelled through the colony. Taiwanese firms were the largest investors in Malaysia in 1990–91 and in Indonesia in 1988 and 1991. South Korean firms switched in 1992 away from North America towards South-East Asia, which accounted for 44 per cent of the total annual investment. The biggest jump in investment occurred in China and Vietnam, which recently normalized relations with South Korea. Singapore has invested in Indonesia and Malaysia, though it still lags behind the other NIEs in terms of its outward investment. This has prompted the former prime minister of Singapore, Lee Kwan Yew, to exhort local firms to become more active abroad. Nevertheless, the NIEs are by now substantial net investors abroad.

Taken together, investments by NIEs in the rest of Asia often exceed those from either Japan or the United States. This is particularly true in Malaysia and Indonesia, though it is also often the case for investment in the Philippines in spite of that country's close links with the United States. Only in Thailand does Japan prevail. Sales of NIE affiliates in these countries are most likely for the moment to be back to the investing country, representing a division of labour within the region which will eventually be reflected in the trade figures. This investment arises partly because of rapidly appreciating currencies and rising labour costs in the NIEs. The Taiwanese dollar rose 50 per cent against the US dollar between 1985 and 1992. The choice of East Asia for such investment stems from the influence of distance and culture on firms' behaviour.

Most of this intra-Asian investment flows from the NIEs to the ASEAN countries (excluding Singapore) and to China, but even the poorer countries are now starting to venture abroad. Malaysia is looking towards China and Indonesia plans a substantial investment in India. All countries in Asia may become eager to venture into Vietnam now that relations are being normalized.

The record of investment by American, Japanese and NIE firms points to the same conclusion in each case: although investment in East Asia can come from any region of the world, affiliates are selling more and more within the region itself. American affiliates often sell in the country in which they are located. Japanese and NIE affiliates often export back to the home country. In all cases, production appears to be orchestrated on a regional basis far more often than on a global one, and this tendency is growing.

Thus, in Asia as elsewhere, general liberalization with very little preferential access may well promote regional integration more than it will global integration. Rather than being an artificial result of regional trade agreements, such integration is the natural consequence of geographical proximity and cultural affinity. This effect is even stronger with FDI than with trade, though eventually these intra-regional investments will exert a powerful influence on the pattern of trade as well. All MNEs, whether from America, Europe and Japan or from the NIEs, are pursuing a regional division of labour in Asia.

Summary of regional trends

In examining trends in direct investment, as far as possible patterns of investment have been distinguished from patterns of multinational production. There will always be large amounts of inter-regional investment for the simple reason that host-country market size is one of the strongest determinants of where firms invest. What North America and Western Europe offer in terms of actual market size, East Asia offers in terms of market potential. For this reason, direct investment is no more intra-regional than is trade. In both cases, however, the evidence suggests that the intra-regional share is growing.

As with trade, we need to distinguish between different types of investment if we are fully to understand its relationship to the process of integration. Intra-industry trade is not the same as inter-industry trade, and market-oriented investment is not the same as investment driven by lower unit labour costs. In spite of all the excitement about the single market in Europe, much intra-European investment represents attempts by firms from one national market to penetrate another national market (see Thomsen and Woolcock, 1993). It represents part of the growth strategy of firms reaching market share limits at home. In North America, there is greater scope for a regional division of labour, although as we have seen, a good deal of what is produced in each country is still sold in that country. East Asia in turn represents the opposite extreme from Europe, where the largest share of investment is driven by lower unit labour costs. This latter type of investment will spur exports from the host country, as Kojima (1978) has argued for Japanese investment, resulting in even greater intra-regional trade in the future.

Because motives for investment can differ so greatly, we have focused in our review on production strategies rather than on investment *per se*. The evidence presented here suggests that although there is still substantial inter-regional trade in final goods, the production of such goods is likely to result from a regional rather than an international division of labour. This regional preference is not mainly the result of political moves towards greater regional integration at the expense of multilateral negotiations. Indeed, in most cases, regional economic integration by MNEs has actually anticipated the political process. Even those firms that are usually considered global appear to be opting for this regional approach, though in their case the outcome is one of multi-regional production. Some day, the pundits on globalization will be right: these firms will be global factories. But for the moment, MNEs are constrained by geography to a much more modest strategy.

The activities of affiliates of American companies engaged in manufacturing provide ample evidence to support the multi-regional hypothesis. The most important sector for FDI is transportation equipment, mostly automobiles. With the exception of minority holdings in Japanese companies, virtually all US intra-firm imports in this sector come from Canada and Mexico. Similarly, in Europe, most of what is produced by affiliates is sold in the European market. There is virtually no inter-regional trade among affiliates in this sector. In other sectors which are less important in value terms, US intra-firm imports are more likely to come from countries other than Mexico and Canada, but in almost all cases, inter-regional exports are less than what is sold locally and regionally. Most sales by affiliates, regardless of the particular host country, are in the local market in which the affiliate is located. There are exceptions, such as Singapore and other small countries, but even when export sales exceed local sales, these exports are usually destined for the rest of the region rather than for other regions. Not surprisingly, regional sales are greatest relative to total sales in Europe, where regional integration is most advanced.

Conclusion

Static comparisons of intra- versus inter-regional trade show that with the exception of Europe trade is mostly inter-regional, but intra-regional trade is growing quickly in these other regions. Similarly, FDI is increasingly focusing on regional markets and to some extent on a regional division of labour. To be sure, there is very little to stop firms from investing in other regions, as has occurred for well over 150 years. But it appears that when MNEs do invest in other regions, they organize their activities on a regional and fairly autonomous basis. This is not true for all sectors, of course. Economies of scale in some industries make such a multi-regional strategy a luxury that few firms can afford. At an aggregate level, however, the statistics on FDI suggest not only that the multi-regional approach is prevalent but that it is also growing. Because such investment by its very nature increases trade flows, we are likely to see an expansion of intra- relative to inter-regional trade for the rest of the 1990s.

Trade and investment will always be influenced by preferential political agreements, just as the composition of trade is affected by the distribution of barriers across industries. But to accredit this rapid growth of intra-regional trade to the formation of customs unions in each region misses the point. First of all, these agreements often follow steps by MNEs towards regionally oriented production, as the Asian case demonstrates. In other words, regional political integration is driven by regional economic integration, not the other way round. Second, many countries have had better political relations with countries outside their region than with nearer neighbours within the region. Thus regional trade has been thwarted by government policies in many regions in spite of the fact that such activity could potentially be the largest share of a country's trade: the role that geography plays in shaping trade and investment patterns has been suppressed by government policies.

Introducing geography into the discussion of regional integration does not fundamentally alter the way we should judge preferential trade agreements. The standard measures of trade creation and trade diversion still apply. But it does suggest that the gains from agreements among neighbours may well be greater than those among countries with little scope for trade. Like medieval monarchs uniting their kingdoms through marriage, trade agreements among dispersed economies may fail to bring about the expected gains if there is little scope for interaction between the two countries. As Bhagwati (1992) argues forcefully, geographical proximity is not a sufficient condition for gains to be realized, but in many cases it may well nevertheless be a necessary precondition.

Because MNEs are such active participants in economic integration and because they materially affect the outcome of that integration, we have tended to focus on their strategies in each major region. We have implicitly assumed that intra-firm trade among affiliates and the parent tends to represent vertically integrated production. It is possible to argue that trade diversion is more likely to occur with such intra-firm trade than with traditional arm's-length trade. With their global scanning capabilities, MNEs may be quicker to spot the cost advantages from producing inside a preferential area. One American firm, Zenith, has closed down a factory in Taiwan and opened one in Mexico; this could be construed as trade diversion, though even in this case there were extenuating circumstances. In spite of this possibility for relocating affiliates, the scope for trade diversion by MNEs is actually quite small. Over one-half of intra-firm manufacturing imports to the United States already come from Canada and Mexico. Intra-firm trade is already largely regional. This conclusion is most strongly endorsed by trends in the motor industry which tend to dominate the total figures, but even in electronics similar results apply. Although American MNEs locate production of certain electronic components in countries like Singapore that are outside the North American region, very little of this output actually makes its way to the United States. Most of it is sold locally or in the regional market.

I am not implying that inter-regional trade is becoming less important. Western Europe is still the largest trading partner of the United States. What I am suggesting is that in those sectors in which MNEs are important, intra-firm trade already appears to be a regional affair. Global firms are not global factories. The evidence of MNE behaviour therefore provides some optimism about possible pro-trade effects from regional integration. Nevertheless, it must be remembered that in other sectors in which MNEs are less important, such as food, clothing and textiles, trade diversion may be more likely. These are precisely the sectors in which firms are least able to offset losses from such diversion.

For this reason, multilateral, non-discriminatory liberalization remains the best outcome. But we should not be surprised if regional agreements proliferate in the near future. In many cases, they are merely redressing political biases against regional trade that existed in the past in spite of the putative regional solidarity professed by governments. Growing regional links may well just be a prelude to the global economy; but for the rest of the 1990s at least, geography is likely to matter more, not less, than in the past.

References

Balassa, Bela and Bauwens, Luc, 1988, 'The determinants of intra-European trade in manufactured goods', *European Economic Review*, 32, 1421–37.

Beckerman, W., 1956, 'Distance and the pattern of intra-European trade', *Review of Economics and Statistics*, 28, pp. 31–40.

Bergstrand, Jeffrey, 1985, 'The gravity equation in international trade: some microeconomic foundations and empirical evidence', *Review of Economics and Statistics*, 67, pp. 467–81.

Bhagwati, Jagdish, 1992, 'Regionalism and multilateralism: an overview', Columbia University Discussion Paper 603, Columbia University, New York.

Caves, Richard, 1971, 'Industrial corporations: The industrial economics of foreign investment', *Economica*, 38, pp. 1–27.

Financial Times, 1991, 'Germans pledge $3 million investment in Mexico', 4 July.

Fuller, Jane and Fraser, Damien, 1992, 'Cadbury Schweppes in Mexico water deal', *Financial Times*, 19 March.

Graham, Edward, 1978, 'Transatlantic investment by multinational firms: a rivalistic phenomenon', *Journal of Post-Keynesian Economics*, 1, Fall, pp. 82–99.

Griffiths, J., 1992, 'Japan to import Mexican Nissans', *Financial Times*, 23 July.

Haigh, Robert, et al., 1989, *Investment Strategies and the Plant-Location Decision: Foreign Companies in the United States*, Praeger, New York.

Hufbauer, Gary and Schott, Jeffrey, 1992, *North American Free Trade: Issues and Recommendations*, Institute for International Economics, Washington, DC.

Jacquemin, Alexis and Sapir, André, 1988, 'International trade and integration of the European Community: An econometric analysis', *European Economic Review*, 32, pp. 1439–49.

Julius, DeAnne, 1990, *Global Companies and Public Policy: The Growing Challenge of Foreign Direct Investment*, Pinter for RIIA, London.

Knickerbocker, Fred, 1973, *Oligopolistic Reaction and Multinational Enterprise*, Harvard University Press, Cambridge, MA.

Kojima, Kiyoshi, 1978, *Japanese Direct Foreign Investment*, Charles Tuttle, Tokyo.

Molle, Willem and Morsink, Robert, 1991, 'Intra-European direct investment', in B. Bürgenmeier and J. Mucchielli, eds, *Multinationals and Europe 1992*, Routledge, London.

Servan-Schreiber, J.-J., 1967, *The American Challenge*, translated from the French by R. Steel, Hamish Hamilton, London.

Tejima, Shijeki, 1992, 'Japanese foreign direct investment in the 1980s and its prospects for the 1990s', *EXIM Review*, 11, 2, Export-Import Bank of Japan.

Thomsen, Stephen and Woolcock, Stephen, 1993, *Direct Investment and European Integration: Competition among Firms and Governments*, Pinter for RIIA, London.

Wijkman, Per, 1990, 'Patterns of production and trade', in W. Wallace, ed., *The Dynamics of European Integration*, Pinter for RIIA, London.

6 COMPETITION, INTEGRATION AND REGULATION IN EC CAPITAL MARKETS

Benn Steil[*]

1 INTRODUCTION

A major objective of the European Community's 1992 single market initiative was the financial integration of the twelve member states. This objective, as developed in the European Commission's 1985 White Paper, was defined to comprise the complete liberalization of capital movements, the unification of national markets for financial services and the establishment of a common regulatory structure for financial institutions.

While important elements of the Community legislative framework for a common financial market remain to be implemented, a tremendous increase in inter-market competition has accompanied major national deregulatory initiatives, the removal of capital controls, advances in trading system technology and the proliferation of derivative instruments. With 1993 having marked the official christening of the single market, it is now a good time to take stock of the competitive shape of the European financial markets and to examine the state of the regulatory framework which has evolved.

While international competition in the retail banking sector has certainly been given an impetus through the establishment of a 'single passport' for EC banks in the Second Banking Coordination Directive, the local character of retail banking services means that integration in this sector will be highly limited for some time to come. The securities sector, however, marked by highly standardized products and an overwhelming dominance of mobile over fixed production factors, is inherently international. This chapter therefore limits its focus to the European capital markets.

As the chapter illustrates, European capital market integration is being driven overwhelmingly by international competition rather than by Community legislation. The Community legislative process allows excessive scope for national protectionist initiatives which act to restrain rather than promote the creation of an efficient European capital market. Likewise, deregulatory measures at the Community level are readily thwarted by national governments

[*] This chapter was originally published in 1993 as an RIIA Special Paper. Only minor changes have been made.

Table 6.1 EC equity markets vs New York and Tokyo, 1992[a]

Stock market	Market capitalization (US$bn)	% of EC's market capitalization	Annual turnover (US$bn)	No. of companies listed
London	980.3	44.1	340.6	1,878
German exchanges[b]	342.2	15.4	399.8	425
Paris	340.6	15.3	115.0	515
Amsterdam	177.6	8.0	45.4	251
Madrid	120.7	5.4	33.8	401
Milan	119.7	5.4	26.8	226
Brussels	66.5	3.0	7.8	164
Copenhagen	33.9	1.5	15.9	257
Luxembourg	12.3	0.6	0.3	59
Dublin[c]	10.4	0.5	3.0	51
Athens	9.8	0.4	1.5	156
Lisbon	9.0	0.4	1.2	100
EC major markets	**2,223.0**	**100.0**	**991.1**	**4,483**
New York	**3,938.1**	**n.a.**	**1,689.0**	**1,969**
Tokyo	**2,486.0**	**n.a.**	**493.3**	**1,651**

[a] Domestic shares only.
[b] Consists of Frankfurt and seven other regional exchanges.
[c] 1990 data.

Sources: *London Stock Exchange Quality of Markets Review* (Spring 1993), *Fortune* (2 December 1991).

determined to maintain competitive positions. While major political initiatives such as the establishment of a single European currency would undoubtedly provide an enormous spur to European capital market integration, it is the markets themselves rather than the legislators who will continue to act as the engine of integration for the foreseeable future.

2 EC CAPITAL MARKET COMPETITION AND INTEGRATION

Equity markets

Market profile

Table 6.1 provides some useful overview statistics for comparison in the twelve major EC national markets, New York and Tokyo.

Market capitalization

Over the course of the past decade, EC equity markets have steadily increased their share of world equity market capitalization, largely at the expense of the United States. EC equity markets in 1992 accounted for approximately 23 per cent of the value of world markets, up from 15 per cent in 1982. The tremendous decline in the Japanese market since January 1990 has meant that Japanese and EC market valuations are now almost equivalent.

National levels of and growth in market valuation differ markedly within the EC. The United Kingdom, with a 1992 market capitalization of $980.3 billion, is predominant at over 10 per cent of world valuation. The French share of world valuation, at 3.6 per cent, grew by over 2.5 times during the 1980s, and now stands at $340.6 billion. German market capitalization is fractionally higher ($342.2 billion), although its growth during the 1980s was far more modest. Amsterdam ($177.6 billion), Madrid ($120.7 billion) and Milan ($119.7 billion) are the next largest markets.

The potential exists for a considerable rise in European share demand in the years ahead, which should boost these figures significantly. At present, most EC national share markets are extremely small relative to the size of their economies, with equity-to-GDP ratios among the lowest in the world. A handful of stocks dominate many of the exchanges: ten stocks comprise about half of the national market capitalization in Germany, Italy, Belgium, and Spain, and the figure reaches 80 per cent for the Netherlands. This compares with concentration values of only 15–20 per cent in the United States and Japan. This may change markedly in the coming years as an ageing European population swells corporate pension reserves. At present, such funds represent less than 5 per cent of private sector savings in France and Germany, as compared with 70 per cent in the United States, while French and German mutual funds invest less than 20 per cent of assets in equity markets. These figures are set to rise considerably against a backdrop of declining European interest rates.

Table 6.2 provides market capitalization figures for nineteen of the world's major markets between 1982 and 1992.

Market turnover

London contributes about 11 per cent of world equity turnover, with 43 per cent of its turnover accounted for by foreign equities. Nearly two-thirds of world foreign equity turnover and over 95 per cent of EC foreign equity turnover takes place in London. About half of this activity was evenly divided between Japanese and German shares in 1990, with French shares accounting for one-eighth. The UK's nearest EC rival, Germany, contributes less than 8 per cent of world equity turnover, with virtually all of it accounted for by domestic shares. French share turnover is just over a quarter of the German level. Table 6.3 provides 1992

Table 6.2 Percentage shares of world equity market capitalization, 1982–92

	1982	1983	1984	1985	1986	1987	1988	1989	1990	1991	1992
United States	56.5	55.9	54.7	48.6	39.2	31.2	28.7	30.0	33.5	37.7	41.2
Japan	17.7	18.4	21.2	22.6	31.1	41.9	44.4	40.6	33.4	30.5	26.0
United Kingdom	7.9	7.4	7.3	8.2	7.8	9.3	8.3	8.2	10.5	9.7	10.3
Germany	3.0	2.9	2.7	4.5	4.4	2.9	2.8	3.6	4.1	3.8	3.6
France	1.3	1.3	1.4	2.0	2.7	2.2	2.6	3.4	3.5	3.5	3.6
Canada	4.5	4.3	4.0	3.7	3.0	2.8	2.6	2.9	2.6	2.4	2.6
Switzerland	1.8	1.7	1.5	2.2	2.4	1.9	1.7	1.9	1.9	2.0	2.1
Netherlands	0.9	1.0	1.1	1.3	1.3	1.0	1.0	1.1	1.4	1.3	1.9
Hong Kong	0.9	0.7	0.9	0.9	0.9	0.7	0.9	0.8	1.0	1.2	1.9
Australia	1.8	2.2	1.8	1.6	1.4	1.2	1.6	1.4	1.3	1.4	1.4
Italy	0.9	0.7	0.8	1.6	2.5	1.5	1.6	1.6	1.8	1.6	1.3
Spain	0.4	0.3	0.4	0.5	0.7	1.1	1.0	1.1	1.3	1.2	1.3
Sweden	0.7	0.9	0.7	0.7	0.9	0.7	1.0	1.1	1.1	1.1	0.8
Belgium	0.3	0.4	0.4	0.5	0.6	0.6	0.7	0.7	0.8	0.7	0.7
Singapore	1.0	1.3	0.9	0.5	0.6	0.5	0.5	0.6	0.8	0.8	0.5
Denmark	0.3	0.4	0.2	0.3	0.3	0.3	0.3	0.4	0.5	0.5	0.4
Austria	0.1	0.1	0.0	0.1	0.1	0.1	0.1	0.2	0.3	0.3	0.2
Norway	0.1	0.1	0.1	0.2	0.2	0.2	0.2	0.2	0.3	0.2	0.2
New Zealand	0.0	0.0	0.0	0.0	0.0	0.0	0.2	0.1	0.1	0.1	0.2
World	100.0	100.0	100.0	100.0	100.0	100.0	100.0	100.0	100.0	100.0	100.0
Europe (EC and EFTA)	17.6	17.3	16.5	22.1	23.8	21.7	21.3	23.6	27.4	25.9	26.2
Big 10	95.3	95.2	95.5	94.5	93.2	94.4	93.6	93.0	92.1	92.3	94.5
G7	91.7	91.0	92.0	91.1	90.6	91.9	90.9	90.2	89.5	89.1	88.5

Source: London Stock Exchange Quality of Markets Review, Spring 1993, Johnson (1992), UBS Phillips & Drew.

Table 6.3 EC equity market turnover vs US and Tokyo, 1992

	Domestic equity		Foreign equity		Total	
	$bn	% of EC turnover	$bn	% of EC turnover	$bn	% of EC turnover
London	340.6	34.4	258.7	95.7	599.3	47.5
Germany	399.8	40.3	6.3	2.3	406.1	32.2
Paris	115.0	11.6	2.8	1.0	117.8	9.3
Amsterdam	45.4	4.6	0.1	0.0	45.5	3.6
Madrid	33.8	3.4	0.0	0.0	33.8	2.7
Milan	26.8	2.7	0.0	0.0	26.8	2.1
Copenhagen	15.9	1.6	0.7	0.3	16.6	1.3
Brussels	7.8	0.8	1.7	0.6	9.5	0.8
Dublin[a]	3.0	0.3	0.0	0.0	3.0	0.2
Athens	1.5	0.2	0.0	0.0	1.5	0.1
Lisbon	1.2	0.1	0.0	0.0	1.2	0.1
Luxembourg	0.3	0.0	0.0	0.0	0.3	0.0
EC major markets	**991.1**	**100.0**	**270.3**	**100.0**	**1,261.4**	**100.0**
New York	**1,689.0**	**n.a.**	**121.0**	**n.a.**	**1,810.0**	**n.a.**
NASDAQ	**891.2**	**n.a.**	**32.8**	**n.a.**	**924.0**	**n.a.**
Tokyo	**493.3**	**n.a.**	**1.3**	**n.a.**	**494.6**	**n.a.**

[a] 1990 data.
Source: *London Stock Exchange Quality of Markets Review*, Spring 1993; *Fortune*, 2 December 1991.

turnover statistics for the major EC national markets, New York, NASDAQ, and Tokyo.

Share issuance

France is the clear EC leader in gross share issuance over the past decade, accounting for 17.5 per cent of the G6 total; over twice the level in Italy and the United Kingdom, and three times the level in Germany. The annual rate of increase in share issuance in France and the United Kingdom, at nearly 25 per cent, was well beyond that in other G6 countries; particularly Japan, where sharp declines in 1990-91 brought the twelve-year average down to zero. Table 6.4 contains G6 share issue figures from 1980 to 1991.

Market integration

Compared with the US securities markets, European markets remain highly fragmented. The United States has eight stock exchanges and seven futures and options exchanges, as compared with thirty-two stock exchanges and twenty-

Table 6.4 Gross Share Issues, G-6, 1980–91

	US		Japan		France		Italy		UK		Germany		G-6 total	
	$bn	%	$bn	%	$bn	%	$bn	%	$bn	%	$bn	%	$bn	%
1980	22.7	51.5	6.75	15.3	5.00	11.3	3.60	8.2	2.22	5.0	3.82	8.7	44.8	100
1981	25.6	46.8	10.82	19.8	5.75	10.5	6.32	11.5	3.81	7.0	2.44	4.5	54.74	100
1982	30.5	57.5	8.65	16.3	5.13	9.7	4.44	8.4	1.84	3.5	2.44	4.6	53.0	100
1983	51.6	65.5	7.11	9.0	6.52	8.3	7.18	9.1	3.49	4.4	2.85	3.6	78.76	100
1984	22.6	45.8	10.07	20.4	6.77	13.7	5.56	11.3	2.14	4.3	2.20	4.5	49.35	100
1985	35.7	50.3	10.04	14.2	9.30	13.1	6.40	9.0	5.73	8.1	3.74	5.3	70.91	100
1986	61.9	48.3	14.93	11.7	19.87	15.5	12.66	9.9	11.4	8.7	7.55	5.9	128.05	100
1987	53.5	32.8	42.38	26.0	26.76	16.4	8.05	4.9	25.7	15.8	6.61	4.1	162.98	100
1988	43.6	27.6	65.97	41.8	26.26	16.6	7.45	4.7	10.29	6.5	4.29	2.7	157.86	100
1989	34.1	15.8	108.77	50.5	38.18	17.7	13.39	6.2	10.44	4.9	10.30	4.8	215.18	100
1990	25.8	17.2	43.05	28.7	40.92	27.3	17.73	11.8	6.69	4.5	15.80	10.5	149.99	100
1991	70.9	42.7	11.55	7.0	42.57	25.6	14.11	8.5	18.82	11.3	8.02	4.8	165.98	100
1980–91	478.5	36.0	340.1	25.6	233.0	17.5	106.9	8.0	102.3	7.7	70.1	5.3	1330.9	100

Sources: Johnson (1992), OECD *Financial Statistics*.

three futures and options exchanges in the EC. In the increasingly competitive environment which is now developing, some consolidation would appear inevitable, although national exchanges will not face the direct threat of extinction until European monetary union becomes a reality. Regardless of whether physical consolidation is occurring, however, we would expect the combination of technology, deregulation and the legislative establishment of the single market to be fuelling a process of capital market 'integration'.

Several recent studies have applied various econometric techniques to measure the degree of EC stock market integration. The primary technique involved comparing the 'excess returns' on equities in different industry sectors across the EC, on the premise that greater integration implies greater correlation in returns.[*] While some evidence of European stock-market convergence was detected for several industry sectors, correlations on intra-EC returns were generally dominated by correlations on US-EC returns, with strong evidence that US excess returns explain most of the excess returns recorded for the major European exchanges (see Fraser et al., 1992; Fraser and MacDonald, 1992). In other words, evidence of EC stock-market integration remains outweighed by evidence of US market influence on European market performance.

Less sophisticated methods do offer some confirmation of a pan-Western European equity market convergence between 1987 and 1991 (see Figure 6.1). In 1987, there was considerable disparity in the performance of the eight largest European markets relative to their mean. Only two showed less than 10 per cent divergence from the mean, while Spain out-performed by 35 per cent and Germany underperformed by 27 per cent. There was a steady convergence through 1991, by which time only one market diverged over 10 per cent from the mean (Italy, which underperformed by 13 per cent). Against a backdrop of the Danish rejection of the Maastricht Treaty, an unexpectedly narrow French approval, multiple devaluations, British departure from the ERM and the Swiss rejection of the European Economic Area (EEA), it is not surprising that 1992 marked an abrupt departure from the course of market convergence, with five countries diverging more than 10 per cent from the European mean. Should the political and monetary turmoil subside, however, evidence of convergence is likely to re-emerge rapidly. Corporate share price to cash flow ratios are showing increasing similarity in major industry sectors across countries, indicating an emerging cross-market consistency in valuing corporate earnings flows.[†]

Besides seeing some measure of market integration in share price data, we

---

[*] 'Excess returns' are defined as the *ex post* returns on a security above and beyond the risk-free rate, approximated by the rate on three-month government Treasury bills.
[†] *The Financial Times*, 1993. Analysis by Warburg Securities indicates that prices of thirty major European stocks generally fall between 3.8 and 5.8 times cash flow, while the comparable range for the major automakers is 2.5 to 3.0.

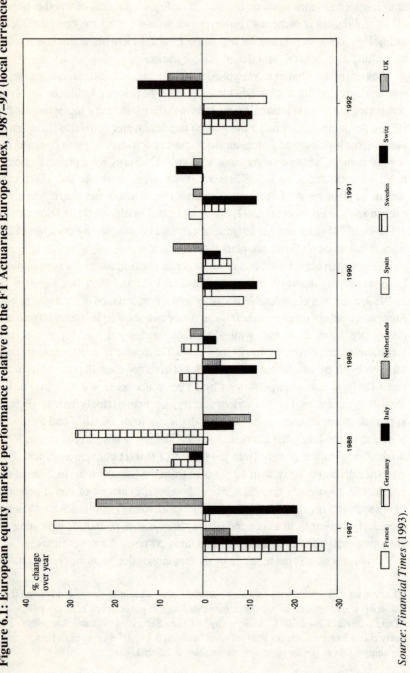

Figure 6.1: European equity market performance relative to the FT Actuaries Europe Index, 1987–92 (local currencies)

% change over year

France Germany Italy Netherlands Spain Sweden Switz UK

Source: Financial Times (1993).

see it as well in the growing 'internationalization' of European exchanges. Foreign equities have increased their share of London turnover from 23 per cent in 1988 to 43 per cent in 1992, while several smaller exchanges are also relying increasingly on foreign shares for trading volume. In Brussels, they constitute almost 20 per cent of turnover. Although turnover in foreign equities is still very low on most continental exchanges, there exists considerable potential for growth. While foreign equity turnover currently represents only 2 per cent of the total on the Frankfurt Stock Exchange, 43 per cent of the companies listed are foreign.

With national proprietary dominance in domestic share trading being steadily eaten away, several exchanges are struggling to maintain a viable trading volume. Europe's fourth largest stock exchange, Amsterdam, is fighting to stem the rapid flight of Dutch share trading to foreign markets, which now account for 40 per cent of such trading. Institutional investors in particular, accounting for 88 per cent of Amsterdam's turnover, are flocking to London's SEAQ International trading system in search of anonymity and lower fees. While Amsterdam's share of large wholesale institutional trades was almost 70 per cent in 1986, by 1991 it had plummeted to 33 per cent. Although the situation is not nearly as dire in Germany, a substantial 12 per cent of German share turnover now takes place in London.

Intra-EC competition has prompted major changes in the way European exchanges operate. A wave of deregulatory measures, designed to reduce trading costs and stem the flow of domestic share trading to London, has swept the continental markets. Turnover taxes have been abolished in Germany and the Netherlands. The Amsterdam and Paris bourses are instituting new large block-trading systems to replicate the attractions of London's SEAQ International. The German government is pushing for a major consolidation of the eight regional exchanges into a single Frankfurt bourse. Trading links between exchanges are being formed to strengthen competitive positions, most notably between the French (MATIF) and German (DTB) futures markets, and the British (OM London) and Dutch (EOE) options markets. Formerly mundane back-office issues such as trade settlement and share registry have now become fundamental to the continued competitiveness of national exchanges, as evidenced by the dramatic resignation of the London Stock Exchange chief executive over the scrapping of the trouble-ridden Taurus paperless settlements system.

Finally, there are the inevitable attempts to use Community legislation to protect national markets rather than to open them. Debate over the Investment Services Directive has featured an initiative by the 'Club Med Group' (France, Belgium, Italy and Spain) to curtail 'off-exchange' competition by mandating that trading in domestic exchange-listed shares take place on a 'regulated market'. With sufficient ingenuity, the definition of a regulated market could be

Figure 6.2: Sources of G6 business financing, 1985–1991 (net flows, in billions of local currency)

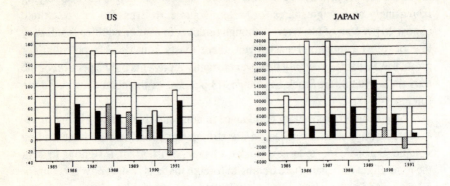

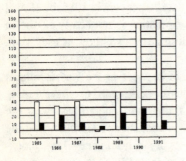

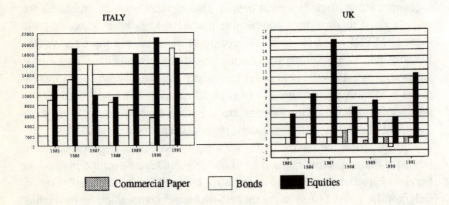

Source: IMF (1992); OECD, *Financial Statistics Monthly*.
Note: Except for Italy, equity financing is in terms of gross flows.

structured to exclude London's SEAQ International. The compromise in the offing will allow investors explicitly to 'opt out' of this restriction, leading one to suspect that the Club Med Group envisions having sufficient regulatory scope for discouraging such opt-outs.*

Regardless of the course which European monetary and political integration may take in the future, continued growth in demand for efficient international markets may be expected to generate much of its own supply. The Eurobond market and London's SEAQ International system are both products of widespread dissatisfaction with the limitations of then existing national markets, while the foreign exchange market remains the world's largest without any need for organized exchanges at all. Nevertheless, there remain significant barriers to an integrated EC equity market which will not be brought down by competitive forces alone. A single European currency is essential for a truly unified market, although the necessary political initiative would appear to be still some way off. A single currency would also greatly facilitate the establishment of an integrated settlements system. Even the development of common accounting and disclosure standards would represent a significant step forward, and should certainly prove less intractable than monetary union.

The European Federation of Stock Exchanges had seriously discussed the establishment of an electronic share-market system called Euroquote, but the project collapsed under the weight of conflicting visions for its development. Political intervention in such schemes is unlikely to be effective, as the desire of each national government to defend its own securities industry would tend to produce a compromise enshrining a networked version of the status quo in a market where survival depends critically on rapid adaptation. A more modest proposal which has been debated for several years is the creation of a 'Eurolist' of over 250 European blue-chip companies whose shares will be cross-listed on all EC exchanges. This initiative would reduce exchange listing charges to a single fee and allow reporting requirements to be fully satisfied on the basis of home country rules.

Despite the tremendous scope for further integration, it cannot be overlooked that the equity markets play very different roles in different member states. Figure 6.2 illustrates the wide disparity in the use of equity market financing in the G6. The contrast between the United Kingdom and Germany is particularly striking. The equity market in the United Kingdom, as in the United States, serves as the market for corporate control, whereas in Germany the combination of concentrated shareholdings, extensive cross-shareholdings, voting-right restrictions, and corporate board structure design operates so as virtually to eliminate opportunities for hostile takeovers. Close, long-standing institutional links between the large German universal banks and the corporate sector

*See the section below on trading concentration in the Investment Services Directive.

Table 6.5 G6 public and private sector outstanding borrowing, end 1990

	Public sector			Private sector			Private sector: financial institutions			Private sector: non-financial institutions			All borrowers		
	D	I	Total	D	I	Total	D	I	Total	D	I	Total	D	I	Total
US $bn	3662.9	0.7	3663.6	1714.4	169.6	1884.0	526.8	64.6	591.4	1187.6	105.0	1292.6	5377.3	170.3	5547.6
%	100.0	0.0		91.0	9.0		89.1	10.9		91.9	8.1		96.9	3.1	
Japan $bn	1694.1	4.3	1698.4	714.8	313.4	1028.2	502.8	67.9	570.7	212.0	245.5	457.5	2408.9	317.7	2726.6
%	99.7	0.3		69.5	30.5		88.1	11.9		46.3	53.7		88.3	11.7	
Germany $bn	371.6	1.1	372.7	604.8	63.5	668.3	603.1	48.7	651.8	1.7	14.8	16.5	976.4	64.6	1041.0
%	99.7	0.3		90.5	9.5		92.5	7.5		10.3	89.7		93.8	6.2	
Italy $bn	617.1	17.5	634.6	127.8	28.5	156.3	123.5	16.3	139.8	4.3	12.2	16.5	744.9	46.0	790.9
%	97.2	2.8		81.8	18.2		88.3	11.7		26.1	73.9		94.2	5.8	
France $bn	370.5	6.8	377.3		83.9			50.9		87.8	33.0	120.8		90.7	
%	98.2	1.8								72.7	27.3				
UK $bn	226.2	4.0	230.2	28.0	123.1	151.1		80.6			42.5		254.2	127.1	381.3
%	98.3	1.7		18.5	81.5								66.7	33.3	

D = Domestic; I = International
Source: Bank for International Settlements (1991).

have obviated the need for the highly developed liquid securities markets which are central to the bank-disintermediated Anglo-Saxon financial structure. While there is certainly evidence of a general movement towards this structure within the Community, particularly in France, the scope for securitization and disintermediation is likely to remain more limited in the Netherlands, Belgium and, particularly, Germany.

Bond markets

Market profile

The nominal US dollar-value share of total outstanding domestic and international bond issues accounted for by EC member state issuers is roughly a quarter, of which Germany accounts for one-third, France one-sixth and the United Kingdom one-eighth.[*]

The amount of borrowing on domestic as opposed to international markets varies markedly among G7 countries. In the United Kingdom, private-sector borrowing is over four times as high in international markets as in domestic markets (very much due to London's dominance in eurobond trading activity), while in Germany domestic bond issues, accounted for almost entirely by financial institutions, exceed international issues by a factor of nearly ten. Regulation in home markets can be significant in determining where corporate borrowers choose to raise their funds, and has played a major role particularly in driving Japanese, British and French firms into international markets.

Given the significant role of public-sector borrowing requirements in the bond markets, and the fact that such borrowing tends to be done almost exclusively in domestic markets, the scale of government borrowing is generally the dominant factor in determining the size of domestic markets. Within the G7, Germany was the only country in 1990 to have a public-sector/private-sector bond issue ratio of under 1.0, while in Italy it was over 4.0 (see Table 6.5).

The role of domestic bond markets as a source of corporate finance also differs markedly among G7 countries. In the US non-financial corporate sector, domestic bonds represent a significant source of finance, amounting to nearly one-quarter of the level of bank credit. In Germany and Italy, on the other hand, the bond markets are virtually dominated by government and bank issues, and non-financial corporations rely almost exclusively on bank credit as a source of debt finance.

[*] International bond issues include both eurobond and foreign market placements.

Market integration

Bonds are inherently more amenable to global trading than equities for a variety of reasons. Most importantly, borrowers may issue bonds in a range of currencies to suit their circumstances, and the investment risk to lenders may be largely reduced to credit risk. Investments in the international equity markets are complicated by the tremendous disparity in disclosure and accounting standards mandated by different national authorities, and are always subject to the risk of exchange-rate fluctuations. Thus reduced barriers to international capital flows may actually produce greater divergence in national equity market performance, as cross-border equity investments can be determined as much and even more by currency diversification or speculation objectives as by corporate performance evaluations. Bonds will then continue to be more readily substitutable one for another across countries, while equities will retain much stronger ties to the idiosyncratic structure and performance of individual national economies. The fact that the bond markets are almost exclusively wholesale also serves as a major impetus to international integration, as regulatory barriers are relatively minimal.

Largely on the basis of statistics from 1987 to 1991, it has been claimed that there is evidence of a trend toward international bond yield convergence (see Johnson, 1992). Looking at the post-Bretton Woods period, since 1973, we find that the standard deviation in G7 long-term government bond yields has declined from a 1977 high of 30 per cent to 1990–91 lows of 15 per cent and 15.8 per cent, respectively. Using more recent data from March 1993, however, we find that the standard deviation is now back over 27 per cent. In the EC (excluding Greece), the standard deviation declined rapidly from 26 per cent in 1988–9 to 14.4 per cent in second-quarter 1992. By the fourth quarter it was back over 22 per cent.

A movement back toward more divergent bond yields should not be surprising given the background of declining G7 and EC monetary coordination. Despite increasing opportunities for investors to shop a truly global bond market, yield convergence should not be expected in the absence of some measure of policy convergence. The trials and tribulations of the EC monetary integration process provide a useful backdrop against which to analyse the behaviour of international bond markets.

Looking back at a period of great stability in the European Monetary System (EMS) Exchange Rate Mechanism (ERM) in 1988–91, we find a considerable rise particularly in the French franc share (1.2 per cent to 2.8 per cent) and Italian lira share (0.3 per cent to 1.5 per cent) of outstanding international bond issues, followed by a rise in the UK pound sterling share (7.9 per cent to 8.4 per cent) after its entry into the ERM in October 1990. These were accompanied by a levelling off of the Deutschmark share at 9.5 per cent. Bond yields among EMS currencies were converging rapidly over this period. These developments were being driven by the markets' growing belief that European monetary union was proceeding apace; a belief strongly reinforced by the establishment in the Maastricht Treaty of hard criteria and a timetable for member states' adoption of a single European currency. The effect was to lend greater weight to the German monetary anchor within the Community, rendering bonds denominated in credibly tethered European currencies increasingly substitutable for Deutschmark bonds. Higher yields on such currencies attracted funds out of Deutschmark assets as the perceived risk of devaluation receded.

Most significantly, ecu bond issuance surged dramatically as borrowers and investors, within and outside the Community, discovered a newly credible debt instrument for a Europe-wide market. In the first half of 1992, ecu bond issuance reached 12.6 per cent of the world total for the period, making the ecu the third largest currency of denomination, barely behind the Japanese yen. The increasing credibility of the single currency programme led to a fall in ecu bond yields below their weighted EC-average yield .

In terms of the value of bonds outstanding, domestic markets in total are roughly eight times the size of international markets. Yet if all were to proceed according to the Maastricht blueprint, the establishment of a single European currency would actually eliminate all domestic markets within the Community, and replace them with a truly integrated single ecu market in which borrowers would have to compete to attract investors. With the removal of currency risk on European bonds, national EC governments, which generally dominate their respective domestic bond markets at present, will find themselves competing for funds directly with other EC governments on the simple basis of yield and credit risk.

The effect of destabilizing events in the second half of 1992, such as the Danish and French referenda and the associated ERM turmoil, was to shatter the growing belief in the inter-substitutability of European bonds, flatten the ecu bond market, drive ecu bond yields back above weighted EC-average yields (see Figure 6.3), and to re-establish the hefty risk premium required on non-Deutschmark bonds. The ecu bond market appears to be staging a hesitant recovery, although it is clear that the long-term prospects for European bond market integration are intimately tied up with the process of European economic and political integration, and will be considerably dampened by evidence of national monetary and fiscal policy divergence.

3 EC CAPITAL MARKET REGULATION

National regulatory regimes

While there is a developing Community-level legislative framework in which European capital markets operate, regulation *per se* remains nationally based. The variety of regulatory structures which coexist in the Community is consider-

Figure 6.3 Ecu bond market, 1992–3

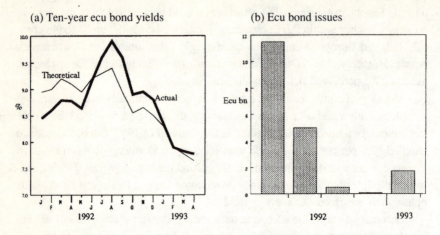

(a) Ten-year ecu bond yields   (b) Ecu bond issues

Source: *The Economist* (1993); Bloomberg, Euromoney Bondware.

able, largely reflecting the diverse historical developments of the financial markets in the individual member states. In the United Kingdom, the regulatory structure which resulted from the 1986 'Big Bang' reforms is a complex one, comprising a web of self-regulatory organizations operating under a statutory umbrella, supervised by a national Securities and Investments Board (SIB). This system may yet undergo considerable changes in response to mounting public as well as industry criticism of self-regulation, particularly in the retail sector, and excessive overlap of supervisory responsibility. The French regulatory structure is more centralized, with authority vested primarily in the finance ministry and the Commission des Opérations de Bourse (COB), whose 'Napoleonic' rule book is heavily codified and detailed. Major regulatory reforms have been undertaken since 1988, including the opening up of the brokerage industry to outside buy-ins and the abolition of fixed commissions. Securities markets in Germany have, to date, been subject exclusively to institutional and local market self-regulation, reflecting both the decentralized character of the federal state and the relative unimportance of the markets vis-à-vis the banking sector. Major changes are in train, however, largely in response to international competitive pressures which have highlighted the exchanges' inability to control practices such as insider trading. The finance ministry has announced the government's intention to establish a German equivalent of the American Securities and Exchange Commission (SEC).

While the European single market programme has prompted some measure of regulatory convergence through the efforts of national governments to enhance the efficiency and soundness of their financial markets, certain national initiatives have had the direct effect of impeding further market integration. Partly motivated by the collapse of the Euroquote project, which had lent an air of permanence to the existing structure of European exchanges, national authorities have become increasingly concerned with promoting and protecting their domestic securities industry (see Federal Trust Study Group, 1993). Italy, for example, passed a measure known as the SIMs law, which from January 1992 required all foreign firms carrying out securities business in Italy to operate through a separately capitalized and incorporated local subsidiary.* The law raises significant financial and administrative barriers to the effective operation of non-Italian financial institutions, and has prompted a formal complaint by the British Department of Trade and Industry (DTI) to the European Commission. While the Italian securities market watchdog, Consob, insists that the law is designed to create 'transparency and order', London-based dealers dismiss this defence as a smoke-screen for a protectionist measure designed to force securities business back to Italy (*Financial Times*, 1992). In the retail banking sector, France tightened a ban on interest-bearing current accounts in direct response to domestic bank protests over a foreign bank's (Barclays') competitive initiative. The fact that these restrictions appeared to be in violation of the Second Banking and (forthcoming) Investment Services Directives did not impede their implementation.

EC securities markets legislation

Principles of EC financial regulation

The Community-level legislative framework for securities market operations is grounded in a concept known as 'competition among rules', which takes the continuing reality of separate and distinct national legal and regulatory systems as given. The principle outlined in the European Commission's 1985 White Paper supporting competition among rules is that of *mutual recognition*, according to which all member states agree to recognize the validity of each other's laws, regulations, and standards, and thereby facilitate free trade in goods and services without the need for prior harmonization. Directly derived from this principle is the Second Banking Coordination Directive provision for a *single passport*, under which credit institutions incorporated in any EC member state are permitted to carry out a full range of 'passported services', detailed in the Directive's annex, throughout the Community (assuming they are authorized to provide such services in their home state). Similar guidelines are laid down for

---

* SIM stands for Società di Intermediazione Mobiliare, the type of firm through which the new law requires securities dealings to be carried out.

the provision of investment services cross-border in the Investment Services Directive. Reinforcing the market-opening effect of mutual recognition is the assignment of *home country control*, which attributes the primary task of supervising a given financial institution to its home country authorities. Home country control provides further assurance that foreign EC firms will not be put at a competitive disadvantage by host country authorities seeking to protect domestic firms.

A second major principle enshrined in the White Paper, that of *harmonization of minimum standards*, acts to limit the scope for competition among rules by mandating member state conformity with some base-level Community-wide requirements. The principle is intended to ensure that 'basic public interests' are safeguarded in a single market with different national rules and standards. Whether this principle facilitates or inhibits the free movement of goods, capital and labour depends wholly upon the manner in which it is applied. It can, on the one hand, facilitate free competition by stopping member states from erecting 'standards barriers' against one another's products and services, while on the other it can inhibit free competition by barring certain practices or products from the market altogether.

The minimum harmonization principle represents a potential source of concern regarding EC legislation, since the Commission has never been explicit either about what sorts of rules do and do not require harmonization, or about how the 'minimum' is to be determined. Reading the Commission's version of history in the White Paper, it is clear that the minimum harmonization principle is not seen simply as a necessary response to negative externalities deriving from free competition among rules, but rather that competition among rules is itself seen as a necessary but regrettable consequence of the Commission's inability to legislate full harmonization.

It is possible to derive some broad principles for determining where capital market regulations need to be harmonized and where they are best left to the 'regulatory market'.* As European financial markets become increasingly integrated, *systemic risk* will become increasingly an international problem, rather than a purely national one, and coordinated approaches to controlling it will become correspondingly more necessary. Systemic risk in truly international markets is akin to acid rain, in that it may be produced in one jurisdiction yet spread its effects through many. In an internationally integrated financial market, *market efficiency* concerns could, in principle, also justify coordinated intervention. 'Prisoner's Dilemma'-type problems can afflict the processes of inter-jurisdictional competition, so that behaviours which are efficient from the perspective of individual jurisdictions will, when aggregated, produce outcomes which are inefficient for the market as a whole. Questions related to the establish-

* See Steil (1992) on the international harmonization debate.

ment of *fair* or *equitable markets*, broadly defined, are, however, not clear candidates for harmonized intervention. First of all, common understandings of 'fair' societies and markets are conspicuously lacking across nations,* but more importantly there is simply no reason to expect 'competition in laxity' to take hold on fairness issues. Just as voters will turn out governments whose policies are perceived to be unfair, so investors will exit markets which are perceived to be rigged or to offer inadequate protection. As the outgoing Chairman of the US SEC pointed out, 'In ... a "buyer's market", countries that do not provide adequate protection for investors just won't see the investments. Therefore, large and small markets will all need to focus on achieving "quality" for the investor in offering trading practices and in the overall safety and integrity of the market.'†

This position is echoed in an *Economist* report on insider trading laws: 'As competition for foot-loose business and for investment capital grows stronger, a market's reputation for honesty is becoming a significant competitive tool' (*Economist*, 1992b). This view is not, however, reflected in the work of the Commission, which appears to see deregulation and supervisory laxity as dangerous but reliable magnets for investment capital.

EC securities markets directives

Five directives explicitly relating to securities markets are now in effect. These directives cover:

- mutual recognition of listing particulars;
- mutual recognition of public offer prospectuses for public offerings;
- major shareholdings;
- insider trading;
- collective investment undertakings (UCITS).

The two most important and contentious directives on securities markets are not scheduled to be implemented until 1996. These are the Capital Adequacy and Investment Services Directives, the main provisions of which we discuss below.

Capital Adequacy Directive

The Capital Adequacy Directive (CAD), the text of which was agreed by EC economics and finance ministers (ECOFIN) in March 1993, is intended to establish harmonized minimum capital requirements for securities operations, just as the 1989 Solvency Ratio and Own Funds Directives did for banking

---

* See *The Economist* (1992a) on a Gallup survey revealing strikingly different national attitudes towards such concepts as 'equality' and 'freedom'.
† Richard Breeden, as quoted in *International Herald Tribune* (1992).

operations. 'Recognized third-country investment firms', the directive specifies, must be 'subject to and comply with prudential rules considered by the competent [national] authorities as at least as stringent as those laid down in this directive'.

The CAD sets minimum initial capital levels for Community investment firms, ranging from 50,000 ecus ($61,500) to 90,000 ecus ($110,500) depending on the general scope of activities, as well as detailed additional requirements to cover specific categories of asset risk. The most significant of these risk categories are *position risk* – broadly defined to include market, credit, and liquidity risk – and *settlement (counterparty) risk.*

Risk and the CAD Capital Requirements

The CAD measures of position risk are crude compared with those mandated by the Securities and Futures Authority (SFA) in the United Kingdom. While the SFA's risk weights account for empirical variations in price volatility between different equity markets and between different national government bond issues, the CAD assigns a flat 10 per cent risk weighting for qualifying equities, and differentiates fixed interest positions according to a simple tripartite classification: central government, other public sector and listed grade corporate, and all others. Simplicity is an understandable feature of multinational agreements, since the complexity involved in reaching accord among numerous national bodies with divergent views and interests generally precludes the detail feasible in purely domestic arrangements. However, it is not clear that simplicity is innocuous in setting capital standards. The zero risk weighting applied to government bonds in the 1988 BIS accord, for example, consistent with a simple focus on credit risk, provides considerable incentive for banks to substitute government debt for business loans in their asset portfolios. Since interest rate risk on the bonds is ignored, the Basle rules may be choking off credit to the small business sector without actually strengthening bank balance sheets. Likewise, the simple 10 per cent risk weighting on equities in the CAD provides no incentive for institutions to prudently monitor volatility levels on their equity holdings or to ensure sufficient sectoral diversification. Despite these not insignificant failings, the CAD requirements on position risk are, on balance, not markedly out of line with those of the United Kingdom, the United States, or Japan, although they may be biased somewhat downwards (see Dale, 1992).

The CAD provisions for settlement risk are intended to cover the risk of counterparty default under the implicit assumption that a trade involves cash against delivery. In this case, the relevant measure of risk is replacement cost, defined as the difference between the agreed settlement price on a security and its current market price. The amount of capital required to be held against an overdue deliverable rises steadily as a percentage of replacement cost, reaching 100 per cent forty-six days after the settlement date. If cash is paid or securities delivered in advance, then the risk deriving from counterparty default is actually much greater than simply replacement cost. While this 'full credit risk' is not covered in the CAD settlement risk provisions, it is indirectly accounted for by the 100 per cent risk weighting assigned to unsecured receivables. This is more stringent than the SEC provision, which allows for an 'amortization' of the receivable over time against capital.

Level playing fields

One of the major stated objectives of the CAD is to create a '*level playing field*' between banks and non-bank investment firms dealing in securities. This objective is consistent with a widely held view that regulators should be regulating activities rather than institutions, so that two institutions of different types engaged in an identical activity should, in respect of that activity, be subject to identical regulation. This view has an alluring ring of fairness to it, and has therefore been useful in underpinning a directive requiring the support of continental member states with universal banking systems.

Limiting systemic risk – threats to the safety and soundness of the financial system – is the *raison d'être* of capital standards. The problem with the level playing field concept is that an institution's trading book, viewed in isolation from its other activities, is not the relevant measure of its contribution to systemic risk. The performance of an institution's trading book influences its ability to carry out its other activities; activities which differ between bank and non-bank investment firms, and which have very different implications for the stability of the financial system.

The composition of bank asset and liability bases can differ markedly from that of securities firms. Banks' primary assets are generally illiquid loans, rather than liquid securities, while a major component of their non-capital funding derives from retail deposits which can be withdrawn on demand. The non-marketability of a large segment of assets means that banks in financial distress cannot be wound down quickly without jeopardizing the claims of depositors and other creditors. At the same time, this ever-present risk to depositors means that any hint of financial difficulty has the potential to provoke a contagious withdrawal of funds from the entire system. While the risk of contagion may be reduced dramatically through government deposit insurance, this comes only at the cost of encouraging excessive risk-taking, particularly by financially tenuous institutions.* Combine these bank-specific risks with their exclusive direct

---

* This is the classic moral hazard problem which featured prominently in the US Savings and Loan disaster.

access to national payment systems and it becomes clear that banks do not merit the same type of regulation as securities firms. The level playing field principle cannot be justified as long as banks are playing with wider boundaries.

Securities firms perform only a subset of the financial activities performed by universal banks, and forbearance from engaging in the full range mitigates their contribution to systemic risk. Securities firms are less liable to large and rapid withdrawals of core non-equity funding, are much less reliant on a lender of last resort function, require no government insurance guarantees, and are a step removed from the payments system. From a regulatory perspective, therefore, ensuring solvency is a considerably more critical objective when dealing with banks than when dealing with securities firms. While this has been explicitly recognized by the Commission,* it is not reflected in the CAD. The CAD permits banks to apply more subordinated debt as capital than would be allowable under the banking directives specifically to support trading book activities – a provision designed to level the capital standards playing field with securities firms. This means, however, that banks which choose to deal in securities are substantially increasing the range of their risky activities without having to increase equity capital as a buffer – thereby increasing insolvency risk – while at the same time maintaining government insurance and lender of last resort backing unavailable to securities firms. From the perspective of maintaining prudential capital standards in universal banks, it is appropriate that the CAD limits on subordinated debt as capital are somewhat more restrictive than those in the United Kingdom, the United States, or Japan. From the perspective of EC securities firms, however, greater-than-necessary subordinated debt restrictions, imposed in the name of a European level playing field, place them at a competitive disadvantage particularly against their American counterparts. The proposed penalties for concentrated positions (those exceeding 25 per cent of own funds) in the CAD's large exposure annex, while perhaps duly prudent for banks, would also appear excessive when applied to the large-scale underwriting activities undertaken by securities firms.† As with parts of the Investment Services Directive, to which we now turn our attention, the CAD reflects a spirit of compromise which, while perhaps admirable in a purely political exercise, may serve to entrench a European status quo which is ill-suited to the most dynamic and integrated sector of the global economy.

---

* See, for example, the London Guildhall speech to the Overseas Bankers Club by Commission Vice-President Sir Leon Brittan, 5 February 1990, quoted in Dale (1992).
† This provision was singled out for particularly strong criticism in a 1992 study commissioned by the International Primary Market Association (IPMA), the general conclusions of which are summarized in the *Financial Regulation Report* (1992).

Investment Services Directive

The text of the Investment Services Directive (ISD) was agreed by ECOFIN in November 1992, and all seven amendments proposed by the European Parliament were rejected by the Commission in March 1993. The ISD establishes the 'single passport' in investment services for specialized securities firms which the Second Banking Coordination Directive (SBD) created for banks. The fact that the ISD will not be implemented until 1996 places securities firms seeking cross-border expansion at a competitive disadvantage vis-à-vis banks in terms of Community-level legal protection against national entry barriers and activity restrictions. It would be wrong to assume that a directive implemented is a directive enforced, yet it is nonetheless clear that national laws with protectionist effects, such as the Italian SIMs law discussed earlier, are more easily maintained in the face of European Commission and Court challenge while the ISD is only slowly working its way into national law.

As with the SBD, the ISD single passport is premissed on a 'minimum harmonization' of essential requirements and standards, which in turn will allow member states to grant mutual recognition and accept home country control. Major exceptions to the home country control provision are in the areas of 'rules of conduct', broadly defined, and investor compensation. Rules of conduct will remain the province of the host country where such rules can be justified as being in the interests of 'the general good'.* In the area of investor compensation, host countries will be permitted to require foreign firm adoption of domestic compensation systems 'where the home Member States have no compensation systems or where their systems do not offer equivalent levels of protection'. The Commission intends eventual harmonization of member state compensation systems, perhaps under a proposed investor protection directive.

According to Commission Vice-President (External Economic Affairs) Sir Leon Brittan, the Commission's original draft proposal for the ISD was far less detailed than the final product which emerged from the political negotiation process.† Not surprisingly, therefore, several key sections of the ISD are political compromises reflecting the determination of member state governments to protect their domestic industry's competitive position, rather than provisions for ensuring a stable and efficient European financial market. The major issues of

---

* Such rules are expected to be non-discriminatory, proportionate to the regulatory function at which they are directed, and not duplicative of home country rules applying to the same entity.

† As reported by Sir Leon at the Federal Trust Conference of 19 March 1993, entitled 'Towards an Integrated European Capital Market'. The Principal Administrator of the Commission's Directorate-General XV affirmed that the same process of increasing detail and complexity characterized the evolution of the Capital Adequacy Directive (Beverly, 1993).

contention in finalizing the ISD – bank access to regulated markets, trade reporting and transparency, and trading 'concentration' – are also the issues of greatest interest to the market, and we discuss each of these below.

Bank access to regulated markets

Whether the significant restrictions on banks' securities business imposed by the US Glass-Steagall Act or Japan's Article 65 are warranted on prudential grounds is a question which has been scrupulously avoided by the EC because of the political need to accommodate universal banking in the single market. Given the importance of securities market activities for major German banks, Germany was adamant that banks be accorded direct access to all EC regulated markets. France, Spain, Italy and Portugal all resisted this provision, which led to a compromise allowing a lengthy transition period at the end of which such access must be accorded. France, Italy and Belgium have until the end of 1996 to allow host country banks to trade directly on their exchanges, while Portugal, Spain and Greece were given until the end of the century. While this is a long way off, it may yet be considerably longer: Article 15 specifically stipulates that such restrictions may be extended by a qualified majority vote in the Council of Ministers. Until the restrictions are lifted, banks wishing to trade directly on these exchanges will be able to do so only through a separately capitalized securities subsidiary.

Trade reporting and transparency

'Transparency' refers to the degree to which investors are able to see the prices at which trades are taking place in a market, as well as information regarding trading volumes and high and low prices over a given period. In order to ensure transparency, trades must be reported and published as rapidly as possible.

A high level of transparency safeguards the 'integrity' of the market by ensuring that investors have rapid access to accurate price and volume information, the latter providing an important indicator of the liquidity of a given security. In the abstract, a fully transparent market would be one which maximizes *operational efficiency*; that is, it would eliminate all rents to be extracted by market intermediaries with private information. Markets are not, however, made 'in the abstract', and full transparency should not be sought without due consideration of how markets actually function.

In the ISD debate over transparency, the French have been its most ardent champion. While one need not question the French commitment to market integrity, it is clear that the primary motivation for their position is simply fear of losing more and more large block trading to London's SEAQ International, where publication requirements are far less stringent than on the Paris Bourse. The reason for such trading migration is that the high transparency in the Paris order-driven central market makes it impossible to liquidate a large position without instantly revealing the intention to the entire market, and thereby driving the price down immediately. The London market is quote-driven, relying on competing market-makers who are willing to take on the risk of such large positions only so long as they are afforded a reasonable period of time in which to unwind them, piece by piece, before trade publication is required (see International Securities Market Association, 1993, appendix on market structures).

Since large positions are more difficult to move in highly transparent markets, they are rendered less liquid and correspondingly more risky to hold. Less liquidity means less trading, and therefore less information brought to the market which is relevant to the pricing of securities. Given such a trading environment, traders will either refuse to take on large positions unless they can offset them against short positions, or seek to divert transactions to 'offshore' markets. Thus, if publication requirements are not relaxed somewhat for a quote-driven marketplace, the *pricing efficiency* of the European securities market as a whole is likely to suffer. In practice, operational efficiency and pricing efficiency are not independent; each can only be maximized in isolation.

Since market transparency is clearly a good, but not unambiguously so, the only question of relevance to transparency should be whether the London market currently has reporting requirements which are sufficiently rigorous to provide the greatest degree of transparency consistent with the need to limit short-run price volatility and to maintain liquidity. This is an exceptionally difficult question to answer, and one on which the ISD does not shed any light. The reporting and transparency provisions, Article 21, represent a political compromise between the United Kingdom and France which, in its present form, is unlikely to have any significant effect on the way the two markets at present do business or on the direction of trade traffic between them. The Commission intends to report on the application of the Article by the end of 1995, and any proposals for amendment will be decided by qualified majority voting in the Council.

Article 21 requires all regulated markets to publish weighted average prices, high and low prices, and aggregate trading volumes at the start of trading and on a rolling basis throughout the trading session. However, wide discretion will be allotted to national authorities to suspend or override the rules in the case of 'very large' trades, 'illiquid' securities, or 'exceptional' market conditions. The criteria for very large trades and illiquid securities are to be set by each individual authority, although they must be 'objective' and made public.

Rather than concern itself with the *harmonization* of reporting requirements, which should logically differ under different market structures, the Commission could better aid the task of creating an integrated European securities market by focusing on the efficient *dissemination* of price and volume data around the

Community. The task of consolidating the data from the various European exchanges would appear to be one which would naturally evoke private sector interest, although it may well be the case that the Commission would be required, perhaps owing to legal obstacles, to pursue a facilitating role.

Trading concentration

The 'concentration principle' enshrined in Article 14 is the result of a French-led 'Club Med Group' initiative, referred to earlier on, to prevent their nationals from transacting in domestic securities away from a 'regulated market'. This provision was at least partially aimed at stopping brokers on their own territory from dealing with one another off-market, but it was primarily aimed at curtailing foreign competition. Northern member states were justifiably concerned that this principle could be invoked either directly to protect southern markets against foreign market trading of their listed securities, or indirectly to restrict the development of off-market derivatives based on exchange-traded products (*Financial Regulation Report*, 1993). The original hope of the principle's framers was apparently that SEAQ International would fail to qualify as a 'regulated market' under the ISD definition, and that they would then be able legally to bar their nationals from trading domestic securities in London.

There are two conceivable economic justifications for a 'concentration principle'. The first is a market failure argument based on asymmetric information between market professionals and individual investors, which leads its proponents to claim that equitable treatment of the latter requires that the markets be 'sufficiently' regulated. The second argument is a market efficiency argument based on the premise that dispersed trading of a security harms the price discovery mechanism, which leads its proponents to claim that trading should be concentrated on one market.

The second argument does not appear to have been central to the debate, probably because it is an exceptionally weak one. Market *integration* rather than *concentration* is what is required for efficient price discovery, and this requires only that effective arbitrage between markets be possible. The first argument in the end resulted in a North-South compromise on the inclusion of an opt-out clause for investors, which would allow investors to derogate from the requirement that their trade be carried out on a 'regulated market'. Member states are to be given extremely wide latitude in determining how cumbersome the opt-out authorization is to be: Article 14 allows authorities to discriminate explicitly between professional and individual investors in formulating the requirements.

It remains to be seen precisely how southern states intend to apply Article 14. Since SEAQ International will, ultimately, almost certainly qualify as a 'regulated market' according to the ISD criteria, the concentration principle will not be easy to exploit for protectionist purposes. It may, however, allow states to curtail off-exchange trading within their own borders, and thereby help domestic exchanges to maintain sufficient volume to survive in a more open international trading environment.

Third country provisions

EC *branches* of investment firms authorized in non-EC countries will not be accorded the single passport rights delineated under the ISD, although full *subsidiaries* of third country firms established in a member state will be passported 'subject to a procedure intended to ensure that Community investment firms receive reciprocal treatment in the third countries in question'. The establishment of branches will remain subject to the rules of individual member states.

The reciprocity provisions in the SBD and ISD are, in the words of former US Treasury Under Secretary David Mulford, a 'club in the closet' which can potentially be wielded against third country institutions. The ISD requires that EC firms operating in third countries be accorded 'national treatment', or non-discriminatory treatment vis-à-vis domestic firms, as well as 'effective market access comparable to that granted by the Community to investment firms from that third country'. The Commission reserves the right to require member states to limit or suspend decisions regarding authorization requests from third country firms where the Commission is unsatisfied with the treatment or access accorded EC firms in that third country. The rights of firms already authorized to operate in the Community will not be affected.

Definitions of 'effective' and 'comparable' market access are not provided in the ISD, and are therefore potentially liable to hijack by protectionist forces. While the Community has refrained to date from brandishing the reciprocity club, this could change if foreign investment firms were perceived to be posing a threat to Community firms comparable, say, to that posed by Japanese automobile manufacturers. The Community has a large target, should it choose to swing at it, in the US McFadden Act restrictions on interstate banking, since it may always argue that the US is not providing 'comparable access' even if it is providing 'national treatment'.

Evaluating the EC securities markets regulatory framework

The EC financial market directives contain major regulatory as well as deregulatory elements. Since competent and prudential regulatory structures have existed for some time in most EC countries, it is the latter which are the more important in facilitating the creation of a stable and efficient European securities market.

It is unfortunate that the most liberalizing provision – the single passport provided in the ISD – will not actually take effect until 1996. Even come 1996, however, enormous scope will remain for effective protectionism. The path from Council approval of a directive to national legal implementation to local enforcement is a rocky one, and the Commission's practical ability to remove obstacles at the national level or below is extremely limited, despite its responsibility for effective and consistent implementation laid down in Article 155 of the Treaty of Rome.

Given the enormous difficulties involved in establishing a regulatory structure for a European financial market built on a foundation of tremendous legal and cultural diversity, it would have been more sensible initially to construct a much more flexible framework than that which has emerged. Member states fear justifiably, however, that if directives are insufficiently explicit the European Court might some day interpret the provisions in a manner which they find unacceptable. This leads to the creation of directives which look more like ceasefire arrangements than essential ground rules for international competition. This characterization is consistent with the picture of the present legislative process painted by the Principal Administrator of the Commission's Directorate-General XV (Financial Institutions and Company Law): 'In the case of the Investment Services Directive it took us over two years to strike a balance between the opposing factions' (Beverly, 1993).

The most sensible solution to this type of dilemma would be to have two different levels of Community legislation: primary and subordinate.* Primary legislation would enshrine broad political objectives on which member states could more readily agree. If the European Court were to be required to take a strict constructionist view of such legislation, and were to be enjoined from disallowing national initiatives which were not expressly prohibited, it would be far less necessary to fear judicial activism than at present. Once primary legislation has been passed, member states could then negotiate the subordinate legislation necessary to meet their agreed objectives. Such legislation, having to deal with the detailed operations of ever-evolving markets, needs to be subject to less stringent amendment procedures than the existing directives.

At present, the Commission is responsible for both initiating legislation and supervising its implementation and enforcement. The latter role would be better served by the establishment of a separate supervisory agency, comprised of industry experts, which would keep the Commission informed of progress and problems in the operation of Community legislation. At such an embryonic stage in the single market's development, it would be unwise to give such an agency powers of enforcement or prosecution: it should serve merely as the Commission's 'smoke alarm', providing advance warning of possible divergences between national practice and Community legislation.

*See Lee (1993) and the Federal Trust Study Group (1993) for complementary perspectives on EC legislation and regulation.

It is clear that the changes advocated above are unlikely to be pursued in the near future, and this means that further directives in the securities field will suffer from the same limitations as the CAD and ISD. While the CAD and ISD do provide a sufficient foundation of prudential requirements to inhibit the feared regulatory 'race to the bottom', they are also infused with political concessions serving to protect national competitive positions rather than to underpin the efficiency and stability of the wider European market. It is clearly the markets themselves rather than the legislators that will continue to provide the engine for integration.

4 EUROPE AND THE WORLD

Intermarket linkages

New York, London, and Tokyo form the regional and time-zone hubs of a globally linked 24-hour market. In the absence of a draconian re-imposition of capital controls, the North American, European and Asian markets will become increasingly integrated. With instantaneous communication and information flows among all the major markets, passive capital and unexploited investment opportunities will not long be kept apart by national borders.

Capital controls have now become virtual poison pills for the major national economies: they can thwart the will of the market for a spell, but only at the cost of seriously damaging a national market's long-term ability to raise capital. The proliferation of standardized derivative instruments is also slipping beyond the control of national authorities. If there is a viable futures or options market to be made, it is of little relevance *where* it is made. Thus, regardless of whether the concerns of the Japanese authorities over the effect of futures trading on underlying cash markets are valid, the efforts to restrict futures trading are self-defeating: more restrictions simply push more trading to Singapore, and the effect on the Japanese cash markets is precisely the same.

International equity issues are among the factors serving to integrate markets worldwide, such issues having reached an all-time annual high of $36.5 billion in 1993. Multi-market offers are being driven by a number of factors, foremost among them the desire of firms trading globally to expand their shareholder base, the growing diversification needs of rapidly expanding institutional investment funds, and the rise in large-scale government privatizations beyond the absorption capacity of domestic stock markets. The boom in global issues is creating genuine international competition among investment firms, as more and more share issues are now destined beyond the reach of favoured national intermediaries. Britain's S.G. Warburg and France's Paribas have emerged as Europe's main challengers to American dominance of international placements, which is currently led by Goldman Sachs and Morgan Stanley.

Among all major economic sectors, geography matters least in capital market services. European exchanges are not limiting their search for strategic alliances in Europe, but are combing the globe for competitive opportunities. Paris's Matif, for example, began listing contracts on the Chicago-based Globex after-hours screen trading system in May 1993, and could eventually be joined by London's LIFFE, Frankfurt's DTB and the Sydney Futures Exchange.

Sharing a common time zone and a single market for goods and services,* European exchanges will generally face more direct competition and establish more strategic alliances within the Community than outside it, yet there is simply no basis for the sort of inefficient 'trade diversion' that many fear in the creation of regional trade blocs. In terms of the Community's legal framework, EC capital markets provide relatively little in terms of preferential arrangements for member state institutions, products, and services vis-à-vis common notions of a regional trade bloc. The principle of 'mutual recognition' does offer advantages to member state firms in terms of direct investment rights and the elimination of administrative barriers in areas such as multi-country securities listings, but these advantages extend also to EC subsidiaries of foreign firms.

Prospects for non-EC investment firms in Europe

Prospects for American investment houses in a single European market look exceptionally good: in fact, American institutions are likely to be among the major beneficiaries of the removal of trade and investment barriers in Europe. US-based institutions already account for two-thirds of global capital market activity, and are firmly established within the Community in virtually all major areas, particularly mergers and acquisitions. Fledgling derivatives markets in Europe are proving bounteous hunting grounds for invading hordes of American traders, ever in search of inefficient markets to arbitrage. Cultural barriers are virtually meaningless in securities trading: as an American equity options trader in Frankfurt commented, 'Who needs to learn German? I'm dealing through a keyboard all day' (*International Herald Tribune*, 1993). This is clearly much less true in the corporate finance area, where local knowledge and sensitivity are still important. Japanese houses, according to many senior European executives, suffer from a yawning cultural gap, overcentralization and a lack of flexibility, and may therefore find it more difficult to exploit European market liberalization in the short run.†

---

* The United Kingdom is generally one hour behind the continent.
† For discussions of third country competitive prospects in the Community, see Smith (1992) and Golembe and Holland (1990).

International cooperation and agreements

Many of the major issues of concern to European policy-makers are also being addressed through national bilateral agreements with third country authorities, and through international institutions working to facilitate information exchange and promote harmonization of regulations and standards. European national regulatory authorities have signed Memoranda of Understanding (MOUs) with third country authorities to provide mutual assistance in enforcing regulations and carrying out investigations. The International Organization of Securities Commissions (IOSCO), the Fédération Internationale des Bourses de Valeurs (FIBV) and the Group of Thirty have all been examining issues relating to cross-border securities transactions. One result has been a set of widely hailed recommendations from the Group of Thirty to move toward rolling settlement and shorter settlement periods. International capital adequacy standards for G10 banks have been established by the Bank for International Settlements (BIS), and have been a subject of serious debate for securities firms in IOSCO deliberations.

While international efforts are clearly needed to address problems in a rapidly integrating global market, the proliferation of standard-setting bodies has the potential to inflate compliance costs unnecessarily. EC financial institutions may soon find themselves having to satisfy three different sets of capital standards: national, EC, and BIS/IOSCO. As the markets become further integrated, then so too must the regulatory efforts of national and international authorities.

5 CONCLUSIONS

Competition in the European capital markets has been intensifying steadily, and may be expected to continue to overwhelm European legislation as the driving force behind capital market integration for the foreseeable future. Major changes are taking place in the structure of national securities markets, reflecting the pressing need for exchanges to adapt to increasing international competition. In the short term, London is likely to continue to draw in trading from other European market-places, and further consolidate its predominance. In the longer term, however, London is very vulnerable to stiffer international competition based on more efficient market structures, superior trading technology, more efficient clearing and settlements systems, and effective strategic international alliances. The most credible competitive challenge may yet come from the rapidly developing electronic proprietary trading systems (PTSs), which are already a significant feature of the US equity trading environment.

It is now widely accepted that the pace of international market integration necessitates greater coordination among national regulatory authorities and a degree of harmonization of essential rules and standards. As our analysis of the developing European regulatory framework highlights, however, international rules and standards do not necessarily enshrine 'best practice'; rather, they often entrench existing practice. International agreements emerge from an inherently political process in which national actors are seeking to protect perceived national competitive interests, regardless of whether these may be reconciled with the stated goals of increasing efficiency and ensuring stability in the larger market. It is vital therefore that the international harmonization agenda be kept focused on those specific areas of regulation where the very existence of competing jurisdictions within an integrated market threatens to undermine effective regulation throughout the market. Economists could make a considerable contribution to the harmonization debate by examining more rigorously the nature and putative sources of systemic risk in financial markets.

References

Bank for International Settlements, 1991, 'International banking and financial market developments', May.

Beverly, A., 1993, 'European influence on regulation', paper presented at a conference entitled *City Regulation Re-examined*, organized by Westminster and City Programmes, 24 March.

Commission of the European Communities, 1985, 'Completing the internal market', White Paper from the Commission to the European Council, June.

Dale, R., 1992, 'Capital adequacy and European securities markets', in A. Steinherr, ed., *The New European Financial Market Place*, Longman, London.

The Economist, 1992a, 'Life, liberty and try pursuing a bit of tolerance too', 5 September.

The Economist, 1992b, 'Escaping through the net', 7 November.

The Economist, 1993, 'The resurrection of ecu bonds', 24 April.

Federal Trust Study Group, 1993, *Towards an Integrated European Capital Market*, Federal Trust for Education and Research, London.

Financial Regulation Report, 1992, 'Implications of the CAD and LED for underwriters in the international primary market', May.

Financial Regulation Report, 1993, 'The common position on the investment services directive', January.

Financial Times, 1992, 'Battle looms over Italy's new securities law', 14 February.

Financial Times, 1993, 'Stock markets slow down on road to convergence', 4 January.

Fortune, 1991, 'Stock trading without borders', 2 December.

Fraser, P., Helliar, C.V. and Power, D.M., 1992, 'European capital market convergence: a disaggregated perspective', discussion paper, Department of Economics and Management, University of Dundee.

Fraser, P. and MacDonald, R., 1992, 'European excess stock returns and capital market integration: an empirical perspective', discussion paper, Department of Economics and Management, University of Dundee.

Golembe, C. H. and Holland, D. S., 1990, 'Banking and securities', in G. C. Hufbauer, ed., *Europe 1992: An American Perspective*, The Brookings Institution, Washington DC.

International Herald Tribune, 1992, 'Compensation becomes a tool in today's market competition', 31 October.

International Herald Tribune, 1993, 'A Wall Street am Main? US options traders flock to Frankfurt', 14 April.

International Monetary Fund, 1992, 'International capital markets: developments, prospects, and policy issues'.

International Securities Market Association, 1993, 'Towards a single European securities market', Zurich.

Johnson, 1992, *New Players, New Rules: Financing the 1990s*, Lafferty Publications, Dublin.

Lee, R., 1993, 'Supervising EC capital markets: do we need a European SEC?', Oxford Finance Group discussion paper, 1, June.

Smith, A., 1992, *International Financial Markets: The Performance of Britain and its Rivals*, Cambridge University Press, Cambridge.

Steil, B., 1992, 'Regulatory foundations for global capital markets', in R. O'Brien, ed., *Finance and the International Economy*, 6, Oxford University Press, Oxford.

7 EUROPEAN MONETARY INTEGRATION AND PROSPECTS FOR MONETARY UNION

David Currie and John Whitley

1 Introduction

The European foreign exchange crises of September 1992 and July 1993 have left the European Monetary System (EMS) gravely weakened. Forced by the markets to accept large realignments of EMS parities, an enormous widening of the normal EMS bands and even the abandonment of the Exchange Rate Mechanism (ERM) itself, European policy-makers find their credibility severely diminished. Moreover, the collapse of the EMS leaves a vacuum at the heart of European monetary policy. Within the EMS, monetary policy outside Germany was directed to maintaining the exchange rate within the required band of variation around the specified Deutschmark parity. With 15 per cent bands of variation, this discipline is removed, increasing the scope for independent monetary policy in individual European countries. But the abandonment of the exchange rate discipline leaves considerable uncertainty about the principles that will determine how monetary policy is to be conducted. The combination of greater scope for independent action and absence of clarity as to how this independence will be exercised leaves the markets uncertain and without a clear anchor. An even larger vacuum exists in the future of European monetary cooperation and integration: the abandonment of coordination through the EMS removes the main mechanism for European monetary cooperation, and allows non-cooperative, beggar-my-neighbour policies.

These issues, the determination of national monetary policy and the broader agenda of European monetary cooperation, should be high on the agendas of national governments and of the European Union. In particular, they should be the concern of the European Monetary Institute, which came into being on 1 January 1994 under the leadership of Alexandre Lamfalussy, formerly head of the Bank for International Settlements. In this chapter, we analyse these issues, starting by considering the lessons to be drawn from the collapse of the EMS and then examining possible ways in which the agenda of European monetary integration can be advanced.

2 The background: the postwar history of monetary policy cooperation

For much of the postwar period up to the early 1970s, policy was coordinated internationally through the mechanism of the Bretton Woods adjustable exchange rate system. (See Tew, 1967; for a more recent survey, see Currie et al., 1989.) This placed the dollar at the centre, with other countries committed to a fixed, though periodically adjustable, parity against it. Nominally the dollar was linked to gold, but in practice the dollar was the lynchpin of the system.

Although it was not always evident at the time, the Bretton Woods system provided a powerful mechanism of international coordination. Countries other than the United States faced a severe discipline on the conduct of monetary and fiscal policy if they were not to lose reserves and find their exchange rate commitment under threat. Although there was scope to escape this discipline by devaluation, this option was used very sparingly. Partly in consequence, major imbalances in economic performance did not arise: inflation trends did not differ greatly when measured in terms of the prices of tradable goods; growth rates were generally high and stable; and current account imbalances tended to be corrected over time.

Two main factors acted to bring the Bretton Woods era to an end. First there was the point that the United States, as the anchor country, was free from this discipline. This allowed it to shift to a more expansionary monetary and fiscal stance, motivated by relatively slow US growth and the financing of the welfare programmes of the Kennedy/Johnson era and the Vietnam War. Laxer US policies at the centre of the system led to a more general relaxation of policy elsewhere which would otherwise have been inconsistent with the fixed exchange rate discipline. The result was a rise in worldwide inflationary pressures in the 1960s and 1970s. The second factor was the difficulty of maintaining the adjustable peg system in a world of increasingly mobile capital. The very expectation of a devaluation was sufficient to trigger a flight of capital on a scale that central banks could not manage. The resulting pressures imparted appreciable instability to the Bretton Woods system.

In consequence, 1971–2 saw the abandonment of the Bretton Woods system and a move to generalized floating. Attempts in the 1970s to return to a rule-based international monetary system were unsuccessful; coordination was limited to the one-off Bonn agreement of 1978. The commitment by Germany to an expansionary fiscal package (in exchange for trade liberalization by Japan and a higher oil tax by the United States) was ill-timed, coinciding with the oil price hike following the Iranian revolution, and gave policy coordination a bad name, particularly in Germany. During this period of floating, exchange rates exhibited appreciable volatility.

The unsatisfactory experience of floating in the 1970s led in two different directions. In the European Community, a Franco-German initiative reinstated a rule-based system in the form of the European Monetary System launched in 1979. Elsewhere the strength of the dollar in the first half of the 1980s meant that the Reagan administration saw no need to coordinate policy internationally, despite concern elsewhere. Instead, the emphasis was on each country putting its own house in order: monetarism in one country was very much the order of the day. The surge in the dollar and the US fiscal deficit led to the emergence of a very large US current account deficit, matched by surpluses in Japan and Germany, which has persisted to the present: these current account imbalances have been very much bigger than in earlier postwar decades, both in scale and in persistence.

The most recent form of international coordination came into its own from 1985, when US concern that the dollar might fall too rapidly from its February 1985 peak led it to enlist the assistance of the rest of the G7 countries. A series of summits, the first of which was held at the Plaza Hotel, New York in September 1985, have sought to coordinate policy, with the main focus being very much on the level of exchange rates and intervention policy (see Funabashi, 1989). By the Louvre summit in February 1987, the dollar was judged to have adjusted sufficiently, and the emphasis thereafter was on stabilizing exchange rates: the Louvre communiqué agreed 'to cooperate closely to foster stability of exchange rates around current levels', and subsequent communiqués have usually re-affirm this commitment. But the impetus behind exchange rate coordination seems to have diminished since 1989, when the Bush administration took office: the different cyclical positions of the United States, Japan and Germany have meant that each government has used monetary policy to pursue domestic, not exchange rate, objectives, so that exchange rate volatility has markedly increased since 1992. More specifically, German short-term interest rates have risen sharply to head off domestic inflation at the same time as the Federal Reserve has cut US short rates to head off recession.

The EMS seemed from the second half of the 1980s to be progressing to a hard form with no devaluation since January 1987. This appeared to be giving to the non-German EMS countries the benefits in terms of borrowed credibility of tying themselves to the Bundesbank's monetary policy (Giavazzi et al., 1988). The result was increasing convergence of inflation rates within the EMS, but growing questions over the sustainability of the EMS parities in view of increasing divergencies in competitiveness. The high German interest rates resulting from German unification and consequent inflation proved too much for all but the core EMS countries. Recession or low growth in other European countries led to doubts about the credibility of governments' willingness to raise interest rates to maintain their EMS parities: September 1992 saw the United Kingdom and Italy withdraw from the EMS and some other countries devalue. Just as the Bretton Woods system collapsed because the United States exported inflation, so the recent pressures on the EMS were exacerbated by the Bundesbank exporting deflation.

3 The rationale for policy cooperation

Policy coordination may be defined as the process whereby countries modify their economic policies in what is intended as a mutually beneficial manner, taking account of international linkages. This emphasizes that the rationale for international cooperation is the presence of important linkages between countries, with the consequence that policy changes in one country will have significant spillover effects onto other countries. Such spillovers may be positive, helping other countries to achieve their policy objectives, or negative. In the presence of such spillovers, the standard analysis of externalities means that uncoordinated national policies are likely to lead to too small (large) a response of policy overall in the international economy in the presence of negative (positive) spillovers (see Cooper, 1969; Hamada, 1976, 1985).

Such policy spillovers abound. Positive or negative spillovers may arise from changes in monetary policy, fiscal policy, the tax regime, trade policy, industrial policy, the framework of regulation, environmental policy and other spheres. Focusing on our main concern, a tightening of monetary policy to curb inflation may work in significant part through an appreciation of the currency, thereby exerting an inflationary effect on other countries whose currencies depreciate. This effect of monetary policy through the exchange rate adds to the efficacy of monetary policy in dealing with country-specific inflationary shocks. But when all countries are tightening monetary policy in the face of worldwide inflationary pressures, this effect will be absent: the result may well be an over-reliance on the monetary policy relative to other instruments (for example, fiscal policy) to curb inflation, and an over-tightening of monetary policy worldwide. (See Currie and Levine, 1985; Oudiz and Sachs, 1984, 1985; Miller and Salmon, 1985.)

These spillovers from monetary policy are likely to be rather important between highly integrated economies, such as the European economies, where the repercussions of the exchange rate change for domestic inflation are appreciable, because of both the importance of imports and the absence of pricing-to-market. But the evidence is that the monetary spillovers between the main three OECD blocs (United States, Europe and Japan) are not large (see Bryant et al., 1989), principally because of the relatively low proportion of trade between the main three blocs. Thus an absence of effective monetary cooperation between the three blocs may not impose great costs.

Of perhaps greater significance is the possible impact of mismatches in the fiscal/monetary mix. The integrated international capital market allows countries to run sustained fiscal deficits while keeping control over inflation through a tight monetary policy (as for example in the United States since 1981, and in Germany more recently). But the combination of tight monetary policy and lax fiscal policy raises world real interest rates. If sustained, such policies may well give rise to appreciable negative spillovers on to the supply performance of other countries. The absence of effective coordination of fiscal policy among the main blocs may well impose high costs.

International cooperation may take different forms. International meetings between the officials and/or politicians of different countries may result in important exchanges of information, improving the understanding of economic trends and policy developments in other countries. (More negatively, such meetings may also serve as public relations exercises, and may result in misinformation if each party communicates their public line at the expense of realism.) Furthermore, with proper preparation, such meetings may also result in one-off bargains between countries to modify their policies in mutually beneficial ways: the Bonn summit of 1978 falls into this category (see Dobson, 1991; Putnam and Bayne, 1987). More far-ranging agreements may lay down rules for the conduct of policy, most frequently in the form of exchange rate guidelines, as in the informal, unpublished guidelines for intervention policy agreed in the G7 meetings from the Plaza Agreement of September 1985 onwards, and in the formal agreements of the Bretton Woods system and the EMS.

Some important analytical ideas flow from these distinctions. The exchange of information about policy may take the form of information either on policy outcomes or on policy rules; in the absence of the further coordination of policy, this gives rise to the distinction between uncoordinated, Nash policy games played in terms of policy outcomes (Cooper, 1969; Hamada, 1976, 1985; Oudiz and Sachs 1984, 1985) and Nash games played in terms of policy rules (Currie and Levine, 1985; Levine et al., 1989). Whereas one-off international agreements will necessarily be discretionary in character, in the sense of Kydland and Prescott (1977), rule-based agreements offer the possibility of deriving benefits from credibility and reputation in the conduct of policy. (See Levine and Currie, 1987a.) There is also the idea that to be agreed, incorporated into formal agreements and monitored for agreed performance, a rule-based system needs to be simple in design: hence the emphasis in the literature on simple rules (Levine and Currie, 1987b; Williamson and Miller, 1987). Finally, in contrast to rule-based cooperation, a one-off agreement may be wide in scope and asymmetrical in the obligations it places on each country (Currie and Levine, 1991): the 1978 Bonn summit, for example, required adjustments by Germany in the macro-economic sphere in exchange for action by the United States on oil taxation and by Japan in liberalizing imports.

4 The collapse of the hard EMS: what went wrong?

Several factors contributed to the collapse of the hard EMS (Portes, 1993 provides a useful overview). A number of countries (Italy, Spain, the United Kingdom) had not made the adjustment to low German inflation and had exchange rates that were arguably overvalued: these were the first to be dislodged from the hard EMS in the September storm, being forced either to devalue or to suspend membership of the system. But the second main wave of speculation in July dislodged countries, notably France, which had adjusted to low inflation and for which no obvious fundamental disequilibrium existed in the exchange rate. A key factor was the cyclical divergence between Germany and the rest of Europe over the preceding five years. The inflationary pressures in Germany resulting from German unification and the consequent rise in interest rates put considerable pressure on other European countries, which despite rising unemployment were forced to match the rise in German rates in order to sustain their ERM parities. The low value of the dollar also added to pressures on the EMS, by allowing countries with currencies linked to the dollar (North America, Latin America, and much of the Asian Pacific Rim) to gain European market share through increased competitiveness. Political uncertainties also played their part: the relative weakness of European governments led the markets to question the willingness of governments to court unpopularity by raising interest rates in a sustained way to protect the EMS parity. Uncertainties over the ratification of Maastricht compounded these doubts: why should governments risk short-run unpopularity if the longer-run goal of exchange rate fixity and EMU might well be off the agenda? Once doubts arose about the commitment of governments to maintaining the EMS parities, the process of speculation snowballed: the more intense the speculation, the greater the price (in terms of higher interest rates and more deflation) that governments had to pay to offset it and therefore the more likely it was that they would abandon the EMS commitment.

A general lesson to be drawn is that the sustainability of a fixed exchange rate system relies on the willingness of the country with the core currency role to accept obligations to look after the system as a whole. The Bretton Woods system came under strain in the late 1960s and collapsed in the early 1970s because the United States adopted more expansionary policies and exported inflation to the rest of the world. Similarly, the hard EMS came under strain in the late 1980s and collapsed in the early 1990s in major part because tight German monetary policy exported recession to the rest of Europe. To say this is not to criticize Bundesbank monetary policy, which was well judged to deal with the problems of the German economy in this period. But a systemic problem with the EMS is the conflict between the needs of the system as a whole and the constitutional obligation of the Bundesbank to focus on the maintenance of low inflation in Germany, without regard for developments in the rest of Europe. Currie et al. (1992) show that the incentive compatibility of the hard EMS arrangement relies on a willingness of German policy-makers to accommodate themselves to some extent to the circumstances in the rest of Europe; but to do this would have been in conflict with the constitutional obligation of the Bundesbank.

In addition, fixed exchange rate regimes may be vulnerable to self-confirming speculative attacks (see Obstfeld, 1986; Krugman, 1979). The scope for such attacks is greater the smaller the access of central banks to international lines of credit, and the lower the degree of cooperation between the monetary policies of the members of the fixed exchange rate regime. The Basle-Nyborg agreement of 1987 increased the reserves available to EMS members, providing unlimited swap arrangements on a three-month basis. But the limits of that arrangement were exposed in the recent exchange rate crises: the Bundesbank was reluctant to lend Deutschmarks on an unlimited scale, for fear of destabilizing domestic monetary growth, its principal policy indicator; and other central banks were reluctant to borrow too heavily on a short-term basis because of the risk of substantial losses if eventually forced to realign the currency. The constitutional obligations of the Bundesbank limited its freedom to adapt its policy to help sustain the EMS, throwing the main burden onto the central banks whose currencies were under pressure and weakening the effectiveness of the defence.

5 Can the hard EMS be restored?

Some may favour a return to the hard EMS, with unchanging central exchange rate parities and narrow bands of variation. But the feasibility of this must be in question. Those who argue for this course view the collapse of the hard EMS as resulting from the pressures of German unification, and see no intrinsic difficulties in the operation of the EMS itself. But, as we have discussed above, other factors also contributed to the collapse: these include poor tactics by the authorities, the pressures placed on the system by the political uncertainties over the Maastricht Treaty, the limitations on the extent of cooperation between central banks, and the lack of responsiveness (for proper constitutional reasons) of the Bundesbank to economic conditions in the rest of Europe. But even if it had been the case that the pressures of German unification were the only factor in the collapse of the hard EMS, it is not possible to put the clock back. The limits of the powers of central banks have been clearly exposed, and the credibility of exchange rate targets severely dented. A return to a hard EMS would require a period of credibility-building, in which international investors will test the targets to the limit. Without the credibility accruing from several years of fixed parities, it seems unlikely that the European central banks would be able to pass that test. What might have held together without the pressures of German unification, provided no other major shock occurred, no longer provides a viable framework for policy.

One proposal to make the EMS less vulnerable is to reintroduce some form of limitation on the freedom of international capital, though not a return to the old-fashioned form of exchange controls that were somewhat ineffective, and in so far as they operated tended to introduce inefficiencies in the allocation of capital. Eichengreen and Wyplosz (1993) propose the introduction of a special reserve requirement against the open, uncovered foreign exchange position taken by banks. The objective of this is to reduce the willingness of the financial system to speculate against currencies. The main idea has a long pedigree: Tobin (1978) advocated a tax on international speculation, and Keynes saw much financial market activity as inefficient. Indeed, it is a longstanding theme in international economics that the three elements of fixed exchange rates, freedom of international capital mobility and national policy autonomy are mutually incompatible.

Tobin originally proposed his tax for a floating exchange rate regime, not a fixed exchange rate regime. The aim was to reduce the volatility of capital movements, thereby reducing fluctuations in floating rates. Even in a floating exchange rate regime, there was the powerful objection that the Tobin tax would reduce stabilizing speculation and thereby have the perverse effect of increasing exchange rate movements: this would depend on the balance between fundamentalists and 'noise' traders in the foreign exchange market. But the usefulness of the Tobin tax to help sustain fixed exchange rates is still more questionable. A large tax would certainly act to restrict capital movements and thereby the scope for speculative attacks on exchange rate parities, but the cost would be a severe distortion in the operation of international capital markets. A small tax would avoid major distortions in the international allocation of funds, but would be insufficient to avert speculative attacks: the experience of the past year is that small (and in some cases large) interest differentials have been insufficient to prevent speculation on a scale that has overwhelmed the capacity of central banks to withstand it, and the same would be true of a small Tobin tax. When markets form a clear view that exchange rates are unsustainable, only a punitive tax will prevent speculation.

Another option is a return to the soft EMS in the form that existed prior to 1987, with narrow exchange rate bands but periodic realignments of central parities. But after recent experience, a soft EMS would be subject to major speculative pressures. In particular, the limits of the exchange rate bands would be quickly tested by the markets, and the pressure could be all the greater because the option to realign would be overt, rather than covert as in the hard EMS. Moreover, a soft EMS suffers from the difficulty of managing realignments, unless they are small enough to avoid any discrete jump in the market spot rate. Like the hard EMS, the soft version may well be subject to waves of speculation that force realignments even when the fundamentals appear correct; and the softness of the exchange rate commitment may exacerbate this problem.

If neither the hard nor the soft EMS can be restored, some have suggested a rapid move to EMU or irrevocably fixed exchange rates (see, for example, Giovannini, 1991; Padoa-Schioppa, 1992), possibly involving France and Germany at the core. But there are political and economic obstacles in the way of this option. At the political level, there is no evident willingness, particularly by Germany, to move rapidly to EMU, involving as it does an acceleration of the timetable agreed at Maastricht. Recent constitutional challenges in Germany to the legality of the Maastricht Treaty have been unsuccessful, but they make more difficult any accelerated move to EMU in anticipation of the Maastricht Treaty. This is particularly so since rapid progress to EMU would require the waiving of the Maastricht fiscal criteria, on which Germany has insisted. At the economic level, divergencies in the European economy are substantial: a rapid move to locked exchange rates might well force a painful adjustment on other dimensions of economic performance, notably in growth and unemployment. Large fiscal deficits, well in excess of the Maastricht criteria, could also cause strains. A rapid move to EMU by a small number of countries, such as Germany, France and the Netherlands, creating a two-tier approach, might be more feasible in that it avoids the severity of adjustment in a full union. The political difficulties persist, however, and there is the added dimension that this two-tier approach could be characterized by competitive devaluation by the floating exchange rate countries on the periphery against fixed exchange rates in the core.

6 The need for European coordination

If a return to a narrow-band EMS, however modified, is not a serious option, what form should EC monetary cooperation take? One response is to argue that the present state of wide exchange rate bands is entirely satisfactory, and that no further steps are required. This view is held most strongly by the UK government, which has consistently viewed with suspicion the Maastricht agenda within Europe. On this view, the EC should go slow on further steps towards monetary integration, which is seen as a diversion, and instead place the emphasis on the completion of the single market (where there is much to do in terms of enforcing directives agreed as part of the 1992 process) and enlargement.

It is correct to argue that the single market and enlargement represent the major prizes that Europe can win in the rest of the decade. The economic benefits of creating an effective single trading area in Europe, especially an enlarged Europe, are very considerable. There are also major political gains from tying in Eastern Europe to the West European economy and thereby bringing stability to a potentially troublesome region. By contrast, the benefits of a single currency in Europe are relatively minor. The European Commission (1990) study of the benefits of a single currency estimated by means of some heroic assumptions the gains of a single currency to be around 0.5–1 per cent of GDP, but even this low estimate may be too generous. In particular, it gave too little weight to the additional adjustment costs incurred with a single European currency in the face of shocks that affect parts of the European economy differentially. The benefits of a single currency may well amount to only a part of one year's growth of the European economy: this is neither insignificant nor a major prize.

If the advantages of moving to EMU are considered, the most tangible benefit is that of a single currency in Europe. The resource benefit from eliminating intra-European currency transactions is not large in itself, being estimated by the Commission to be in the range 0.25–0.5 per cent of Community GDP (European Commission, 1990). Larger output gains are seen as accruing from the elimination of currency risk, estimated (perhaps generously) by the Commission at around 2 per cent of Community GDP. Allowing for induced investment and adjustment to a higher capital stock resulting from these efficiency gains applies a multiplier to these gains; and assuming constant returns to capital taken alone, as in the new endogenous growth literature, gives permanent gains to growth. These calculations are pretty soft, and perhaps should not be taken too seriously, but it is clear that the potential benefits could be significant.

What, then, are the disadvantages? The traditional approach to the issue of monetary union is provided by the literature on optimal currency areas. This suggests that the benefits of eliminating currency exchanges in a monetary union will be larger the greater the degree of intra-union trade; while the costs of abandoning exchange rate flexibility will be smaller the higher the degree of labour mobility, the higher the degree of nominal wage and price flexibility, the more diversified the industrial structures of the constituent economies, and the larger the proportion of common, rather than country-specific, shocks. Applied to Europe, this analysis yields a fairly mixed answer. Labour mobility is clearly rather low in Europe, much lower than in the United States. But Europe qualifies rather better on the other criteria. An important reason for the progressive abandonment of the nominal exchange rate instrument in Europe in the 1980s was the view that it is an ineffective means of obtaining adjustments in relative competitiveness except in the rather short run: nominal exchange rate changes tend to lead rather quickly to higher inflation, so that over a two- to four-year horizon gains in competitiveness are eroded through higher prices and wages. Our reading of the optimal currency literature is that it provides a compelling case neither for, nor against, monetary union.

But this analysis presupposes that the benefits of the single market can be obtained without monetary coordination in Europe, that is, with the present system of effectively floating exchange rates. If this is not so, and we discuss below the reasons why it may not be, then the case for monetary coordination and possibly a single European currency becomes much stronger. For if the maintenance of an open trading regime in Europe depends on greater monetary coordination, there are substantial dangers in the present loose arrangement of exchange rates varying within very wide bands.

Table 7.1 Repercussions of a French interest rate cut (% deviation)

	1994	1995	1996	1997
Output				
France	1.2	2.4	3.1	3.3
Germany	–0.2	–0.1	0.0	0.0
Italy	–0.2	–0.2	–0.2	–0.1
United Kingdom	–0.1	–0.1	0.0	0.0
Exports				
France	3.1	3.5	2.6	1.7
Germany	–0.5	–0.4	–0.1	—
Italy	–0.1	—	0.3	0.3
United Kingdom	–0.2	–0.1	—	0.1
Price level				
France	2.3	3.8	4.7	5.2
Germany	–0.1	–0.2	–0.3	–0.3
Italy	–0.2	–0.4	–0.4	–0.4
United Kingdom	–0.2	–0.3	–0.3	–0.4

The danger with the present loose exchange rate arrangement is that it may encourage protectionist responses within the member countries. Such responses are likely to be covert, not overt, but may well take the form of postponing the implementation of parts of the single market directives. When such protection is challenged, the defence will be that an open trading system requires stable exchange rates, and is placed under impossible strains if countries can obtain an arbitrary competitive advantage by means of a beggar-my-neighbour devaluation.

An objection to this line of argument is that there is no connection between free trade and fixed exchange rates: after all, the world economy has survived with floating exchange rates, often exhibiting wide variations, while maintaining a reasonably open trading environment. But this may be too complacent: the big postwar push to open up trade in manufacturing goods came in the 1950s and 1960s under the Bretton Woods fixed exchange rate regime, and the move to floating rates in the 1970s saw a rise in protectionist tendencies around the world, as had occurred in the 1930s with floating exchange rates. It is true that the rise in the dollar in the first half of the 1980s to its peak in February 1985 did not lead to protection in the United States; but that period did see an enormous increase in lobbying pressures for protectionist measures which, to its credit, the Reagan administration resisted. The fluctuations in the dollar in the 1980s increased considerably the risks of worldwide protection, and led to the US Omnibus Trade Bill of 1988, which contains very considerable powers for unilateral trade protection by US administrations.

This issue can also be examined using macroeconometric models of the international economy. We simulated our international model, GEM, to investigate the consequences of unilateral policy measures by one country on its partners. In particular, we examined the consequences of the French government abandoning its *franc fort* policy and cutting interest rates, as many commentators have argued that it should. The relaxation of policy is quite mild: a two percentage point reduction during 1994 and beyond in short-term interest rates below that assumed in our forecast. The result is an initial 15 per cent decline in the franc and a gain in French GDP of over 3 per cent after four years at the cost of a 5 per cent rise in prices (see Table 7.1). The spillover effects on the other European countries from this policy change are likely to be quite small, because the negative effect on demand in other countries arising from the increased competitiveness of the franc is offset, at least in part, by the positive effect of higher demand in France resulting from lower interest rates. This is confirmed by the results reported in Table 7.1: output falls in the other countries, but by only 0.1–0.2 per cent. However, the effect on other countries' export sectors is rather larger. Overall, this policy change raises output among the four European countries reported.

On the basis of this simulation, the spillover effects arising from monetary policy changes, although negative, are quite small. However, with large fiscal deficits, a more likely policy response is for the authorities to combine a reduction in interest rates with a tightening of fiscal policy, to give a better balance between monetary and fiscal policy. With this policy combination, the rise in French output, and hence the positive part of the spillover to other countries, is smaller. The consequence is a larger fall in output in other European countries, concentrated on the export sector (see Table 7.2). Although the spillovers are still modest in size, they are sufficient to cause concern in the tradable sectors of the other European countries. This policy change by the French authorities is sufficient to trigger a fall in the franc comparable in size to the competitive gain secured by sterling devaluation, and this may increase pressure for a competitive, possibly protectionist, response.

A third simulation examines the consequences of a coordinated and general reduction in European interest rates (see Table 7.3). This results in a general rise in output among the major four European economies. The rise in prices is quite subdued, largely because intra-European exchange rates do not move much, so that there is an absence of significant inflationary pressures from the exchange rate.

7 A role for the European Monetary Institute?

These model simulations suggest that there are significant policy spillovers between the European economies. This in turn suggests that uncoordinated

Table 7.2 Repercussions of French fiscal and monetary rebalancing (% deviation)

	1994	1995	1996	1997
Output				
France	0.8	1.5	1.9	2.0
Germany	−0.3	−0.2	−0.1	−0.1
Italy	−0.2	−0.3	−0.2	−0.2
United Kingdom	−0.1	−0.1	−0.1	0.0
Price level				
France	2.3	3.8	4.6	5.1
Germany	−0.1	−0.2	−0.3	−0.4
Italy	−0.3	−0.4	−0.4	−0.4
United Kingdom	−0.2	−0.3	−0.4	−0.5
Exports				
France	3.0	3.3	2.5	1.6
Germany	−0.8	−0.8	−0.5	−0.4
Italy	−0.4	−0.4	−0.2	−0.1
United Kingdom	−0.3	−0.3	−0.2	−0.1

policies may result in undesirable outcomes for the European economy, and creates scope for a coordinating role. An obvious candidate to assume this role is the precursor of the European Central Bank, namely the European Monetary Institute (EMI), which came into being in Frankfurt in January 1994 under the leadership of Alexandre Lamfalussy. This is an institution in search of a role: the Maastricht Treaty, and the discussions surrounding it, gave only shadowy form to the second stage of the transition to EMU and hence to the role to be played by the EMI. But the collapse of the hard EMS creates a policy vacuum which the EMI will seek to fill.

What substance can the EMI give to the coordination of policies in Europe? It would be a mistake for it to seek to move back to the old narrow-band EMS, for the reasons outlined above. Instead, it should seek to coordinate monetary policies in Europe within the present wide-band EMS. This means that exchange rates cannot be the focus of the coordination process: instead, the focus must be on domestic policy objectives. While the EMI will play a role in coordinating policy among all the European countries, its success will in practice depend on coordinating policy between Germany, France and the United Kingdom. Two main obstacles stand in its way: the marked policy differences between the countries, notably between the United Kingdom and the others, and the absence of any formal powers on the part of the EMI to coordinate policy, arising from

Table 7.3 Repercussions of a general European interest rate cut
(% deviation)

	1994	1995	1996	1997
Output				
France	0.3	0.8	1.2	1.2
Germany	0.5	0.9	1.0	0.7
Italy	0.2	0.4	0.5	0.4
United Kingdom	0.4	1.0	1.4	1.4
Exports				
France	0.6	1.0	0.9	0.5
Germany	0.9	1.0	0.7	−0.1
Italy	0.6	1.1	1.2	0.7
United Kingdom	0.4	0.5	0.3	−0.2
Price level				
France	0.3	0.5	0.6	0.6
Germany	0.2	0.4	0.7	1.0
Italy	0.3	0.4	0.5	0.5
United Kingdom	0.4	0.7	1.2	1.7

the shadowy nature of Stage Two of EMU. It will require considerable guile and political agility for the EMI to succeed.

One immediate stumbling block concerns the choice of domestic target or targets on which to coordinate. The principal alternatives involve the use of monetary targets, inflation targets or nominal income targets. It seems clear that the Bundesbank will press strongly for the use of monetary targets, which the Bank of England will oppose on grounds of the historical instability of UK money demand functions because of the effects of financial deregulation. The use of monetary targets poses certain technical questions. These include the definition of the European money supply: it is not sufficient to aggregate normal national definitions of money, since these omit holdings by residents of other European currencies, which should be included in any sensible definition of the European money supply. Other issues concern the stability of the relationship between the European money supply and European macroeconomic aggregates, including inflation and nominal income. There is also the matter of the very different arrangements for money market intervention by the authorities in the different countries: here the main difference is between the United Kingdom, with the special role given to the discount houses, and other countries where the use of 'repo' instruments is much more common.

If it is wise, the EMI will avoid any stark choice between these different domestic monetary targets. What it might establish is an arrangement in which monetary aggregates, along with other relevant indicators, are monitored in the short term with a view to targeting inflation or nominal income growth in the medium term. With different emphases, such an arrangement is consistent with the practices of the Bundesbank, the Banque de France and the Bank of England. As monetary cooperation develops and experience accrues, so the focus may change, moving to emphasize monetary aggregates if they prove to be stable indicators for the European economy, or to inflation or nominal income targets if financial deregulation generates too much instability of monetary aggregates. The important point is that the monetary transmission mechanism differs between member states, with respect to the immediate instruments of monetary policy, the channels through which these instruments influence final objectives of policy such as output and inflation, and the speed and magnitude of these influences. Any framework that the EMI adopts needs to have sufficient flexibility to allow for these differences.

One technical approach that allows for this flexibility is suggested by Garratt and Hall (1992), who show in the British context how a composite indicator can be derived from a range of relevant indicators of inflation with an explicit set of weights (which could vary over time) using a filtering approach. This indicator is shown to be robust with respect to the measure of inflation used and takes account of the main external inflationary shocks that may occur. Comparison of the composite indicator with the target rate of inflation allows the authorities to judge whether monetary policy needs to be tightened or eased. The individual indicators used in the British context include changes in the narrow and broad money supplies, the real short-term interest rate, changes in the nominal exchange rate, the level of the real exchange rate, the yield curve spread and the government deficit ratio, but the relevant indicators could vary from country to country. Similar work has been carried out by Henry and Pesaran (1993) using a VAR (Vector Auto Regressive) model. This approach offers a general framework that can allow for differences across countries in the way in which monetary policy operates, but by specifying explicitly the weight assigned to individual indicators gives content to inflation commitments that might otherwise appear vague and without credibility. (For further discussion, see Currie and Dicks, 1992.)

An implication of this approach is that the EMI should aim to focus on the coordination of outcomes, notably convergence to low and stable inflation, not convergence in policies. The latter is a fruitless task, given the important differences across countries in the relevance and impact of different monetary policy instruments.

The EMI will also need to reach judgments on the conduct of fiscal policy in the member states, even though fiscal policy lies outside its formal remit. This is because the conduct of fiscal policy affects final objectives, such as inflation and nominal income. (This is reflected in the inclusion of the government deficit ratio in the weighted composite indicator derived by Garratt and Hall.) In judging the appropriate monetary stance, the EMI will need to take account of, and comment on, fiscal policy across the European Community.

8 Progress to EMU?

Monetary coordination by the EMI makes sense irrespective of possible progress towards EMU. But it also provides a possible route to EMU. The EC has already seen substantial nominal convergence, at least among the major economies. If the EMI succeeds in maintaining and enhancing this, then it is quite feasible that a number of member states will satisfy the Maastricht guidelines on inflation and long-term interest rate convergence. Although Italy and Belgium will find it impossible to meet the debt criterion, if it is interpreted strictly, fiscal consolidation over the next few years could also bring a number of other countries into line on the fiscal convergence criteria. The exchange rate criterion can also be met very easily if the current wide 15 per cent bands are interpreted to be the normal EMS bands. It is therefore possible that in the second half of the 1990s sufficient countries will meet the Maastricht criteria to allow progress to EMU.

The key point is that progress to EMU does not depend on a return to narrow exchange rate bands and the hard EMS. With convergence, the EMI can be transformed overnight into the European Central Bank (ECB), with the powers to control monetary interventions to fix exchange rates irrevocably. At the technical level, this process presents few problems. It is, of course, possible, indeed likely, that market rates will diverge from central parities at the time when exchange rates are locked, and care will be needed to ensure that exchange rates are locked at levels that reflect fundamentals, not temporary fluctuations.

It is quite a separate question whether there will be the political will to move towards EMU. That may well depend on the track record of the EMI in coordinating policy. If it has established authority and confidence in its role, there may be a willingness to give it some additional powers to coordinate policies. A key test of the EMI will be its ability to manage its relationship with the major countries, notably Germany, France and the United Kingdom. There is no particular reason why it need come into conflict with the Bundesbank, since the goal of low and stable inflation in each country will be a shared one. However, there may be points of difference on timing and the weight to be given to different objectives. A greater point of issue may arise with the Banque de France, if the French authorities maintain their attachment to a largely fixed parity against the Deutschmark, which may come into conflict with an inflation objective.

The experience of coordination to achieve nominal convergence may offer other benefits. A German concern over progress to EMU is that Germany will be required to surrender sovereignty over monetary policy to a group of policy-makers from other countries that may be less concerned about inflation than the Bundesbank. But the period of domestic nominal targeting may be helpful in distinguishing those countries that are genuinely concerned with containing inflation and those that are not. Some, like Paul de Grauwe (1993), argue against a long transition period to EMU. He sets out a case where independent monetary policy can lead to different inflation rates and hence put pressure on a fixed exchange rate transition path.

There are, however, two reasons why a long transition period might be beneficial, in our view, especially if there is no attempt to fix exchange rates. The first is that the current divergences among several of the European economies would imply severe adjustment costs if monetary union were to proceed rapidly. The second is that by allowing the effects of independent monetary policy actions to be observed in inflation outcomes it will soon become clear which countries are committed to monetary union. The 'hard-on-inflation' countries will be those which self-select themselves for membership of the union. Those which are soft on inflation will not converge and will be excluded from full membership. This should help to avoid the reservations of the Bundesbank that its anti-inflation stance could be diluted in a full union. The ideal size of the group, in the eyes of Germany, to proceed towards monetary union is likely to be determined by the trade-off between losing dominance in too large a group or losing influence over its effective exchange rate in too small a group.

The role of the EMI would be to minimize the potential spillovers in monetary policy which might occur through independent monetary policies which tend to export either inflation or recession. More generally, the lessons from the literature on international policy coordination are that the mutual exchange of information as a coordination mechanism is important and that coordination of fundamentals, including fiscal policy, is the key. (See, for example, Currie et al., 1989.) The EMI's success may depend on its effectiveness in marshalling and communicating relevant information to the policy-makers, and in its ability to persuade them to modify, where necessary, the balance of their monetary and fiscal policy.

Eventually, if the process goes well, there may be a willingness on the part of sufficient countries to go further and surrender monetary sovereignty to the EMI in its new role as the ECB. Recent events have not removed EMU from the European agenda: indeed, they may have forced the Maastricht process away from an over-reliance on a fragile exchange rate arrangement to a more stable and viable path towards EMU.

References

Bryant, R., Henderson, D., Holtham, G., Hooper, P. and Symansky, S., eds, 1989, *Empirical Macroeconomics for Interdependent Economies*, Brookings Institution, Washington DC.

Cooper, R.N., 1969, 'Macroeconomic policy adjustment in interdependent economies', *Quarterly Journal of Economics*, 82, pp. 1–24.

Currie, David, 1991, 'European monetary union: a rocky road from Maastricht?', *International Economic Outlook*, 1, pp. 10–51.

Currie, David and Dicks, Geoffrey, 1992, 'UK macroeconomic policy with or without Maastricht', *Economic Outlook*, 16, pp. 29–35.

Currie, D. A., Holtham, G. and Hughes Hallett, 1989, 'The theory and practice of international policy coordination: does coordination pay?', in Ralph Bryant et al., eds, *Empirical Macroeconomics for Interdependent Economies*, Brookings Institution, Washington DC.

Currie, D. A. and Levine, P., 1985, 'Macroeconomic policy design in an interdependent world', in W.H. Buiter and R.C. Marston, eds, *International Economic Policy Coordination*, Cambridge University Press, Cambridge, pp. 228–68.

Currie, D. A. and Levine, P., 1991, 'The international coordination of macroeconomic policy', in D. Greenaway, M. Bleaney and I.M.T. Stewart, eds, *Companion to Contemporary Economic Thought*, Routledge, London, pp. 482–506.

Currie, David, Levine, Paul and Pearlman, Joseph, 1992, 'European monetary union or hard EMS?', *European Economic Review*, 36, 1185–1204.

de Grauwe, Paul, 1993, 'Monetary union in Europe', *The World Economy*, 16, pp. 653–62.

Dobson, W., 1991, *Economic Policy Coordination: Requiem or Prologue?*, Institute for International Economics, Washington DC.

Eichengreen, Barry and Wyplosz, Charles, 1993, 'The unstable EMS', *Brookings Papers on Economic Activity*, 1, pp. 51–124.

European Commission, 1990, *One Money, One Europe*, Brussels.

Funabashi, Y., 1989, *Managing the Dollar: From the Plaza to the Louvre*, Institute of International Economics, Washington DC.

Garratt, Anthony and Hall, Stephen, 1992, 'A proposed framework for monetary policy', *Economic Outlook*, 17, pp. 36–41.

Giavazzi, F., Giovannini, F. and Pagano, K., 1988, 'The advantages of tying one's hand: EMS discipline and central bank credibility', *European Economic Review*, pp. 1055–82.

Giovannini, Alberto, 1991,'Is European economic and monetary union falling apart?', *International Economic Outlook*, 1, pp. 36–41.

Hamada, K., 1976, 'A strategic analysis of monetary interdependence', *Journal of Political Economy*, 84, pp. 677–700.

Hamada, K., 1985, *The Political Economy of International Monetary Interdependence*, MIT Press, Cambridge, MA.

Henry, Brian and Pesaran, Bahrem, 1993, 'A VAR model of inflation', *Bank of England Quarterly Bulletin*, 33, pp. 231–9.

Krugman, Paul, 1979, 'A model of balance of payments crises', *Journal of Money, Credit and Banking*, 11, pp. 311–25.

Kydland, F. E. and Prescott, E. C., 1977, 'Rules rather than discretion: the inconsistency of optimal plans', *Journal of Political Economy*, 85, pp. 473–91.

Levine, P. and Currie, D. A., 1987a, 'The sustainability of optimal cooperative policies in a two-country world', *Oxford Economic Papers*, 39, pp. 38–74.

Levine, P. and Currie, D.A., 1987b, 'The design of feedback rules in linear stochastic rational expectations models', *Journal of Economic Dynamics and Control*, 11, pp. 1–28.

Levine, P., Currie, D.A. and Gaines, J., 1989, 'The use of simple rules for international policy agreements', in B. Eichengreen, M. Miller and R. Portes, eds, *Blueprints for Exchange Rate Management*, Academic Press, London and New York.

Miller, M.H. and Salmon, M.H., 1985, 'Policy coordination and dynamic games', in W.M. Buiter and R.C. Marston, eds, *International Economic Policy Coordination*, Cambridge University Press, Cambridge.

Obstfeld, Maurice, 1986, 'Rational and self-fulfilling balance of payments crises', *American Economic Review*, 76, pp. 72–81.

Oudiz, G. and Sachs, J., 1984, 'Macroeconomic policy coordination among the industrial economies', *Brookings Papers on Economic Activity*, 1, pp. 1–64.

Oudiz, G. and Sachs, J., 1985, 'International policy coordination in dynamic macroeconomic models', in W.H. Buiter and R.C. Marston, eds, *International Economic Policy Coordination*, Cambridge University Press, Cambridge.

Padoa-Schioppa, Tommaso, 1992, 'The September storm: EMS and the future of EMU', *International Economic Outlook*, 2, pp. 4–8.

Portes, Richard, 1993, 'EMS and EMU after the fall', *The World Economy*, 16, pp. 1–16.

Putnam, R. and Bayne, N., 1987, *Hanging Together: Cooperation and Conflict in the Seven-Power Summits*, Sage for the RIIA, London.

Tew, B., 1967, *International Monetary Cooperation 1945–67*, Harkinson, London.

Tobin, James, 1978, 'A proposal for international monetary reform', *Eastern Economic Journal*, 4, pp. 153–9.

Williamson, J. and Miller, M.H., 1987, *Targets and Indicators: A Blueprint for the International Coordination of Economic Policy*, Institute for International Economics, Washington DC.

8 PUTTING 'TRADE BLOCS' INTO PERSPECTIVE

David Henderson

1 'Trade blocs', liberalism and cross-border integration

In this chapter I assess the significance of (so-called) 'trade blocs' as an influence on the evolution of the world economy, and on the conduct of international economic relations. The argument refers to, but does not try to summarize, other chapters of this book, and it draws at various points on previous publications of mine.

The presentation is part analytical and part historical, but under both heads it has the same theme or point of reference. This theme is *the shifting balance between liberalism and interventionism* in international economic policies, and hence in the character of the world trading and investment system. The course of events, and the evolution of official policies, are charted from this point of view – that is, as a story of the changing fortunes of economic liberalism in the realm of cross-border transactions.* It is in this light that the impact of 'trade blocs', past and prospective, is considered: the question at issue is how far, and in what respects, they may cause the system as a whole to become more liberal or less.†

The same issue can be posed in a different though closely related way. Economic liberalism goes together with, and promotes, closer economic integration across frontiers and boundaries. Viewed as a process (as distinct from an end-state), integration can be defined as a tendency for the economic

---

* This forms the central theme of my essay on the evolution of the world trading system (Henderson, 1991), which covers the period from the end of the Second World War to the beginning of the 1990s, and on which I have drawn here.
† The main single principle which a liberal trade and investment regime embodies is that of *non-discrimination*. As far as trade is concerned, this implies that there are no differences in treatment (i) between goods and services which are produced domestically and those produced abroad; (ii) within domestic production, between goods and services for export and those that go to meet domestic demand; and (iii) within overseas production, between goods and services produced in different countries.

In relation to direct investment, non-discrimination implies that enterprises receive the same treatment, and are subject to the same laws and rules, irrespective of both the location of their head offices and the nationality or regional affiliation of their owners and directors.

significance of political boundaries to diminish;* and in so far as policies affecting cross-border transactions reflect the liberal principle of non-discrimination, this tendency is strengthened. In a regime that was fully liberal, there would be no politically derived barriers or deterrents to cross-border transactions: for various reasons, such as differences in language and culture, frontiers and boundaries might well continue to have economic significance, but this would not be attributable to the policy regime (or regimes) directly affecting trade and investment flows.† Thus liberalism and closer integration go together; and conversely, illiberal trade and investment policies are a source of disintegration within the system. Hence the main issue can be alternatively stated, in terms of whether 'trade blocs' – or more precisely and more neutrally, *regional integration agreements* – on balance have the effect of promoting a greater degree of cross-border economic integration in the world economy as a whole.

In considering the issue, the impact of 'trade blocs' has to be distinguished from, and weighed against, that of other influences which are at work – i.e., other agencies, and other mechanisms, through which official policies in relation to cross-border transactions are decided and put into effect. All such policies may affect the balance between liberalism and interventionism in the international sphere, and with it the extent of economic integration. These two sets of influences – 'trade blocs' versus the rest – are compared below under three related headings. Section 2 reviews the notion of 'trade blocs', and their attributes and status in the world economy of today. Section 3 is historical. It summarizes the ways in which, over the past half-century since the end of the Second World War, the international economic policies of governments have affected the extent of integration within the world economy. The effects of regional integration agreements form part of this wider story. Section 4 looks at the possible future evolution of the world trading and investment system – i.e., at the prospects for cross-border economic liberalism – with particular reference to the international policy regimes of the European Union and the United States.

2 'Trade blocs' in the world of today

The term 'trade blocs' is not well-defined. In this section I begin by comparing some rival interpretations of it, and then comment on the extent to which the present-day world economy is characterized by 'blocs'.

---

* The general topic of international (or more strictly, cross-border) economic integration is the subject of Henderson (1992).

† Under the heading of cross-border integration, it is not only trade and investment flows that are relevant, but also international and interregional migration. This aspect is not considered here. Some of the issues that it raises are taken up in Henderson (1994).

2.1 What makes a 'trade bloc'?

It so happens that three recent and independent sources provide rival interpretations of the notion of 'trade blocs', with correspondingly different listings of the 'blocs' that are currently to be found on the world scene.

The first interpretation, and the most restrictive of the three, is that suggested by Jim Rollo in Chapter 3 of this book. He asserts (p. 35) that 'The European Community is the one true trading bloc in the world at this moment'. By contrast, Martin Wolf (1994, p. 13) takes the view that, while the GATT lists no fewer than 65 regional trading arrangements, 'the world has only two significant trading blocs, defined as zones of preferential trade'. These are specified as being (i) Western Europe, centring on but extending beyond the EC, and (ii) North America – i.e., Canada, Mexico and the United States, grouped together as members of the NAFTA. A third and broader interpretation is to be found in a recent paper by Deepak Lal (1993, p. 350), in which the author's starting point is that 'trading blocs' can take either of two forms – 'common markets or regional free trade areas'. On this definition the number of currently existing blocs would be greater, and their ranks would not be confined to Western Europe and North America.

This diversity of views reflects differences in the criteria that the three authors have implicitly adopted. Rollo arrives at his figure of just one 'true trading bloc' by in effect imposing two qualifying conditions: first, that the constituent participating units should be sovereign national states; and, second, that these states should have agreed at any rate to form a customs union, so that they no longer operate their own independent trade regimes. In order to constitute a 'bloc', countries have to have grouped themselves into what may be termed a *trading entity*. The first of these conditions rules out the United States, since its constituent states are not sovereign. The second excludes, for the time being at least, not only the NAFTA but also the other regional integration arrangements that are to be found outside Europe and North America, since none of these is as yet a trading entity (though the four Mercosur countries have agreed to form a customs union as from the beginning of 1995). Hence only the EC is left.

Lal's definition also implicitly incorporates the first of these conditions: his 'trading blocs' likewise comprise groupings of sovereign states. But by admitting free trade areas into the category of 'trading blocs', as well as customs unions, he is relaxing the second condition: his 'blocs' are not necessarily trading entities.

In one respect, Wolf is more elastic than his fellow-authors, since he raises the possibility that a single national state, which constitutes a trading entity, could itself be viewed as a 'bloc'. Thus he notes that in North America the establishment of the NAFTA 'does not create much change in the "bloc" that existed beforehand, the United States itself'. Along these lines, one might think of the US, and possibly some other national states also, as 'quasi-blocs'. This puts in question the first of Rollo's qualifying conditions, accepted also by Lal, that a 'bloc' has to comprise more than one sovereign state.

Although this line of thought would make it impossible to define the notion of a 'trade bloc' at all precisely, it draws attention to an aspect of reality that is sometimes overlooked. Economically speaking, national frontiers are not the only ones that count. The concept of closer economic integration is general: it does not refer only to integration across the frontiers of sovereign states or trading entities. In this connection, all political boundaries may possess or acquire significance. It is not to be taken for granted, nor is it the case, that full economic integration necessarily prevails within national states – for example, there are now important respects in which integration is less close in Australia, Canada and the US than it has become within the European Union.* It is further the case, as will be seen later, that elements of disintegration within national states or trading entities may come to affect international economic relations. Hence the full story of the progress of integration, and the changing fortunes of economic liberalism, has to include events and relationships within trading entities as well as between them.

Wolf's approach is less restrictive than that of Rollo, in that by classing North America (the NAFTA members) as a 'bloc', he extends the notion beyond trading entities. He thus sets aside Rollo's second condition. On the other hand, he is more restrictive than Lal, since he limits the existing number of 'blocs' to two only. He does this by bringing in the additional criterion of size. For him, smaller free trade areas or customs unions do not qualify as 'trading blocs', because their actions and policies have too slight an impact on the rest of the world: they are not 'significant'. By the same token, smaller national states could not, in contrast to the United States, be viewed as 'quasi-blocs', because changes in their trade regimes have little effect on other national economies.

This appeal to different authorities does not yield a single agreed answer to the question of what constitutes a 'trade bloc'. The differences are not surprising, however, in that they reflect the complexities of the present world situation. It is because of this complexity – the wide variety of situations, agreements and tendencies that is to be found within the world economy – that the notion of

---

* In relation to Australia, precisely this point was made not long ago by an official agency, the Industries Commission: the 1991/92 OECD economic survey for Australia referred to the Commission's judgment that 'in the absence of reform, trade between Member states of the EC, when the measures proposed for 1992 are fully implemented, would be less restrictive than between the States and Territories of Australia' (OECD Economic Surveys, *Australia*, OECD, Paris, 1992). In the case of Canada, a recent newspaper article notes that the country 'is still without a solution to the pervasive inter-provincial non-tariff barriers that stifle growth and the free flow of goods, services and capital within its own borders' (*The Financial Times*, 6 June 1994).

'trade blocs' is not only ill-defined but also open to question: it suggests a degree of convergence, of uniformity, that neither exists nor is in prospect.

2.2 'Trade blocs' today: myths and reality

It is often now suggested or assumed that 'trade blocs' have become, or are in the course of becoming, a dominant feature of the world economy. More specifically, reference is made to the supposed existence or prospect of three large and well-defined regional 'blocs' – one in Europe; the second in North America, possibly to be extended further southward into Latin America; and a third in East Asia or (if Australia and New Zealand are counted in) the western Pacific region.* Neither of these assertions is valid. Looking at the world economy as a whole, there is no standard pattern or model of 'trade bloc' which constitutes a prevailing norm on which there is a clear and widespread tendency to converge. Rather, there exists a broad spectrum of regional agreements, which covers varying forms and degrees of integration. At the same time, there are both areas of the world and substantial numbers of individual countries for which such arrangements have not been made or are at present of little importance.

This diversity is likewise apparent among the three geographical areas listed above: there are substantial differences between them with respect to both the existing degree of cross-border integration and the prospects for taking integration further by agreement between governments.

In the western Pacific only the Australia-New Zealand Closer Economic Relations Agreement takes the member countries any significant distance towards integration, though it has not established a single trading entity. None of the five leading economies of the region, as measured by value of trade in goods and services – China, Japan, Hong Kong, Korea and Taiwan – is a member of a regional integration agreement, while the ASEAN member countries are still in the early stages of forming what is only a free trade area. It is true that trade has been growing fast within the region, but this has not been the result of formal agreements to lower trade barriers: to use the language of Vincent Cable's chapter, economic integration in this case has been largely market-led, rather than politically driven.

The other two areas, North America and Europe, are alike in that in each there is to be found an outstandingly important regional integration agreement. However, the two situations are markedly different one from another, and are likely to remain so. It is true that the NAFTA represents a clear move towards closer integration, which may over time embrace more countries. But the three existing member countries do not form a trading entity: they have not entered

*The argument here, and at one or two further points below, draws on Richard Blackhurst and David Henderson (1993).

into a customs union; they do not concert their actions and policies in relation to trade issues which fall outside the agreement; and they did not act together in the recent Uruguay Round negotiations. By contrast, the EU is long-established as a trading entity, while within it economic integration has also been extended, most notably within the single market programme, to other dimensions of cross-border transactions including not only capital flows of all kinds but also the movement of persons. Moreover, the EU, in ways that are reviewed in Jim Rollo's chapter, is systematically pursuing closer integration with non-member European countries; and under this heading there are publicly announced intentions for enlarging the membership of the Union: here, political as well as economic integration is explicitly involved. In the case of the NAFTA there are no such plans, no corresponding broadly agreed strategy both for enlargement and for still closer integration with well-defined groups of neighbouring countries.

Thus the world economy today is far from being divided into a number of geographically distinct but otherwise similar 'blocs'. There is no common and widely diffused pattern for regional agreements; the various existing agreements are highly specific and diverse; and there are important countries and areas, particularly though not only in Asia, for which such agreements have so far been of little or no importance. Only in Europe and North America have regional agreements brought extensive preferential liberalization between groups of countries which account, in each case, for a substantial proportion of world output and trade; and as between the two sides of the Atlantic, the main respective agreements are widely different.

All the same, the significance of regional agreements has increased in recent years, and it is not surprising that concerns should be expressed about their possible effects on the interests of non-members and on the open multilateral system of trade and investment. In this connection, however, it is not so much the spread of regional agreements as such that is in question, nor their general properties, but rather the policy regimes of the two largest trading entities, the European Union and the United States.*

2.3 A dual pre-eminence

Where international economic relations and the world trading and investment system are concerned, the EU and the US share a dual pre-eminence: contrary to what is sometimes suggested, the notion that there exists a 'trilateral world economy', in which Japan (or 'the Pacific') constitutes a roughly equivalent third partner alongside Europe and North America, is mistaken. There is no such 'third

---

*This section draws on Henderson (1993).

force'. Cohesion, economic size, and politico-economic responsibilities combine to place both the EU and the US in a situation unmatched by any other country or group of countries in today's world.

As far as cohesion is concerned, both are trading entities, which is not true of 'the Pacific' or 'Asia'. Within Asia, both Japan and China are also large economies and trading entities, but neither approaches the EU and the US (which themselves are closely comparable) in size of GDP or trade flows. However, the sheer size of their respective economies and external trade flows is not the only reason why the EU and the US are at the same time comparable with one another and pre-eminently influential within the international system. An additional and decisive factor, linked to economic size but going well beyond it, is that both are at the centre of extensive regional integration agreements which may well be subject to further enlargement. Both the EU and the US, and more especially the former, have in this respect an inescapable strategic or leadership role, extending clearly in the one case, and arguably in the other, across an entire continent. This is true of no other country or grouping of countries.

This situation is not, of course, entirely new. The United States has been for a long time the world's largest trading entity, while the original European Economic Community (EEC) had established itself as the second largest, and as the world's leading regional integration agreement, by the end of the 1960s. But developments over the past decade or so have at the same time enhanced the role of the EU and changed the orientation of the US. In both cases, the result has been to increase the significance of regionalism within the system.

In Europe, there have been three main developments: first, the closer economic integration within what is now the Union which has resulted from the establishment of the single market; second, the creation of the European Economic Area (EEA), now probably to be followed by the extension of EU membership to Austria, Finland, Norway and Sweden; and, third, the moves towards closer integration with countries in Central and Eastern Europe, most notably through the 'Europe Agreements'. All this has increased, and is increasing, the area, the economic size and the extent of integration of the EU, and hence its weight in the world economy and in international economic relations. As a result, the regime of the Union is unavoidably a matter of greater concern to nonmember countries, both within and outside Europe.

For the United States, the most notable development has been a new readiness to enter into regional integration agreements embodying preferential liberalization. The main instances have been the Free Trade Agreement with Israel of 1985, the US-Canada Free Trade Agreement of 1988, and now the NAFTA, which itself may be subject to further extension southwards. These moves towards regionalism have not altered the status and role of the United States as one of the two great trading entities: American trade and investment policies are still decided in Washington, and their influence on the system has not diminished. But the new orientation of policies has increased the extent to which what happens to the world system depends on developments within regional agreements.

Two aspects in particular of these recent changes in Europe and the United States are worth noting. First, what happens at the world or multilateral level now depends, even more than was the case a decade ago, on the policy stances of the 'big two' and their capacity to reach agreement with each other: clear recent evidence of this is to be found in the long-drawn-out history, and more particularly in the tense and laborious final stages, of the Uruguay Round negotiations. As trading entities, the EU and the US, taken together, now loom larger than before.

Second, the past and prospective enlargement of the EU, together with the creation and possible further enlargement of the NAFTA, have inevitably increased the concerns of countries which are not parties to either agreement that decisions may be taken within the agreements which are contrary to their interests. These countries have two main concerns: first, that market access for outsiders may become more restricted; and, second, that non-members may be more subject than before to the exercise of pressures and coercion, whether from the EU or the US, in relation to their trade and investment regimes. I return to this aspect in Section 4 below.

All this has to be viewed against a wider background, in which influences on the system other than regional integration agreements are given their due place in the analysis and the narrative of events.

3 Regionalism and other influences: developments over the past half-century

In the five decades since the end of the Second World War, the extent of international economic integration has greatly increased. The trend has not been uniform across countries or sectors, and the full story is a complex one, but the broad direction of change has been clear. While technical developments have played a part in events, the main influence has been the policies of governments. Closer integration has chiefly resulted from decisions by national governments to make international transactions freer, or to permit them to become so.

In making and giving effect to decisions that bear on the trade and investment regime, governments may act through one or more of three modes or channels. These are: (a) *unilateral*, where no other government is directly involved; (b) *regional*, where a group of governments within a designated area makes decisions affecting relations between their own economies, and between the group as a whole and the countries outside it; and (c) *multilateral*, where a group of governments, which may or may not have geographical ties, makes decisions which affect their economic relations not only with one another but with the rest of the world (or with other Contracting Parties to the GATT). The relative importance of these three elements has varied. Hence the influence of regional integration agreements on the system has to be viewed and judged in the context of developments under all three headings.

The drama here has two sets of actors, and falls into two distinct periods of time. The two groups concerned are: (i) the 24 countries which until the spring of 1994, when Mexico was admitted, had for some time made up the membership of the OECD; and (ii) the rest of the world. The first period covers roughly forty years, from the end of the Second World War to the mid-1980s, while the second comprises the decade that has since elapsed. In both periods, and for both sets of countries and governments, the evolution of international economic policy involved all three modes of operation – unilateral, regional and multilateral.

3.1 The evolution of policies in the OECD area

Among the OECD member countries, international economic policies during this half-century have been (a) broadly similar, and (b) characterized by a varying blend of liberal and interventionist elements. The prevailing theme or pattern, both within and across countries, has been one of *heavily qualified liberalism.*

During the first period of four decades, two sub-periods can be distinguished. In the first of these, which extends to the early 1970s, the liberal aspect was clearly dominant: there was a far-reaching liberalization of the trade and payments regimes of these countries. Over the next decade or so, the balance between liberalism and interventionism became more even. On the side of liberalism, the main developments to note are the conclusion of the Tokyo Round of trade negotiations and the growing trend towards liberalization of international financial transactions. On the other side of the balance, OECD countries generally, including the EC and the US, came to rely increasingly and as a matter of course on measures of selective protection. These comprised in particular (a) (so-called) voluntary export restraint agreements (VERs), (b) anti-dumping actions, and (c) specific subsidies. In this respect, as also (with one or two exceptions) in relation to agricultural production and trade, the policies of the OECD countries have tended increasingly to become – and still remain – a source of disintegration within the system.

Throughout the period, until the mid-1980s, actions were taken by the OECD governments under all three headings – unilateral, regional and multilateral. But only in Western Europe, with the creation, consolidation and enlargement of the EC, and the establishment in consequence of the EFTA, was there a strong specifically regional component to liberalization (and in some respects, to interventionism also). Outside Europe the extent and influence of regional agreements was slight. Even within Europe the regional aspect, though important, was by no means the whole story. European governments, sometimes through the EC as a newly created trading entity, were fully involved in the various multilateral agreements which did much to liberalize the system, and they also acted unilaterally in relation to a wide range of issues.

As Alasdair Smith notes in Chapter 2, a great deal of work has been done on the question of whether and in what ways the regional integration agreements of this period in Western Europe, and in particular the establishment and subsequent evolution of the EEC, are to be viewed as liberalizing or restrictive – as promoting integration in the world economy as a whole, or limiting it. Broadly, the verdict has been positive, in that trade liberalization within the EC went together with a continued parallel growth in trade with the rest of the world. This in turn is largely accounted for by the fact that, far from turning inward after its formation, the EC itself became more liberal, largely through its involvement in the Dillon and Tokyo Rounds within the GATT. Only with respect to agriculture, in the Common Agricultural Policy (CAP), is there clear reason to think that the effect of establishing the EC as a trading entity was illiberal, in that the CAP was a more protectionist outcome than would have resulted if the six member states had never been grouped as a trading entity. But despite this and some other reservations, the evidence suggests that the formation of the EC was itself a part of the story of liberalization in the OECD area, not only as between the member countries but also more broadly.

Since 1985, in ways that have been summarized in the previous section, regionalism has become a stronger and more pervasive influence on the course of international policies within the OECD countries, not only in Europe but also in North America and Australasia. To a greater extent than before, international integration has been going ahead on regional lines. At the same time, however, the unilateral and the multilateral elements have also been present, and in two significant areas of recent liberalization both have been in evidence. One of these areas is financial markets, where international flows of all kinds have now been substantially freed from national regulations on the part of OECD governments; the other is foreign direct investment.* More recently, as Vincent Cable notes in

---

* A recent OECD report (OECD, 1992) contains the statement: 'No one can fail to be astonished by the extent of Member countries' progress since the beginning of the [1980s] towards greater liberalisation and the removal of restrictions and obstacles to direct investment flows to and from other countries and more significantly still, in their broader regulatory approaches to such investment.' As noted below in the text, progress on similar lines has been made, over much the same period, by a growing number of non-OECD countries.

Chapter 1, the conclusion of the Uruguay Round negotiations, with the decision to create a new World Trade Organization, bears further witness to the continued relevance of the multilateral approach. Policies thus remain subject to the influence of all three modes of action, even though the regional aspect is now more conspicuous, and more extensive geographically, than was the case in the earlier postwar decades.

During this more recent period the two main further ventures into regionalism have of course been (a) the creation of the single market within the EC, and (b) the establishment of the NAFTA. With regard to the former, the evidence so far suggests that, as with the earlier stages of regional integration within the EC, internal liberalization has not been associated with a greater degree of protectionism vis-à-vis the rest of the world: fears that a 'fortress Europe' would be created have so far proved unfounded. Nor is there reason to think that as a result of the formation of the EEA, and the further enlargement of the EU that seems now about to take place, the Union will become less liberal in its trade and investment regime. This is not to say that the regime is a fully liberal one, even leaving aside the CAP: more on this later. The point here is that in recent years, as earlier, internal liberalization has in general gone together with maintaining, and in some respects increasing, the degree of openness of the EC in relation to other countries. Where protectionism remains strongly entrenched, or may actually have increased in intensity, the causes are not to be found in the programme of internal liberalization.

As to the NAFTA, a broadly similar but possibly more cautious verdict may be warranted. In the recent GATT volume on regional integration (Anderson and Blackhurst, eds, 1993) the editors note (p. 7) the conclusion of the chapter that reviews the agreement:

> NAFTA will, on balance, be trade-liberalizing despite some clearly restrictive or discriminatory measures, including some Byzantine rules of origin. It will be even more liberalizing if the Uruguay Round concludes successfully, because that would reduce the preferential margin for trade within NAFTA through lowering most-favoured nation trade barriers.

Since this was written, two further developments have taken place. First, the Uruguay Round tariff reductions have been agreed (even though not yet fully ratified), so that the above conclusion is reinforced. On the other hand, the final outcome provides, in addition to the main Agreement, three supplemental agreements relating respectively to environmental standards, labour standards, and 'import surges'. These additions were made at the insistence of the United States, in response to pressures from the trade unions and from within the Congress; and they could well limit the extent to which in the event trade is freed between

Mexico and the other two partners to the Agreement. As will be seen, it is possible that such provisions could increasingly become a feature of trade agreements.

3.2 The non-OECD world

In the non-OECD countries, the evolution of policies has been quite different, and the influence of regionalism has till recently been negligible. In this context also, the mid-to-late 1980s mark a new phase in the evolution of international economic policies; but the new phase is one of unilateral liberalization, rather than regionalism.

Among the developing countries, as compared with the OECD group, a much greater diversity of trade, payments and investment regimes has been a continuing feature. But from the early post-Second World War years there was a clear tendency within the group, in marked contrast with the OECD member states, to move in the direction of greater trade protectionism and closer control over international transactions in general. In this, governments acted largely on their own; and as noted by Vincent Cable, such attempts as were made in this period by groups of developing countries to establish regional integration agreements came to virtually nothing. In these countries the policy initiatives which actually influenced events, whether in a liberal or (more typically) an interventionist direction, were with few exceptions unilaterally decided and put into effect.

From about the mid-1980s, a remarkable change has taken place in the trade regimes of a growing number of developing countries – as also, more recently, in some of the former communist countries of Central and Eastern Europe. Substantial liberalization has taken place and is still continuing, while a parallel and equally striking development has been the change in attitudes towards, and in regulations affecting, private foreign direct investment. In both these areas of policy – as also, in some cases, in relation to exchange controls and freedom of capital movements – non-OECD countries have been consciously moving in the direction of closer integration into the world economy. Although in some instances this tendency has been partly linked to actual or proposed regional agreements – as in the case of the Europe Agreements – such agreements have in general, at any rate up to now, played a minor part in this recent process of liberalization. As in the previous four decades, the actions that have counted have been largely unilateral, though the past few years have seen a supporting role, mainly within the Uruguay Round, for the multilateral approach as well.

Viewing the half-century as a whole, across both groups of countries, the impact of policies has been on balance – though with many exceptions and qualifications – to make the system more open and liberal, and the world economy more closely integrated. Actions taken through all three main channels have contributed to this outcome; and these include the establishment of regional integration agreements which up to now appear to have had mixed but generally positive effects. Outside Europe, the contribution of 'regionalism' to the evolution of international economic policies has so far been small: unilateral and multilateral modes of action have been dominant. However, Europe is a major and continuing exception, with the weight and influence of the EU still growing, while the significance of regional agreements has recently been increasing not only within the European continent but outside it. Further, despite what has happened in recent decades, there is no assurance that new regional agreements, or the new features that may be added to existing ones, will conform to the past pattern of qualified liberalism. Given the increasing scope and influence of regionalism, any disintegrating effects that it might bring would be a matter of concern, particularly for countries outside the main agreements. Such future possibilities, like the past effects of regionalism, have to be viewed in the wider context of changes in the world economy and the evolution of international economic policies more generally.

4 Looking ahead: the prospects for a liberal world economy

4.1 A path of opportunity

To an extent that was wholly unforeseen before the event, liberalism has gained ground across the world over the past 15 years or so. In all the OECD countries, economic policies have moved in a market-oriented direction, most notably through deregulation, privatization, tax reform, and measures to reduce the size and improve the efficiency of the public sector. As to the international policies of these countries, the extent of trade liberalization during this period has with a few exceptions been very limited; but with respect to capital flows and private direct investment there has been far-reaching liberalization. Outside the OECD area the idea of a command economy has been wholly discredited, and a large and still growing number of countries have engaged in programmes of reform with the intention, and the effect, of reducing the extent of central direction in their economic systems and enlarging the sphere of competitive markets. Within these programmes, as has been seen, substantial steps have been taken to establish freer trade and investment regimes. For many of these countries, it has in effect been decided that they should now become part of the world economy.

These events have opened up a new prospect. It has become possible to think in terms of a continuing evolution, with the participation of virtually all countries, towards closer integration of the world economy through progressively greater freedom for cross-border trade and investment flows. This would bring substantial gains in world prosperity; and these gains would be widely shared, by rich and poor countries alike. Nor would the benefits from further systematic liberalization be counted in terms of prosperity alone, since a world in which the principle of non-discrimination in international transactions was generally observed would by virtue of this be more orderly and less subject to frictions.

If such a process of change occurs, all three channels of policy are likely to be involved; and within the mix, new or enlarged regional integration agreements could form part of the story of continuing liberalization. In assessing this possibility, separate consideration has to be given to two different categories of agreement in the world of today: first, the two predominant 'blocs', the EU and the NAFTA; and, second, the various smaller agreements that exist, or may be established, outside them.

As regards this latter category, there is some reason to suppose that, at any rate outside Europe and North America, the existing and newly established regional integration agreements, and further ventures along the same lines, will on balance serve to make the system as a whole more rather than less liberal. The main point here is well made by Anderson and Blackhurst. They note that a common motive now for joining an existing agreement, or for becoming involved in the creation of a new one, is the wish on the part of the countries concerned to consolidate, and to take further, a programme of market-oriented reform. Membership of the agreement may then be viewed, with good reason, as 'a means of reducing the risk that political pressures from interventionists at home will in the future cause a reversal of [the] reform process' (1993, p. 3). This is not just speculation: such a motive was clearly present when Spain and Portugal decided to apply for membership of the European Community; and in both cases membership went together with substantial liberalization which extended to the trade and investment regimes of both countries. More recently, the same was true of the Mexican decision to seek entry into the US-Canada Free Trade Agreement. In related cases – the Mercosur agreement may prove to be one of them – where the participating countries wish to establish a new arrangement as part of a wider reform process, there are grounds for expecting that the newly created 'bloc' will not be protectionist: the same reasoning that leads such a group to reduce or eliminate barriers within the region provides the rationale for a wider opening of markets. As Anderson and Blackhurst (1993, p. 4) put it, 'The fact that a key motivation of excluded countries to join an existing [regional integration agreement] is their desire to safeguard their ability to pursue outward-oriented development policies suggests that [such agreements] can make a positive contribution to the liberalization of global trade'.

However, this line of thought is valid only within limits. For one thing, it remains to be seen how strong and sustained the commitment to liberalism on the part of non-OECD countries will prove to be. More fundamentally, the argument applies only to smaller agreements which have not become firmly established, rather than to the two predominant existing 'blocs'; and by comparison with the EU and the NAFTA, these other recent and prospective agreements are relatively small affairs. The important questions for the future of the system relate to the external policies of the two predominant 'blocs' – and within the NAFTA, to the trade and investment regime of the United States. It is unlikely that the entry of new member countries into the EU or the NAFTA, even if these countries are themselves liberal (as now in the case of the Czech Republic in Europe, or Chile on the American continent), will influence in a liberal direction the policies of either the EU or the US: a more probable outcome, now as in the past, is that newcomers will have to adapt to the already existing trade regime of the 'bloc' concerned. The case of the entry of Spain and Portugal into the EC is in fact a good illustration: such effects that this may have had on the trade regime of the Community were not only slight, but quite possibly on balance anti-liberal. Liberalization did indeed take place; but it was liberalization within the EC, and in the trade and investment regimes of Spain and Portugal, not in the EC's relations with the rest of the world.

Hence the argument comes back to the central point made at the end of Section 2 above. The main single influence on the way in which the world trade and investment system now evolves, and on the extent to which international economic integration will proceed further, is the external policies of the EU and the United States. This, however, is not so much because they are 'trade blocs' – though the EU is a 'bloc', and the United States can be viewed as one – but rather because they are by such a wide margin the largest and most influential trading entities. As such, theirs are the unilateral decisions that chiefly count. At the same time, these decisions are subject to influence by other national governments and trading entities.

4.2 The EU, the US and others

Although there are important differences between the European Union and the United States, arising chiefly from their differing political and constitutional status, the two respective trade regimes have much in common, and within them the present balance between liberal and interventionist elements is similar. Both the Community and the United States have over the years taken unilateral steps towards liberalization, and both have participated fully in successive GATT rounds and in liberalization which has been carried through within the OECD. Both are formally committed to further progressive liberalization, and to acting in ways that will strengthen the open multilateral trading system. At the same time, and notwithstanding the strong criticisms which each is apt to make of protectionism on the other's part, they are interventionist in much the same ways and for much the same reasons. Both operate well-established systems of selective protection which are broadly similar to one another;* both have brought official pressure to bear outside the GATT, in particular on Japan, with a view to influencing specific trade flows; in both, ideas are now being canvassed for further regulation of international trade, in ways that would increase the extent of disintegration within the international system; and in both, public opinion, within official circles as well as more broadly, is influenced by pre-economic conceptions of what is involved, and what is at stake, in international transactions.

Although it is not the concern of this chapter to review the possible evolution of these two trade regimes, it is worth noting two related and fairly recent developments which may, both singly and together, reinforce the interventionist elements and tendencies in each of them.

The first of these developments is the amazing and sustained economic success, and with it the rapidly growing participation in international trade, of a group of East Asian economies which now includes that of the Republic of China. In both Europe and North America,† businesses are increasingly having to take into account the opportunities and problems which these changes are bringing with them. As part of the reaction to this challenge, there may well be increasing pressure to retain existing forms of selective protection against imports from East Asia, and to develop new instruments for the same purpose. Looking further ahead, it is possible to foresee a situation in which Japan will no longer be the only country which has matched or surpassed the living standards, and in some areas at any rate the technical prowess, of the industrial countries of Europe and North America which for long were the richest, the most advanced, and – going beyond economics – the most powerful in the world. Major changes are thus in prospect, not only in the volume and composition of international trade, but also in the numbers, and the relative economic status, of the world's most prosperous countries: new members can now be anticipated for what has long been a select economic and political club. Experience suggests that this may raise problems for the existing members. Over the past four decades, both West European countries and the United States have found it difficult to adjust to, and to accommodate, the economic transformation of Japan: in reaction to it, their

---

* The main shared forms of protectionism are (i) the special regimes which have been created for 'sensitive' products – in particular, textiles and clothing, motor vehicles and steel, and (ii) the systematic use of anti-dumping actions. Another aspect of interventionism in which there are close parallels is agricultural policies, as Tim Josling has noted. In this area 'the similarities between the EC and the US are more striking than the differences' (Tim Josling, 'Agricultural trade issues in transatlantic trade relations', *The World Economy*, vol. 16, no. 5, September 1993, p. 555).
† In this paragraph the term 'North America' refers to the United States and Canada only – i.e. excluding Mexico.

governments have resorted to a range of illiberal actions. If this precedent is anything to go by, and if the East Asian dynamism is maintained, further interventionist pressures, and possibly initiatives, are to be expected. The fast-growing East Asian economies, and other countries outside Europe and North America which achieve rapid export growth, have reason to be concerned about access to markets in the EU and the NAFTA, as also about official pressure from Brussels and Washington to limit exports, and to expand imports, in ways that supersede market processes.*

A second development with interventionist implications is the increasing concern, on both sides of the Atlantic, with defining, and enforcing within the trading system, minimum international standards relating to (i) terms and conditions of employment and (ii) the environment. The recent side additions to the NAFTA have been noted above; and both the United States and France have now given official support to the idea that the setting of internationally agreed labour standards should be part of the agenda for the new World Trade Organization. So far the EU as such has not moved in this direction; but existing regulations, national and EU-wide, already limit the extent to which full integration of labour markets exists within the Union;† and as Wolf (1994, p. 47) has remarked, 'The logic that leads to [internal] harmonisation of labour standards demands their world-wide extension'.

It is therefore easy to imagine how, in both the 'big two', the trend towards more liberal trade regimes, which has broadly prevailed over the past half-century, could now be halted or even on balance reversed. If and in so far as the EU and the US were to retain their existing modes of selective protection, or to extend them in the ways that some are now proposing, this would in itself affect unilaterally the balance between liberalism and interventionism in the world as a whole. It would also influence the extent to which future regionalism went together with liberalization. There would clearly be a direct influence, in that new members of the EU, and possibly also of an enlarged NAFTA, would be joining agreements which in important respects were becoming less liberal rather than more. There could also be an indirect influence, in that countries remaining outside the two 'blocs', including those in other regional agreements, would have less to gain from external liberalization, and might themselves be more influenced by protectionist arguments and pressures.

---

*In the EU, the Commission and the Council have recently taken measures to simplify and speed up the procedures relating to anti-dumping actions, while the number of Commission staff engaged in administering these actions is to be doubled.
†The possible disintegrating effects of enforced uniformity can be seen at their starkest in post-reunification Germany. They have arisen there from the premature convergence, through non-market influences, of the wage systems in east and west.

However, such a change in course is not at all inevitable. In both the EU and the United States there are to be found today, as in the past, ideas and interests which lend support to free trade, while the official commitment to liberalization is likely to remain. As before, the balance between liberal and interventionist forces may remain fairly evenly poised, not always tilting consistently in one direction.

In this situation, the actions of the 'big two' could well be subject to influence by the conduct, arguments and pressures of other countries or groups of countries within the system: the scope for such influence should tend to increase, as a result of (i) the growing relative economic importance of many of these countries, and (ii) their closer integration into the world economy. Much may therefore depend on the way in which international economic policies now evolve in the rest of the world – in particular, in Russia, the leading Latin American economies, the now advanced and still fast-growing smaller economies of Asia, and the three largest Asian economies, namely China, India and Japan. Further liberalization on their part, together with a commitment to strengthen the multilateral trade system (and the WTO), would improve the prospects for trade liberalism within the EU, the United States and the NAFTA.

4.3 Regionalism within a liberal international order

Since closer integration and economic liberalism go together, the path of opportunity outlined above would also be the path to a liberal international economic order. Such an order has prevailed in history only once, during the half-century or so preceding the outbreak of the First World War. It is now possible to visualize, not just as an abstract idea but as a reference point for actions and policies, a 21st-century counterpart. If established, this second liberal order should in one respect be more securely founded than its predecessor, because of the now widespread – and still growing – recognition that the key to prosperity is not to be found in the occupation or control of territory. This makes it possible for international economic policies to be kept more effectively separate from the assertion of state power.

In such an order, regional integration agreements could have a well recognized and accepted place. In particular, groups of countries that have close political and cultural ties may want to establish arrangements which provide (i) for the free movement of people within the region, together with restricted rights of entry for outsiders, and (ii) wider opportunities in each member country for nationals of other countries within the region, as distinct from those outside it, to acquire residence rights and citizenship. Such arrangements, though discriminatory, are compatible with a liberal trade and investment regime; and they reflect the long-established principle, for which good supporting arguments can be found, that questions of entry, residence and citizenship fall within the competence of national sovereign states.

In relation to trade and capital flows, as already noted above, the creation or extension of regional integration agreements might actually form part of the liberalization process. For this to be the case, such agreements would have to embody liberal norms, so that the removal of barriers within the region went together with (i) a readiness to liberalize further with respect to the rest of the world, and (ii) observance of the principle that trade and capital flows across international boundaries, like their counterparts within each national state or region, should be subject to legal norms rather than coercive official interventions. Whether and how far future regional agreements will conform to this pattern will depend, as in the past, on developments within the main national states and trading entities. Present and future regionalism can be compatible with liberalism, and even a partial expression of it, if and in so far as it coincides with, and reflects, a general acceptance of liberal principles in international economic relations.

Two questions that can be asked about the future of the world trading and investment system are, first, will it become more open and more liberal; and, second, will the extent and influence of 'trade blocs' increase? Contrary to what is often suggested, these two questions are largely distinct. The future of the multilateral trade and investment system, and of international economic integration, will chiefly depend, not on the extent to which regional integration agreements become more extensive or more deep-rooted, but rather on how far liberal rather than interventionist influences affect the evolution of external economic policies in the leading national states and trading entities, including in particular (though not only) the European Union and the United States. Regional agreements will largely reflect this balance, rather than determining it either at national level or in the world as a whole. That part of the current debate which portrays regionalism on the one hand, and liberalism or multilateralism on the other, as warring principles is misguided. A truer antithesis, and a more fundamental one, is between liberalism and interventionism.

References

Anderson, Kym and Blackhurst, Richard, eds, 1993, *Regional Integration and the Global Trading System,* Harvester Wheatsheaf, Hemel Hempstead.

Blackhurst, Richard and Henderson, David, 1993, 'Regional integration agreements, world integration and the GATT', in Anderson and Blackhurst, eds, 1993.

Henderson, David, 1991, 'The world trading system', in John Llewellyn and Stephen Potter, eds, *Economic Policies for the 1990s,* Blackwell, Oxford.

Henderson, David, 1992, 'International economic integration: progress, prospects and implications', *International Affairs,* September.

Henderson, David, 1993, 'The EC, the US and others in a changing world economy', *The World Economy*, September.

Henderson, David, 1994, 'International migration: appraising current policies', *International Affairs*, January.

Lal, Deepak, 1993, 'Trade blocs and multilateral free trade', *Journal of Common Market Studies*, 31, 3.

OECD, 1992, *Foreign Direct Investment Policies and Trends in the OECD Area*, OECD, Paris.

Wolf, Martin, 1994, *The Resistible Appeal of Fortress Europe*, published by the Trade Policy Unit of the Centre for Policy Studies, London, together with the American Enterprise Institute for Public Policy Research.